Franz Xaver Kroetz

Plays: 1

Stallerhof, Request Programme, The Nest, Tom Fool, Through the Leaves, Desire

Franz Xaver Kroetz was born in Munich, West Germany in 1946, the son of a government tax official. He grew up in Bavaria and worked as an actor during the sixties, taking minor roles in small theatres, including Rainer Werner Fassbinder's antitheater. *Game Crossing*, his first play, was written in 1968 whilst his two one-act plays, *Stubborn* and *Working at Home* premiered in 1971 at the Munich Kammerspiele. *Working at Home* was acclaimed as 'the most important play of 1971' by Theater Heute, although the accompanying scandal caused the theatre to be placed under police protection. Over the next few years Kroetz wrote a series of plays, the most successful of which is *Stallerhof* (1972). By 1973 Kroetz was Germany's most performed living playwright. He joined the Communist Party (DKP) in 1972, but left in 1980. Three seminal plays followed: *The Nest* (1974), *Through the Leaves* (1976) and *Mensch Meier* (*Tom Fool*, 1977). In the eighties Kroetz turned to acting and directing, achieving celebrity in the TV hit *Kir Royale*. His recent play, *Das Ende der Paarung* premiered in 2000 at the Berliner Ensemble directed by Claus Peymann.

Stallerhof (1971) deals with stunted emotions in a dysfunctional, impoverished rural home and a doomed illicit relationship.

Request Programme (1971) is an extraordinary silent play showing the last moments in a woman's life before her suicide.

The Nest (1974) shows the near-fatal action that an employee takes in order to fulfil the wishes of an employer, which jeopardises his family.

Tom Fool (1977) is the story of an insecure Munich assembly-line worker, his housebound wife and their teenage son, a silent observer. It was a huge success, having its world premiere in four simultaneous productions in 1978.

Desire (1994) deals with the last of all taboos, a serial sex offender's release after many years and the effect on his family and girlfriend.

Through the Leaves (1976) explores a failed relationship between a female butcher and her factory worker lover. 'A gripping and convincing study of emotional need' (*Sunday Telegraph*).

Anthony Vivis has been a freelance translator since 1983. His many stage translations include works by Brecht, Büchner, Fassbinder, Hauptmann and Strauss. He has had work produced at the RNT, the RSC, the Royal Court, the Bush and the Traverse theatres.

Katharina Hehn has lived in London since 1965 and works as a freelance author and translator. Alongside translations of Kroetz, Brecht and others, she has published numerous articles on German literary and theatre history.

FRANZ XAVER KROETZ

Plays: 1

Stallerhof
translated by Katharina Hehn

Request Programme
translated by Katharina Hehn

The Nest
translated by Katharina Hehn

Tom Fool
translated by Estella Schmid and Anthony Vivis

Desire
translated by Anthony Vivis

Through the Leaves
translated by Anthony Vivis

introduced by Moray McGowan
Professor of German, Trinity College Dublin

Methuen Drama

Published by Methuen Drama 2004

1 3 5 7 9 10 8 6 4 2

First published in 2004 by
Methuen Publishing Limited

A CIP catalogue record is available from the British Library

ISBN 0 413 77401 5

Typeset by SX Composing DTP, Rayleigh, Essex

Contents

Chronology

Unless otherwise stated, all titles are plays listed under the year of their premiere (dates in brackets are those of composition, where known to be different).

1946   25 February: Franz Xaver Kroetz born in Munich; the only child of a civil servant and housewife. Baptised and brought up a Catholic; claims last attended confession aged 14.
Begins writing in his early teens.

1961   Kroetz's father dies of cancer. Kroetz breaks off schooling in business studies; works as builder's labourer; attends acting school in Munich and the Max-Reinhardt-Seminar in Vienna. First role in student production of Nestroy's *Der Talisman* (1964). Begins writing plays.

1967   Small roles as actor and director in fringe theatres (e.g. R.W. Fassbinder's 'antiteater') and in 'Bauerntheater' (rural theatres, usually playing peasant farces for a partly tourist audience). Range of temporary employment: van driver, nursing assistant, and (supposedly) banana slicer.
Als Zeus zum letzten Mal kam oder: Die Nacht der weißen Segel (*When Zeus last came, or: The Night of the White Sails*; unperformed) and the experimental novel *Tiroler Elegien* (*Tyrolean Elegies*); both first published 1983.

1968   *Julius Cäsar* (Collage, based on Shakespeare), Büchnertheater, Munich fringe theatre, directed by Kroetz.
Oblomov, adaptation of Ivan Gontcharov's novel, Büchnertheater.

1969   *Hilfe, ich werde geheiratet!* (*Help, I'm being married off!*), peasant farce: Ludwig-Thoma-Bühne in Rottach/Egern, Bavaria.

1970   Awarded dramatist scholarship by Suhrkamp
        publishing house, which allows him to concentrate
        on writing.

1971   *Heimarbeit (Working at Home*, 1969) and *Hartnäckig
        (Stubborn*, 1970) at Münchner Kammerspiele. Minor
        scandal over sex and abortion scenes, fuelled by
        right-wing press. Actors Hans Brenner and Ruth
        Drexel begin long association with Kroetz's work.
        Beginning of Kroetz's artistic and media
        breakthrough.
        Michis Blut (Micky's Blood, 1970), pro T (former
        Büchnertheater), Munich, directed by Kroetz.
        Wildwechsel (Game Crossing, 1968), Städtische Bühnen
        Dortmund.
        Awarded Ludwig-Thoma-Medal of the City of
        Munich.

1972   *Männersache (Men's Business*, 1970), Landestheater
        Darmstadt.
        Stallerhof (1971), Deutsches Schauspielhaus Hamburg.
        Role as Beppi founds Eva Mattes' acting reputation.
        Dolomitenstadt Lienz (Lienz, the Dolomite town, 1972),
        Kammerspiel Bochum.
        Kroetz joins the Deutsche Kommunistische Partei
        (DKP), campaigns and stands for the party
        unsuccessfully in various elections.
        Globales Interesse (Global Interest/s), an anti-capitalist
        agitprop play performed in the context of the
        Munich Olympics, Residenztheater Munich.
        Oberösterreich (Upper Austria; translated and performed
        at the Edinburgh Festival 1975 and on BBC radio as
        Morecambe), Städtische Bühnen Heidelberg.
        Awarded writing scholarships, firstly by the Baden-
        Württemberg Ministry of Culture, secondly by the
        West Berlin Kunstpreis jury.

1973   *Wunschkonzert (Request Programme*, 1971),
        Württembergisches Staatstheater Stuttgart.

R.W. Fassbinder's film of Kroetz's *Wildwechsel* shown on German TV. Kroetz distances himself from the film, claiming it distorts his intentions.

Oberösterreich at the Volkstheater Rostock becomes first Kroetz play to be performed in the German Democratic Republic (East Germany). A TV version of the play is withdrawn by the West German ZDF station for political reasons.

Kroetz visits Moscow with DKP delegation.

Maria Magdalena (1972), freely adapted from Friedrich Hebbel's play of same name, Städtische Bühnen Heidelberg.

Münchner Kindl, subtitled 'a Bavarian ballad', performed as part of a 'Tribunal' against property speculation, organised by the DKP.

Die Wahl fürs Leben (*Life Choice*), radio play, WDR Cologne.

Awarded the West Berlin Critics' Prize.

The Tyrol schoolteacher Agnes Larcher is dismissed from her post for reading *Stallerhof* with her fourteen-year old female pupils.

1974   Hanover Dramatists' Prize for *Sterntaler* (*Pennies from Heaven*).

Der Mensch Adam Deigl und die Obrigkeit (1972) (*Adam Deigl and the Authorities*), adapted from novel by Josef Martin Bauer, TV play, Bayerischer Rundfunk.

In August, David Mouchtar-Samorai's production of *Stallerhof* at the Bush Theatre, London, relocating the play in a Northumberland hill farm, launches his career as a director and Kroetz's reception in Britain. The sparse brutality of the production creates tenacious myths of Kroetz the 'brutalist' whose plays feature 'Bavarian peasants, inarticulate almost to the point of animality' (Martin Esslin, *TLS*, 7 October 1977).

Kroetz buys farmhouse in Bavarian hamlet Kirchberg. He begins to market his plays as his own theatrical agent.

1975   *Lieber Fritz* (*Dear Fritz*, 1971), Staatstheater
       Darmstadt.
       Geisterbahn (*Ghost Train*, 1971): David Mouchtar-
       Samorai's production at Bush Theatre, London on
       13 May precedes the German-language premiere at
       the Ateliertheater am Naschmarkt, Vienna that
       October.
       Das Nest (*The Nest*, a version of which dates from
       1967), Modernes Theater, Munich.
       Weitere Aussichten . . . (1974) (*Prospects . . .*), Städtisches
       Theater Karl-Marx-Stadt (now Chemnitz). TV
       version, directed by Kroetz, awarded Wilhelmine-
       Lübke Prize.
       Muttertag (*Mothers' Day*), TV play.

1976   Mülheim Dramatists' Prize for *Das Nest*.
       After Suhrkamp refuse, in 1974, to publish his
       glowing account of a visit to a GDR collective farm,
       'Sozialismus auf dem Dorf' ('Socialism in the
       Village'), Kroetz leaves Suhrkamp and publishes
       Weitere Aussichten . . ., an anthology of plays, prose
       and interviews, with Kiepenheuer und Witsch in
       Cologne. By 1979 he is back with Suhrkamp, though
       he leaves again in 1994 when the publishers refuse
       'on grounds of literary quality', to publish *Ich bin das
       Volk*.
       Herzliche Grüße aus Grado (*Greetings from Grado*;
       originally TV play, 1972), Düsseldorfer
       Schauspielhaus.
       Reise ins Glück (*Journey to Happiness*, 1975), Theater am
       Neumarkt, Zurich.
       Mitgift (*Dowry*), TV play.

1977   *Sterntaler* (*Pennies from Heaven*, 1974; music by Peter
       Zwetkoff), Staatstheater Braunschweig.
       Ein Mann ein Wörterbuch (*One man, one Dictionary*, 1973;
       revised version of *Männersache*), Ateleier am
       Naschmarkt, Vienna.
       Agnes Bernauer (1976; assistance: Hans Dieter

Schwarze), based very loosely on Friedrich Hebbel's play of same name, Leipziger Theater.
Verfassungsfeinde (*Enemies of the Constitution*, originally TV play), Staatstheater Dresden.
Chiemgauer Gschichten. Bayerische Menschen erzählen. (*Tales from Chiemgau: Bavarians tell their Stories*): edited interviews.
Kroetz begins to work professionally as an actor again, and continues to act periodically in TV and films from now on.

1978　*Mensch Meier* (1977) (*Tom Fool*) has German premiere at four theatres simultaneously, after world premiere at small provincial theatre in Brazil.

1979　Kroetz plays lead role of Kurt in TV version of *Das Nest.*

1980　*Der stramme Max* (1978) (*Sturdy Max*), Recklinghausen. Kroetz leaves the DKP, dissatisfied with its dogmatism, uncritical allegiance to the Soviet Union and GDR, and with its faith in technological progress despite environmental consequences.
Bilanz (*Balance sheet*; originally radio play, 1972), Torturmtheater Sommerhausen.
Die Wahl fürs Leben (*Choice for Life*; originally radio play, 1973), Theater rechts der Isar, Munich.

1981　*Wer durchs Laub geht...* (*Through the Leaves*, 1976; second revised version of *Männersache*), Marburger Schauspiel.
Nicht Fisch, nicht Fleisch (*Neither Fish nor Fowl*, 1980), Düsseldorfer Schauspielhaus.
Kroetz visits Calcutta for performance of five of his plays in a Kroetz series.
Der Mondscheinknecht (*The Moonshine Lad*), novel. Part Two follows in 1983.
Gute Besserung (*Get Well Soon*; originally radio play, 1972), theatre k, Munich.

1983   *Frühe Prosa, frühe Stücke (Early Prose, Early Plays)*
        published: volume of work from the latter 1960s
        which confirmed Kroetz's roots in avant-garde
        experiment with form as well as in social realism or
        peasant literature.
        Jumbo Track (1979), rock musical for young people,
        co-authored with political cabaret group Floh de
        Cologne, at Landestheater Tübingen.

1984   *Furcht und Hoffnung der BRD (Fear and hope in the FRG,*
        1983), with Alexandra Weinert-Purucker. Premiered
        simultaneously at Schauspielhaus Bochum and
        Düsseldorfer Schauspielhaus. Published version
        includes notes and diary entries recording Kroetz's
        crisis of self-doubt as a writer, which continues
        throughout the 1980s.

1985   *Bauern sterben (Dead Soil)*, Münchner Kammerspiele,
        directed by Kroetz. Provokes accusations of
        pornography and blasphemy, fuelled by sensational
        reports in *Bild*, Germany's largest-selling tabloid.
        Beppi im Glück, adaptation of *Stallerhof* and *Geisterbahn*
        into a single play, at Munich Volkstheater.
        Nicaragua-Tagebuch (Nicaraguan Diary): subtitled
        'Roman', novel, and as much about Kroetz's creative
        crises as about the country he visited in 1984.

1986   Kroetz's role as gossip columnist Baby Schimmerlos
        in Helmut Dietl's TV series *Kir Royal* about the
        Munich jet set makes him a hugely popular actor
        and restores his media presence. He puzzles and
        upsets those who had seen him as a scourge of the
        right by writing for *Bild*; subsequently, he also gives
        interviews to German *Playboy* and writes for *Die Welt*,
        the right-wing broadsheet.
        Der Weihnachtstod (Death at Christmas), extended version
        of a scene in *Furcht und Hoffnung der BRD*.
        Der Nusser (untranslatable dialect term for an
        incompletely castrated pig, 1985), adapted from

Ernst Toller's *Hinkemann*, Residenztheater, Munich.
First of a series of productions Kroetz directs there,
including Felix Mitterer's *Stigma* and Brecht's *Herr
Puntila und sein Knecht Matti.*

1987   *Heimat (Homeland*, 1975), podium theatre, Freiburg.
Der Soldat (The Soldier, 1968; early version of
Hartnäckig) premiered by a Munich youth theatre.

1988   *Zeitweh (Times Pain*, 1986), Theater 'Die Färbe', fringe
venue in Singen.
Gerd Kühr's opera *Stallerhof*, with libretto by Kroetz,
premiered in Graz.

1991   *Bauerntheater (Peasant Theatre*, 1989), Schauspiel Köln,
Kammerspiele.
Brasilien-Peru-Aufzeichnungen (Brazil-Peru-Notebook): like
Nicaragua-Tagebuch, reflections as much on Kroetz's
creative and personal crises and dissatisfaction with
his homeland as on the places visited.

1992   Kroetz marries Marie-Theres Relin (daughter of
stage designer Veit Relin).

1994   *Der Drang (Desire*, 1992), revised version of *Lieber Fritz*,
Münchner Kammerspiele.
Ich bin das Volk (I am the People,1993), Wuppertaler
Bühnen.
Bertolt-Brecht-Prize of the City of Augsburg.

1996   Kroetz's adaptation of Büchner's *Woyzeck*, which he
directs at the Hamburger Schauspielhaus, is a critical
and popular disaster.
Der Dichter als Schwein (The Writer as Swine),
Düsseldorfer Schauspielhaus.
*Heimat Welt. Gedichte eines Lebendigen (Homeland World.
Poems of a Living Man)*, Kroetz's first collection of
poetry.
From 1996 Kroetz and Marie-Theres Relin alternate

summers in Germany with winters in Teneriffe, since two of their children are asthma sufferers.

1997   Kroetz's production at the Düsseldorf Schauspielhaus of Schiller's *Wilhelm Tell* in the comic Volksstück tradition is a critical and popular success.

1998   Kroetz abandons rehearsals for *Furcht und Hoffnung in Deutschland* (revised version of *Furcht und Hoffnung der BRD*) at the Düsseldorfer Schauspielhaus, declaring he will not direct in Germany again (he does, in 1999: his adaptation of Anton Hamik's *Der verkaufte Großvater* at the Munich Volkstheater).

1999   *Die Eingeborene. Stück für großes Kasperletheater* (*The Native. Play for Grown-up Puppet Theater*, 1997), Vienna Akademietheater.

2000   *Das Ende der Paarung* (*End of the Mating*, 1996), directed by Claus Peymann, Berliner Ensemble.

2004   *Die Trauerwütigen* (2001) (*The Griefcrazed*), rehearsed reading at Berlin Schaubühne.
       Haus Deutschland. Drei Stücke published (*Haus Deutschland. Made in Deutschland. Deutschland sucht dich* [*Germany wants you*]).

Introduction

The work

'Man muß sich wehren, wenn man ein Mensch sein will.'
'You must resist, if you wish to be human.'[1] What is it in
people, their relationships, their language, their socio-
economic and other circumstances, which disables or inverts
their power to resist? Where and how does resistance begin?
How might drama represent those disabling circumstances
without reinforcing them, and how might drama articulate
those energies of resistance without simply, implausibly,
asserting them?

The work of playwright Franz Xaver Kroetz has engaged
tenaciously with these questions – at once political and
aesthetic – since he emerged onto the German theatre scene
in 1971. By the early years of the twenty-first century, his
fifty-odd plays had been translated into nearly forty
languages and had had countless productions worldwide,
long ago belying his, and their, sometime image as Bavarian
curiosities. Despite his repeated crises of artistic self-doubt
and despite his forays into acting, directing, journalism, and
talk-show celebrity, Kroetz has returned again and again to
writing drama. While his work's view of the balance
between determinism and free-will, or of that between the
social and the existential, in shaping the human condition,
has fluctuated, his work has remained focused firstly on the
impact of these forces on individuals and on the micro-
structures of relationships and families: social exclusion,
communication failure, self-destructive violence, displaced
aggressions, the loss of job, health, identity and self-worth.
Secondly, it has focused on the moments and energies of
resistance against these fates. The result is an extended
exploration of the tension between the human being as
object of social forces and the human being as active subject
struggling for self-determination.

This sustained humanist project, at times undermined by
its own sentimentality as well as beleaguered by changes in

theatrical fashion, has been pursued in an oeuvre in which form, and in particular the craft of dialogue, has been of prime importance. As Kroetz remarked in 1976, with an aphoristic sharpness which reflects less a political incorrectness about disability (though he has few inhibitions about being politically incorrect) than his intense awareness of stage effectiveness and his drastic use of metaphor: 'The theatre is the most pitiless mother of dialogue. It strangles its ill-formed children on the very boards of the first night's performance'.[2] This interplay of humanist social criticism and an uncompromising quest for stageworthy form and for the powerful stage image has characterised his most memorable work throughout his writing career.

This career can be divided into four phases, though with many overlaps, continuities and contradictions. In the first, the late 1960s, Kroetz was furiously experimenting in a wide variety of forms, only one of which was the apparently social realist dramas for which he later became famous, such as *Wildwechsel (Game Crossing)*, *Heimarbeit (Working at Home)*, or *Der Soldat (The Soldier)*, later revised as *Hartnäckig (Stubborn)*. Much of his other, very different work of the period was only published much later, when Kroetz became willing to admit the complexities and contradictions of his artistic career: an adaptation of Ivan Goncharov's novel *Oblomov* (1968; dates are those of first production); an iconoclastic Shakespeare collage *Julius Cäsar* (1968); the absurdist *Als Zeus zum letzten Mal kam oder: Die Nacht der weißen Segel (When Zeus last came, or: The Night of the White Sails)*; experimental prose such as the 'novel' *Tiroler Elegien (Tyrolean Elegies)*; popular farces for the rural 'Bauerntheater' such as *Das Schaf im Wolfspelz (Wolf in Sheep's Clothing)* and *Hilfe, ich werde geheiratet! (Help, I'm being married off!* 1968); and an early version of *Das Nest (The Nest)*, a play usually associated with Kroetz's most earnestly didactic period in the mid-1970s.

Kroetz's breakthrough, and the beginning of his second phase, came in April 1971, with the twin premieres of *Working at Home* and *Stubborn* at the Munich Kammerspiele, beginning a decade in which he became the German theatre's most performed living playwright. These plays

were initially understood as grim records of the material and
linguistic poverty of the socially disadvantaged and
marginalised who formed a substantial minority behind
what was then the still intact façade of the
'Wirtschaftswunder' (Germany's post-war economic
miracle), a facet of West German society revealed at the
same time in works like Jürgen Roth's *Poverty in the Federal
Republic* (1974). Kroetz's plays were seen as part of the trend
for 'new Realism' or the 'new Volksstück', social realist
drama with a regional milieu defined through the language,
which enjoyed a brief critical success around 1970.
However, unlike the plays of his fellow 'new Realists',
Martin Sperr (*Hunting Scenes from Lower Bavaria*, 1966) and
Rainer Werner Fassbinder (*Katzelmacher*, 1968), which tend
to focus on the group dynamics of prejudice and violence,
most of Kroetz's plays of this period are domestic dramas, in
which the figures direct the aggressions their social
experience has generated – but their impoverished language
cannot accurately articulate – towards themselves, their
families or their unborn children. Thus domestic murders
and attempted or successful abortions are central motifs, for
example in *Game Crossing* (1971) or *Michis Blut* (*Micky's Blood*,
1971). Shocking stage images, such as the masturbation and
defloration scenes in *Stallerhof* (1972), ensured these plays
notoriety, further fuelled by Kroetz's often intemperate
pronouncements. In *Working at Home*, the straitened material
and psychological circumstances of Martha, Willi and their
children are so threatened by the conception of a third
child, fathered by another man, that Martha attempts an
amateur abortion with a knitting needle. The child is born
deformed. Willi's accusatory aggression drives Martha to
leave. Willi strangles the child. Order now having been
restored, Martha returns and the play ends with the couple
once more about to have sex. The cycle appears to be
beginning again. Similarly bleak, brutal plots are to be
found throughout the plays of this phase.

     Kroetz's antecedents are Georg Büchner's *Woyzeck* with
its foregrounding of the little man as possible and proper
subject of drama, Gerhart Hauptmann's exploration of the

fateful effects of milieu and socio-economic circumstances, Marieluise Fleißer's dramatisations of the transmission of societal power structures through gender relationships and Ödön von Horváth's tracing of the perversion of consciousness in and through a language which internalises and naturalises ideology. In contrast, Brechtian 'Verfremdung', distancing or making the familiar strange by displacement, as a strategy for energising the audience, is not central to Kroetz's work, even when, from 1972–1980, he was an enthusiastic Communist Party member.

Kroetz's early plays were seen as epitomising the 'Sprachlosigkeit' (more accurately rendered as 'inarticulacy' than as 'speechlessness') of a linguistically, spiritually and materially deprived sub-proletariat, an over-simplification for which Kroetz himself was substantially responsible, for example through his use of the term in his foreword to *Working at Home*, the first of his plays to receive wide critical and public attention. (FXK 63–65)[3] 'Sprachlosigkeit' is characterised by the figures' inability to resolve their difficulties discursively, resorting instead to violence. The language they do use leans heavily on pre-fabricated phrases, clichés and maxims, hindering them from recognising their own needs or those of others. In this, the plays build on Horváth's dramatic portraits of the linguistic dispossession of a whole class, the 'Kleinbürgertum' or petit-bourgeoisie, whom Horváth, like Ernst Bloch, saw as the fertile humus for fascism (e.g. *Tales from the Vienna Woods*, 1930). The silences in Kroetz plays, too, seemed to function like Horváth's as moments where the stage figures' struggles between unconscious and conscious, between authentic self and ideologically determined self are made clear to the audience.

So closely did Kroetz's dialogues seem to fit Basil Bernstein's then fashionable model of language competence – of a middle-class 'elaborated code' and a working-class 'restricted code' – that one analysis declared roundly that Kroetz 'unmistakeably proceeds from the contemporary discussion about language barriers and class-specific language use'.[4] This is unquestionably untrue: Kroetz's highly crafted dialogues result not from sociolinguistic theory but from empirical observations reshaped according to his acute sense of dramatic effectiveness.

Moreover, just as Bernstein's theories were criticised for unintentionally confirming the hierarchy of class by neglecting the creative and affective potential of working-class speech, so too Kroetz came to reject the label 'Sprachlosigkeit' attached to his early plays, both for the fatalism it implied and for the way it neglected the elements of humour, struggle and solidarity present even in the bleakest of his plays. In 1971 in the preface to *Geisterbahn* (*Ghost Train*) he already noted that the pauses in his dialogue were not only moments of communication failure; they could also signal 'possibilities of human understanding' beyond the verbal. (GS 160)[5]

These plays are characterised too by Kroetz's ability to extract both dramatic interaction and precisely observed detail of human behaviour from dialogues which, in a play such as *Micky's Blood*, are the tersest of utterances, each a handful of words long, flanked by pauses. They are characterised by the way in which both acts of violence and taboo-breaking scenes of defecation, masturbation and crude (though never 'earthy') sex are depicted matter-of-factly, and by how, despite all this, the universal human impulses towards companionship, happiness and harmony can become visible even in the blackest deprivation.

Kroetz's image as a quasi-documentary dramatist was persistent. Even after the decline of the 1960s' fashion for documentary literature on grand political themes, critics and audiences in the early 1970s still believed they saw 'authenticity', a direct relationship with social reality, in Kroetz's early work. This was encouraged by his pronouncements that this work was, indeed, drawn from newspaper reports and from observation: 'Invention, I hope, hardly plays a role.'[6]

However, this is misleading, as Kroetz himself would later admit. Firstly Kroetz's plays of this phase manifestly are not concerned with 'Randgruppen' alone, social outsiders (a misunderstanding attributable, perhaps, to the narrow social experience of some theatre critics, but also partly encouraged by Kroetz himself): Erwin, the father in *Game Crossing*, is a lorry driver, Rustorfer and Erl in *Stubborn* are publicans, Otto in *Lieber Fritz* (*Dear Fritz*, 1975) a market gardener, Fräulein Rasch in *Wunschkonzert* (*Request Programme*, 1973) a clerical worker; *Männersache* (*Men's Business*, 1972) concerns a factory worker and a shopkeeper. Secondly, these plays are in any case much more than social reportage. Though often described as 'Mitleidsdramaturgie', the dramaturgy of pity, they are also imaginative restatements of personal experience: 'I hadn't felt pity for others, I had suffered myself, and portrayed that in my early plays', Kroetz remarked. (FXK 172).

The motif of 'Heimarbeit', piecework labour performed in the home, whether filling seed packets, making Christmas decorations or threading rosaries, which occurs in *Working at Home, Ghost Train, The Nest, Sterntaler* (*Pennies from Heaven*, 1977), *Agnes Bernauer* (1977) and *Heimat* (*Homeland*, 1986), is of course a social fact, an extreme example of economic marginality. But it is also a metaphor for exploitation and an effective piece of stage business, and moreover it articulates the socially isolated and insecure world of Kroetz in the late 1960s, drifting between unskilled casual jobs, rare engagements as an actor, and unsuccessful attempts as a writer. The same applies to the motif of handicap in *Working at Home, Stubborn, Stallerhof* and *Dear Fritz*: it is a social reality too often suppressed from public consciousness and from the stage, and it is also a metaphor for social exclusion, and an expression of the rejection Kroetz experienced before 1971. Beyond that, the motif of handicap as an image of a humanity tragically denied and denying its own ideal nature recurs from Kroetz's earliest texts, such as 'Koreanischer Frühling' ('Korean Spring') to his two-part novel *Der Mondscheinknecht* (*The Moonshine Lad*, 1981 and *Der Mondscheinknecht. Fortsetzung*, 1983), whose central character is the polio victim Anton Kreuzberger, and to *Der Nusser* (untranslatable reference to an incompletely castrated pig, 1986), Kroetz's adaptation of Ernst Toller's play *Hinkemann* (1922) about a soldier returning from World War I maimed by the loss of his genitals. On the dust jacket of *The Moonshine Lad*, Kroetz remarks: 'I believe we are all handicapped.' Thus motifs that, in his dogmatic socially critical phase, Kroetz insisted were social documents, can also be read as stage metaphors for the human condition.

In other respects too, these plays are much less monochrome than often assumed. Even the apparently naturalistic sparseness of the dialogue represents a radical formal innovation. Though it has parallels with the social realism of Edward Bond's *The Pope's Wedding* and *Saved* (and Bond wrote the programme notes for the 1974 Half Moon Theatre, London production of *Working at Home* in a translation by his wife Elisabeth Bond-Pablé), Kroetz's distillation of intensely dramatic interactions out of apparently banal exchanges punctuated by pauses is often closer to the early Harold Pinter. Both the rhythmic pattern of the scenes, and the dialogue, though based on a Bavarian lower-class sociolect, are highly crafted. The transcribed interviews in *Chiemgauer Gschichten. Bayrische Menschen erzählen* (*Tales from Chiemgau. Bavarians tell their Stories*, 1977), which might have confirmed the authenticity of Kroetz's stage dialogue, share some syntactic features with the plays but are noticeably different. Linguistics scholars, indeed, have observed that pauses and silences, often cited as symptomatic of the 'Sprachlosigkeit' of Kroetz's figures, are as prominent, empirically speaking, in middle-class as in working-class language.[7] This may be another way in which Kroetz's plays could appeal to an audience in the established theatre without this audience necessarily recognising that they were also watching versions of themselves.

Though, in 1972, barely a year after his breakthrough, Kroetz was already declaring this phase of his work over, the originality of these early dramas, the scandals which some of them attracted, and the bellicosity of his pronouncements (and indeed their frequency: Kroetz was probably also the most *interviewed* living German playwright of the 1970s) belied the brevity of this phase and shaped public images of the dramatist and his work long after it was over.

At the same time, though, Kroetz had rapidly become convinced that 'das Extreme' of his early work, whether understood as an extremism of theme, treatment or dramatic form, had prevented real audience confrontation with the political points he wanted this work to make. Now therefore, in the third phase of his work, from *Oberösterreich* (*Upper Austria*, 1972) through *The Nest* and *Der stramme Max* (*Sturdy Max*, 1980) to *Nicht Fisch, nicht Fleisch* (*Neither Fish nor Fowl*, 1981), he aspired to portray 'typical' members of West German society and moments of awakening political consciousness. The result was dramas of the pressures and contradictions of West German capitalist society as they manifest themselves, primarily, in the petit-bourgeois nuclear family: the married couple, with or without children. These figures represent people 'integrated into the supermarket society of a modern economy'[8], a working-class whose 'Verkleinbürgerlichung' (Kroetz)[9], a largely unquestioning adoption of petit-bourgeois and middle-class aspirations and consumer behaviour, meant they were no longer proletarian. The plots become less violent, the staging less starkly voyeuristic: with the single exception of *Pennies from Heaven*, no play between 1972 and 1981 contains scenes of fatal violence, and the sex scenes move under the covers of the marriage bed. From the deprivation of *Heimarbeit* it is a long way to *Sturdy Max*, in which Anna and Max send their daughter Sabine to an expensive boarding school to compensate for her working class origins.

These plays of Kroetz's third phase established him as the dramatist of the habits of thought, speech and consumption of the West German everyman. The male protagonists of the plays from *Upper Austria* to *Neither Fish nor Fowl* all experience a socially grounded threat (typically, unemployment or the economic consequences of a pregnancy) that disorientates them sufficiently for them to recognise, often for the first time, the alienated nature of their lives. This alienation reaches, as Heinz remarks to his wife Anni in *Upper Austria*, from the workplace into the marriage bed: 'But sometimes, when the two of us are together, 'cause we're being intimate, it's like at work [. . .]'

You do something, someone who just happens to be oneself, like, and millions of others have done it before, just the same.' (GS 400) Moreover, their prosperity stands on shaky foundations, vulnerable to the economic cycles of capitalism and exposed to the hazards of a profit-oriented industrial economy: Kurt in *The Nest* and Max in *Sturdy Max* risk the health of their families or themselves in a desperate defence of their spending power, since that is how their male identity is defined.

But in contrast to the early plays, the characters' improved socio-economic situation and articulacy mean that when faced by crisis, they are better able to realise and at least begin to resist the other-determined nature of their lives. This enlightenment is as much moral as political (e.g. *The Nest*) and conservative attitudes often underlie the plays' social criticism. This applies for example to the perspectives on gender, even though the women figures (notably Martha in *Tom Fool*) often show greater insight, sensitivity, decisiveness and capacity to resist than the floundering men. Nonetheless (or hence?) these plays were among the most performed in the German theatre of the mid-1970s. Kroetz insists on working class characters' right to the identity crises that, since Goethe's *Sufferings of Young Werther* (1774), had been customarily reserved for the sensitive bourgeois individual. Arguably, this rehabilitation, in Kroetz's work, of an archetypal bourgeois theme in socially critical guise aided his success with a West German public whose disillusion with the political demands made on literature in the late 1960s was advanced but still not complete.

In his fourth phase, from around 1980 onwards, Kroetz continues to portray existential crises as social, therefore man-made and changeable, as phenomena affecting representative figures whose problems have concrete social and economic origins. But the optimistic, rationalistic tenor has been increasingly supplemented or even replaced by more pessimistic tones. He still rejected, as in his dogmatic DKP phase, the artistic search for self-realisation at the expense of social reality and social solidarity. But he now acknowledged that his work, full of 'injuries, ruptures, moments of desperation, depression, loneliness, loss of dignity, inferiority complexes, wounds'[10], had always also been about himself, 'my own, biographically located, existential shipwrecks, which I try to grasp and to represent as social phenomena.'[11] He now insisted, too, that political art, *above all*, should not neglect form: 'Whoever, in the heat of battle [. . .] throws away form, in order to fight better, throws away a part of his weapon. Art without teeth is no art. Art without form too.' (FXK 172).

Kroetz continued to address key social issues such as technology and identity in *Neither Fish Nor Fowl*, unemployment in *Furcht und Hoffnung der BRD* (*Fear and Hope in the FRG*, 1983), the crisis of peasant identity in the face of agricultural modernisation in *Bauern sterben* (*Dead Soil*, 1985). But he also sought to escape the 'Wohnküchen-Gasherd-Realismus' ('living-room/gas-cooker realism': Kroetz) of his family plays, in part through a return to the radicality of the forms and motifs of his early work. His novel trilogy *The Moonshine Lad* (1981 ff.), portraying the progression of a crippled peasant boy to skilled typesetter and trade union activist, exemplified the synthesis of the subjective and the political Kroetz now sought.

In his phase of DKP membership from 1972–1980, Kroetz the political radical, constrained perhaps by his initial eagerness to conform to the aesthetic conservatism of orthodox social realism, was actually writing the most formally conventional of his plays. Since 1980 the formal radicalism of his early work has re-emerged, but linked now to the understanding of social mechanisms provided by his study of Marxism and to the ability to portray them economically and with little trace of didacticism.

From the early stages of his career, when the young Kroetz exhibited the artistic youth's revolt against parental pressure to conform and, in his early DKP phase, the longing to identify with and be subsumed in the masses, Kroetz's anger against society had an expressionist intensity. Hermann Bahr described Expressionism as 'the soul's struggle with the machine [. . .] Man is crying out for his soul [. . .] And Art cries too, into the deep darkness, crying for help, crying for the spirit. That is Expressionism'.[12] In all Kroetz's work humanity cries out against its dehumanisation: 'the soul's struggle with the machine' becomes explicit in the Huxleyan fantasies of Otto Meier in *Tom Fool*, Max in *Sturdy Max* or especially Edgar in *Neither Fish nor Fowl*, and in the very form, an episodic 'Stationendrama', of *Dead Soil*. In 1982, commenting on a variant of *Neither Fish nor Fowl* which ends with Edgar's wife Emmi pregnant, Kroetz remarks that she has 'the whole of future humanity in her belly', like the archetypal Expressionist woman-figure pregnant with the 'New Man'.[13]

Kroetz is not simply a latter-day Expressionist. Changed historical circumstances and his tangible if not always consistent grasp of Marxist dialectics militate against that. But expressionist forms seem to offer a possible way out of one-dimensional naturalism. Moreover, since he formally broke with the DKP and its faith in progress in 1980, another aspect of his complex make-up has become much more apparent, one that he shares with many Expressionists: the conservative rejection of modernity that is part of 'the soul's struggle with the machine'. It becomes explicit in the 1980s, for example in *Dead Soil*'s demonisation of urban society: 'The city is the butcher.'[14] Kroetz's humanism has always had a traditionalist streak, visible in the more sympathetic portrayal in *Neither Fish nor Fowl* of the fecund, motherly Helga than the childless careerist Emmi, or in *Dead Soil*'s requiem for the lost rural 'Heimat': 'Without soil, you die.'

Zeitweh (*Times Pain*), *Der Dichter als Schwein* (*The Poet as Swine*, 1988), *Bauerntheater* (*Peasant Farce*, 1991), and his travel notes, e.g. *Brasilien-Peru-Aufzeichnungen* (1991), address the crisis of the active human subject through often self-mocking portrayals of a writer's crises of political impotence and aesthetic stagnation. Faced with the initial triumphalism of German unification and its immediate aftermath, Kroetz's response was the sarcastic cabaret of scenes of a reviving racist nationalism, *Ich bin das Volk* (*I am the People*, 1994). Suhrkamp refused to publish the play, heightening Kroetz's sense that, whether through artistic exhaustion or political

inopportunism, there was no place for him in the new
German cultural landscape. But after another prolonged
period of self-doubt, Kroetz re-emerged towards the end of
the 1990s with another group of works whose formal and
thematic variety suggests that his creative career is still
developing.

Of these *Die Eingeborene* (*The Native*, 1999), stands out as a
notably productive development in Kroetz's work, both a
continuation of his return to the aesthetics of the
'Holzschnitt' – the woodcut, a reference to the drastic visual
style of the early modern pamphlet – in *Dead Soil* and an
extension of his aesthetic range. Kroetz subtitles the play
'Stück für großes Kasperletheater' ('Play for grown-up
puppet theatre'), whereby the deliberately ambiguous
'groß' may also mean large-scale. The German puppet
tradition has always been more than a children's
entertainment, retaining affinities to the dark realism of the
unbowdlerised versions of Grimm's fairy tales. Prior to
Goethe, for example, the Faust legend was very largely
transmitted via puppet plays. In *The Native* Kroetz turns to
the puppet theatre, which his stage directions describe as
'garish and bright, colourful and fast, short and to the point'
(EdP 96)[15], as a means to achieve authenticity through
artificiality, that is, through a form in which emotional and
social experience can be recognised as real without being
rejected as naturalism or kitsch. The Gretel puppet Irmi, a
single mother struggling to support her son Torsten whilst
finding economic and emotional sustenance for herself,
experiences prostitution and casual sales jobs, and is
buffeted between rejection and possessive abuse in her
sequence of relationships with three Kasperls (that is, fool
figures from the puppet theatre): Kurt, a wily old man dying
of throat cancer, Toni, emaciated and about to die from
AIDS, and Hugo, impoverished, stupid, terminally ill with
stomach cancer. By the end of the play, Torsten is dead too,
and Irmi is pregnant again, a circularity that echoes that of
one of the earliest of Kroetz's plays, *Working at Home*.
Familiar Kroetzean themes of social rejection and the
symbiosis of tenderness and aggression within relationships

are coupled here with the inescapable awareness of
mortality. The stage directions call for a set of wildly
painted, stage-height backdrops following each other in
rapid succession like the illustrations to a ballad and for
hand puppets moving to a pre-recorded soundtrack. The
premiere at the Akademietheater in Vienna in 1999 put
human actors in outsize heads of painted sacking. In either
case, the clownesque starkness, its grotesquely exaggerated
representation of the frailties of the body, allows the author
to address fundamental themes but prevents sentimental
identification.

Arguably, *The Native* finds the form in which Kroetz's
often imitated but, at its best, unmatched combination of
theatrical elements achieves again the disturbing tensions of
his early work: sparse, often ugly, yet musically precise
dialogue; a social realism alert both to the lives of the
forgotten and to aspects of most people's everyday lives they
would usually rather forget; graphic bodily – scatological
and sexual – detail which is both part of that social realism
and also always part of a formal project, a quest for
haunting, disturbing theatrical images, moments which
discomfort and challenge their audience.

By contrast, the still more anti-naturalistic, savagely comic
Die Trauerwütigen (*The Griefcrazed*) would seem like the satyr
play to the tragedy *The Native*, were it not for its political
anger under the sarcasm. It was written at the height of the
BSE crisis of 2001 and in the midst of the drawn-out and
often grotesque debate about a German Holocaust
memorial, but first performed only as a staged reading in
2004: unsurprisingly, as it calls for a cast of 'robust adult
eagles', 'young eagles in the nest', 'old tired eagles' sitting in
a birdcage with mirror, bells, perches, birdbath and feeding
tray, and a calf, mooing pitifully outside the cage.
Punctuated by repeated variations on the stage direction
'shits from the perch', the eagles rant obsessively, switching
bewilderingly between Holocaust guilt, the ritualisation of
contrition and the problems of what to wear for its official
ceremonies 'in order to support the symbolism': 'If you wear
Versace you can't say Treblinka'. (EdP 72–73)

In his early work, Kroetz avoided sentimentality through the stringency of the setting and dialogue. This sentimentality always threatened to swamp his 'Kleinbürger' plays of the latter 1970s with their more loquacious, psychologically more rounded, identificatory characters; the plots, where (as in the case of *The Nest*) they were more than everyday, were often melodramatic and potentially kitsch. *The Native* avoids this pitfall through its tension between a social realist plot as grim as anything from the Kroetz of the early 1970s and the grotesque puppet form. *The Griefcrazed* avoids it through the wholly bizarre milieu of the eagle cage, the formal insistence on an accurately observed and performed framework of avian behaviour which is nonetheless 'a closed system, difficult to understand [. . .] not really penetrable for us humans' (EdP 54), a distancing framework within which a discourse which moves seamlessly from the Holocaust to BSE, from neo-Nazi views to the anthropomorphism of animal lovers is exposed in its lethal sentimentality.

Since the early 1980s, Kroetz has been embarked on a long and not always successful search to regain the theatrical power of his early work. *The Native* and *The Griefcrazed* offer very different but equally exciting examples of how he may recover it. We can be sure, as one study of Kroetz concludes, that 'his writing will continue to seek the preservation of "das Menschliche" ("the human") in the face of all obstacles.'[16] We have not heard the last of this remarkable contemporary voice.

The playwright: Franz Xaver Kroetz 1946–

The startling impact of plays such as *Stallerhof* or *Working at Home* at the beginning of Franz Xaver Kroetz's career, with their rural or sub-proletarian settings and sparse, seemingly impoverished dialogue, came together with Kroetz's virulent attacks, in his first interviews, on both the established theatre and on much of modernist and avant-garde literature, to create an image of a writer who had somehow sprung untutored from proletarian or rustic origins. This image proved tenacious, partly encouraged by Kroetz himself. The reality is rather more complex.[17]

Franz Xaver Kroetz was born in Munich on 25 February 1946, the only child of comfortably middle-class parents: his mother was a housewife, his father a middle-ranking civil servant and, on retirement, a tax consultant. Though the family lived in rural Simbach on the Inn from 1946–51, they then moved back to the Munich suburb of Obermenzing where Kroetz spent the rest of his childhood and youth. The harsh, deprived rural world of *Stallerhof* is thus not his own. He was brought up a Catholic, but claims he last attended confession aged fourteen, and he left the Church before he was twenty. His drama has always drawn on Catholic motifs, though less so than that of other contemporaries such as Felix Mitterer or Werner Fritsch, and far more as part of the South German mental landscape than as an issue of faith or dogma.

Kroetz always aspired to an artistic career, read avidly and eclectically and wrote obsessively from his early teens. This brought a familiar pattern of conflict with a father ambitious for his son to make a solid career. When Kroetz's father died of cancer in 1961, Kroetz broke off his schooling at the 'Wirtschaftsgymnasium' (secondary school with a business studies emphasis), took labouring jobs and attended acting school in Munich and the Max-Reinhardt-Seminar in Vienna, neither of which he completed, though he learned to ride, fence, and quote passages of Schiller from memory. His first role was in a student production of Nestroy's *The Talisman* (1964).

On leaving acting school, Kroetz's life had three interconnecting strands which all fed into his later work: Firstly, from 1966/67 he was active in the Munich fringe theatre scene, acting for example in Rainer Werner Fassbinder's 'antiteater' production of Marieluise Fleißer's *Pioneers in Ingolstadt* in 1968 and staging his Shakespeare collage *Julius Cäsar* and an adaptation of Ivan Goncharov's novel *Oblomov* at the Büchner (later pro T) theatre. Though the late 1960s were a period of heady politicisation in West

German society, when a new upsurge of radicalism seemed
to presage the demise of the liberal-democratic consensus,
Kroetz was here part of an anti-bourgeois rebellion that was
artistic and not political. 'Indeed, we explicitly rejected
politics, found it primitive and unimportant [. . .] Our
expectations of art shrunk back as though bitten by an adder
any time we came anywhere near reality.' (FXK 166).

Secondly, at the same time Kroetz was also acting and
directing in, and writing for, the 'Bauerntheater', theatres in
rural Bavaria which performed both peasant farces for a
partly tourist audience and works by more serious authors of
the South German tradition such as Ludwig Anzengruber.
For these theatres, Kroetz wrote the peasant farces *Wolf in
Sheep's Clothing* and *Help, I'm being married off!* Though hardly
his 'artistic birthplace' as he once claimed[18], the
'Bauerntheater' provided a counterweight to the
experimental excesses of the Munich fringe scene, solid
practical stage experience at a time when the established
theatres were closed to him.

Thirdly, between 1966 and 1970 he was necessarily
supporting this unpaid or modestly rewarded artistic work
with a broad range of irregular and casual jobs: van driver,
nursing assistant, builder's labourer, swimming pool
attendant, lorry driver and (supposedly) banana cutter. This
experience of proletarian and sub-proletarian life
undoubtedly informed many of his plays; he still draws on it
in *The Native* in 1999. But at the time Kroetz always saw
himself as an artist in waiting, writing through the night and
at weekends. Thus a conflict grew between the art he was
trying to practice and the reality he was experiencing, and
as an unskilled, casual labourer, this was disproportionately
the reality of those who had failed to establish a foothold in
the affluent society: 'With my head I was an artist and
otherwise a proletarian.' (FXK 167) As a result, when
Kroetz began to be listened to after his breakthrough in
1971, his aggressively proletarian, anti-intellectual,
utilitarian stance was an expression not just of anger over
conditions at the sump of the affluent society, nor just of
scorn for the theatrical establishment – though the anger

and the scorn were real enough – but also rejection of his own immediate past. All these influences fed into his work which both reflects and revolts against them: formal experiment and its angry rejection, the rural 'Volksstück' and its radical subversion, the economic, physical and psychological burdens of unskilled labour.

When he was awarded a six-month dramatist scholarship by the Suhrkamp publishing house in 1970, he immediately abandoned these other occupations to concentrate on writing, returning to acting and later directing only gradually in the later 1970s. His breakthrough came with the twin premieres of *Working at Home* and *Stubborn* at the Munich Kammerspiele in April 1971. The premiere itself was accompanied by protests and a minor scandal, fuelled by the conservative press, over the sex and abortion scenes. Kroetz's notoriety was accelerated by the attention of the media, hungry for the sensational copy provided by his plays and his freely given interviews, with their intemperate, often mutually contradictory claims about his life and artistic intentions. The Kroetz of the early 1970s was both an angry man and a gifted self-publicist. In the immediate aftermath of the student movement and its assaults on all bourgeois cultural institutions, such attacks were common. But Kroetz's utterances expressed an unusually drastic utilitarianism. The subsidised theatre in West Germany, 'a stinking boil' paid for from the workers' taxes, should either articulate their interests or be shut down.[19] Works of art that did not serve the interests of the masses were 'intellectual excrement'.[20]

Though critics were initially divided on his work's significance, his presence in the subsidised theatre too was rapidly cemented by this theatre's comparable hunger for new plays, which he was able to feed with the backlog of unperformed work accumulated since the late 1960s. A flurry of premieres followed, most notably that of *Stallerhof* at the Deutsches Schauspielhaus Hamburg in 1972. With his remarkable ear for dialogue, for the rhythms underlying apparently banal exchanges, Kroetz was particularly adept at maximising his market value by adapting his stage plays for radio and TV and vice versa.

Almost immediately, Kroetz began to declare himself
dissatisfied that 'das Extreme', the extreme images in his
early plays, were leading them to be seen as portrayals of
inarticulacy and of fatalistic cycles of violence and apathy,
denying their figures any opportunity to escape their fate,
and allowing bourgeois audiences to consume them as
exotic, voyeuristic exhibitions. Symptomatically, in 1973, he
distanced himself from R.W. Fassbinder's film of *Game
Crossing*, claiming it distorted his intentions. In 1972,
frustrated at how the cultural establishment had been able,
after a brief initial shock, effortlessly to absorb his plays,
Kroetz joined the Deutsche Kommunistische Partei (DKP)
as a 'protection against the embrace of the bourgeoisie'
(FXK 169). In choosing the DKP from the various radical
left-wing parties active in West Germany at the time, he
chose the one furthest from the anarchist tendencies
widespread in the Munich fringe scene. Now distancing
himself firmly from apolitical aesthetic experimentation, he
declared that writing was a poor substitute for action, and
he would abandon it altogether: 'I'd rather sit in Bonn in
the Federal Parliament', he declared in 1973 (WA 585)[21],
or he would write only agitprop plays in future. But in fact
little of his work fits this category apart from the quasi-
documentary dramas *Globales Interesse* (*Global Interest/s*, 1972)
and *Münchner Kindl* (1973: the title refers to a variety of beer).
A historical drama on the banned West German communist
party of the 1950s, *KPD lebt!* (*KPD lives!*) was often
announced but never materialised. Instead, the mainstream
of Kroetz's actual work during his DKP phase portrayed
ordinary average members of West German society, in a
succession of 'Kleinbürger' plays from *Upper Austria* (1972) to
Sturdy Max (1980).

His work began to be performed in the GDR, and also,
occasionally, to experience political difficulties in the West:
in 1973, for example, the TV version of *Upper Austria* and an
accompanying studio discussion were withdrawn shortly
before the broadcast. But in East and West, in fact, his
extremely vocal criticism of West German capitalist society
in essays and interviews often influenced responses more

than the actual tenor of the work itself, which, as in the case of *Upper Austria*, could be surprisingly conservative. In the latter 1970s, Kroetz was comfortably the most widely performed living German playwright. He continued to strike radical positions in the media. But he also drove a Mercedes, bought and began to convert an idyllic farmhouse in the Bavarian hamlet Altenmarkt, and became an entrepreneur by setting up as his own theatrical agent.

The reception of his work became complex, as public expectations established during his earlier phase, some of whose plays, such as *Dear Fritz* or *Ghost Train* were still only reaching the stage in the mid 1970s, clashed with his more recent political intentions and aesthetic practice. He also developed a reputation for closely observed, sympathetic studies of themes less obviously associated with the angry young iconoclast. His TV adaptation of *Weitere Aussichten . . .* (*Prospects . . .*,1974), a monologue of an old woman clearing her flat to move into a residential home, became a tour-de-force for the actress Therese Giehse and won the Wilhelmine-Lübke Prize.

Kroetz campaigned actively and stood for the DKP unsuccessfully in various elections in the 1970s. But as the decade progressed, several factors loosened and then severed his commitment to the party and the aesthetic positions he associated with that membership. Firstly, along with many critics he came to realise that the strengths of his early work lay not in their social realism alone. Secondly, he came to accept that the aspiration of his DKP phase, to write plays with politically progressive, positive messages, was misplaced. Thirdly, precisely his engagement with Marxist dialectic led him to reject both the DKP's rhetoric, which he had made his own, and the party's East European model of socialism. In 1974, he had left Suhrkamp, West Germany's most prestigious publishing house, rather than see his admiring report on a GDR collective farm 'Sozialismus auf dem Dorf' ('Socialism in the Village') go unpublished. Ten years later, in 1985, long back with Suhrkamp, he rejected the same report as 'dreadfully dishonest'.[22] He became equally disillusioned with the

DKP's dogged adherence to a vision of progress based on environmentally blind endorsement of technological development. In 1980 he left the party, and in the course of the 1980s, he grew ever more pessimistic about progress, though he continued to reject those forms of nihilistic gloom which can be used to justify inaction, associating himself with parties from the DKP to the Social Democrats and the Greens according to the issue at the time.

His willingness, after this political self-liberation, to accept a more pluralist aesthetics in place of the never very convincing puritanical singleness of purpose he had cultivated in his DKP years, was underlined in 1983 by *Frühe Prosa, frühe Stücke (Early Prose, Early Plays)*. This volume of previously unpublished work from the latter 1960s confirmed that his roots lay in avant-garde formal experiment as well as in social realism or peasant literature. Having begun acting again in the late 1970s (including playing the male lead in the TV version of *The Nest* in 1979), he toured a production of *Neither Fish nor Fowl* through small provincial theatres in 1983, playing Edgar, the more rebellious, less political of the two male leads, and living on the road in a motor caravan. In the following decades, acting and directing seem repeatedly to have offered him a flight from creative crisis as a writer.

In 1981, a visit to Calcutta, where five of his plays were performed in a Kroetz series, signalled a growing awareness that his work could address a world audience and its concerns, not just a German, let alone Bavarian one. At the same time, his series of journeys to third world countries generated texts, such as *Nicaragua-Tagebuch (Nicaraguan Diary*, 1985) that focus as much on the author's creative and personal crises and dissatisfaction with his homeland as on the places visited. In *Brasilien-Peru-Aufzeichnungen (Brazil-Peru-Notebook*, 1991) he rejects his own work as 'a pathetic sandpit [. . .] I despise what I write.' These crises form the theme of a series of plays with writer protagonists – *Times Pain* (1988), *The Writer as Swine* (1996) – of which the most successful is the bitter comedy *Peasant Theatre* (1991).

His production of *Dead Soil* at the Munich Kammerspiele

in 1985, which sought to revive and outdo the stark power
of his early work, provoked accusations, reminiscent of those
against *Working at Home* and *Stallerhof*, of pornography and
blasphemy, fuelled by sensational reports in the tabloid
newspaper *Bild*. From 1986 onwards, Kroetz's role as gossip
columnist Baby Schimmerlos in Helmut Dietl's TV series
Kir Royal about the Munich jet set made him a hugely
popular actor and restored his media presence. While
insisting that 'I am and remain an anti-fascist and an anti-
capitalist', Kroetz puzzled and upset those who had seen
him as a scourge of the right by now himself writing for *Bild*
and for the right-wing broadsheet *Die Welt*.

In 1989/90, the collapse of the GDR followed by
German unification temporarily turned popular and media
attention away from the issues, such as unemployment in
capitalism or the threat of nuclear or ecological disaster,
which had occupied Kroetz's political energies in the 1980s.
'Men like me are no use to the new Greater Germany', he
remarked bitterly (*Brazil-Peru-Notebook*). In 1994 *I am the
People* engaged critically with the post-unification rise of
Neo-Nazism; but Suhrkamp, to whom he had returned in
1979, refused it 'on grounds of literary quality', forcing him
to change publishers again.

In the mid-1990s, Kroetz was in particular crisis as a
writer, and particularly active as a director. His adaptation
of Büchner's *Woyzeck* at the Hamburger Schauspielhaus in
1996 was a critical and popular disaster, his treatment of
Schiller's *Wilhelm Tell* as a 'Volksstück' comedy in 1997 an
almost equally emphatic success. Though in 1998 he
abandoned rehearsals for *Fear and Hope in Germany* (revised
version of *Fear and Hope in the BRD*) at the Düsseldorfer
Schauspielhaus, declaring he would not direct in Germany
again, by 1999 he was back, successfully directing Anton
Hamik's grotesque peasant farce *The Bartered Grandfather* in
Munich.

In the late 1990s, Kroetz appeared to find a new lease of
creative life, with plays that combined formal innovation
with a return to themes and motifs of his early work, such as
The Native. Play for Grand Puppet Theater (1999) or represented

an entirely new departure, such as *The Griefcrazed*, written in
2001 at the height of the BSE panic and provocatively
melding racism, holocaust hypocrisy and the obsessive
concerns of animal lovers in a wild rant for a cast dressed as
eagles squatting on, and shitting from, a birdcage perch. In
2004 the trilogy *Haus Deutschland. Drei Stücke* was published,
suggesting that Kroetz's contribution to German drama is
far from over.

The plays

Stallerhof

More than any other play by Kroetz, *Stallerhof* (1972)
shaped its author's reputation, in Germany and
internationally. The first production at the Hamburg
Schauspielhaus in 1972 contained an iconic image,
reproduced throughout the German media from the
tabloids to the quality magazine *Der Spiegel* and still a staple
illustration for histories of the post-war German drama: at
the play's climax, on the sparse set between the straw bales,
the naked, silent Beppi (played by Eva Mattes, her career
launched by this role) half-innocently, half fearfully awaits
the carbolic-acid abortion her mother, Stallerin, has
threatened. Meanwhile Stallerin, through some
combination of religious or ethical scruples, cowardice, love
or humanity, abandons her abortion plans and, back bent in
the universal pose of peasant labour, begins scrubbing the
floor. This is one of many moments in the play where
negative and positive, pessimistic and optimistic, brutal and
tender, mingle in unresolved and thus dramatically
fascinating tension.

In the 1970s, the play's power to offend was considerable:
the premiere provoked scandals matching those over
Working at Home/ Stubborn the previous year, and in 1973, the
Tyrol teacher Agnes Larcher was dismissed from her school
for reading *Stallerhof* with her fourteen-year old female
pupils. At the same time, for audiences used to the

wordiness that was a characteristic common, for all their differences, to popular comedy, documentary drama and Brechtian political theatre, *Stallerhof*'s sparse dialogue punctuated with silences came almost as much as a shock as did its scenes of defecation, masturbation and explicit sex between Sepp, a farmhand in his late fifties, and the thirteen-year old, possibly mentally disabled Beppi. It was, though, some time before *Stallerhof*'s dramatic quality was recognised as lying not only in its shocking themes or even its author's aggressively uninhibited manner of portraying them, but also in its formal innovations and its precisely composed dialogues and scenic rhythms.

The first English-language production by David Mouchtar-Samorai at the Hampstead Bush Theatre in 1974, which transferred the play's language and milieu to a Northumbrian hill farm, propelled Kroetz onto the British theatre scene with comparable force. The production's stark power came at a cost: the play's positive impulses of resistance, humanity and tenderness were here so overshadowed by its negative images of nasty, brutish lives that many reviewers thought the abortion was in fact carried out, and several years later at least one critic assumed all of Kroetz's figures to be 'Bavarian peasants, inarticulate almost to the point of animality'.[23]

Stallerhof is sometimes translated as *Farmyard*. The German title refers to the farm of a couple whose surname Staller is itself inseparable from the cowshed, Stall, which represents their wealth, their profession and their fate. The play deploys what is potentially the plot of a popular romance: the forbidden love of farmhand and farmer's daughter. But where the romance might comfortably court its audience's approval by challenging a convention that in fact no longer has real social power, Kroetz goes much further. This is most obvious firstly in the age difference between Sepp and Beppi and the latter's possible disability; secondly in the very direct and sometimes – though, crucially, not always – brutal way the sexual relationship is represented; thirdly in the portrayal of topics either distasteful (diarrhoea) or taboo (masturbation). But it also applies to the stripping away of all bucolic traces from the staging and the language, which leave the audience no scope to enjoy the play as a rural entertainment.

However, more subtly, the play also challenges a second set of expectations, by not simply condemning the Sepp figure, by not simply denouncing Staller and his wife for the way their upbringing of Beppi has more impoverished than empowered her, and by insisting on the positive energies to be found in negative circumstances. Sepp and Beppi attempt, despite their disadvantages and the taboos on their relationship, to fulfil their needs for tenderness and self-realisation, and the play observes moments of awakening and self-assertion amidst the crushing blows dealt by deprivation. In Sepp, these energies are present in his halting attempts to entertain Beppi with tales which transparently convert his inferiority and object status into that of a superior, active subject, or with entertainments (visits to pub or fairground) whose would-be worldliness is part of their part-comic, part-pathetic demonstration of his limited horizons. Sepp's abuse of Beppi is a first, halting step out of apathy: helpless and misdirected, certainly, but undertaken. While objectively speaking Sepp's role in the relationship could, and today probably would, be construed as paedophile grooming as well as statutory rape, Kroetz challenges comfortable moral positions by refusing to condemn.

Beppi is shown from the beginning as having more real and potential ability, assertiveness, independence and eagerness to learn than is recognised by her parents, by Sepp or – to judge by many of the reviews of the early productions of the play – by critics. She is a victim, but not just a victim. The dramatically productive complexity of the Beppi figure is evident from the first scene, a masterpiece of exposition which, in barely two dozen lines, makes manifest in the microcosm of a nuclear family the socio-economic, linguistic, psychological and educational structures which determine and perpetuate behaviour and expectations. The scene also establishes the play's central dynamic – one frequently found in Kroetz's work – between apathy and resistance. Beppi attempts to read her aunt's postcard. Each error, some of which result demonstrably from the non-standard language she has learned from her parents, is greeted with a slap from her mother. Even when Beppi reads the card word-perfectly, Stallerin's response is not praise but an impatient order for her to return to her household tasks. Thus Beppi's awakening curiosity beats fruitlessly against the closed door of her parents' conviction of her backwardness and their own limited linguistic and socio-economic horizons.

Yet Beppi persists, her questions not yet choked by this response, despite the fact that we can, in this first scene, assume a pre-history of much the same treatment from her parents. Sepp is the driving force in, and must (since Kroetz is not arguing that Beppi 'leads him on') bear the responsibility for the sexual transgression. But Beppi, in her sexuality as in her life as a whole, begins to develop and express her own needs and desires: much, indeed, to the inexperienced Sepp's alarm. Awakened woman as sexual threat to man: a feminist critique of *Stallerhof* as of much of Kroetz's work can of course identify underlying motifs such as this as evidence of his perpetuation of gender stereotypes. But Kroetz is not condoning Sepp's actions in offering us the chance to understand them. Moreover, Sepp vanishes from the play at the end of the second act, while Beppi's experience is much more strongly foregounded as the play develops.

Staller and Stallerin are in one sense prisoners of their language, which reveals them to be hemmed in by the powerful social controls of the moral precepts both of religion and of the wider society, as well as the economic pressures of running a small farm at the time when the peasantry is in rapid decline (a theme Kroetz would return to in *Dead Soil* in 1985). But their dialogues, especially those where they lie in bed debating Beppi's future and the fate of Beppi's child, are not simply fatalistic: the pre-formed clichés that shape their consciousness and legitimate their actions are sometimes turned against themselves, in snatches of dialogue where one cliché is pitted against another until

an outcome emerges which supports the impulse the figure
had inchoately desired. Stallerin's decision not to abort
Beppi's child may be cowardice, or it may too be an
assertion of her natural humanity against the pressure of
social norms. This reversal of the original decision to abort
is explained neither to Beppi nor indeed to the audience, an
ambiguity sustained in the play's conclusion, the onset of
Beppi's labour. Responding to the figures' fates as though
they were real people, one must surely ask in what sense an
extra child will improve their lives? But read as a stage
metaphor, Beppi's birth pangs signify the onset of a better
world. Conflicting signals of this kind ensure the play's
lastingly productive irritation.

   Stallerhof's place in theatre historiography seems assured,
and its periodic stage revival (e.g. Düsseldorf 1988,
Hamburg 1997 or Vienna 2002, or combined with *Ghost
Train* into a single play, Munich 1985) has defied those
critics who thought it sensationalist, trivial, wilfully
pornographic, a tail-end product of 1960s iconoclasm. The
appearance of Gerd Kühr's opera *Stallerhof* (1988), with a
libretto by Kroetz employing inserts from Luther's bible
translation, even suggests the play is becoming a modern
classic. *Stallerhof*'s sociological accuracy had already been
questioned by critics in the 1970s, who saw it as an
anachronism in the age of modern farming and a Germany
integrated, down to its last backwater, in the media society.
Yet ironically, at that very time studies such as Jürgen
Roth's *Poverty in the Federal Republic* (1974) were suggesting
that this was not the case, in so far as they documented
significant rural poverty in 1970s West Germany despite
two and more decades of national prosperity. But of course
the play is not simply a social document; it is also an artistic
distillation of social and existential experience. Freed of the
tunnel vision that sees Kroetz's early work solely as social
realist studies of semi-rustic 'Randgruppen', one can also
recognise that a play like *Stallerhof* has certain affinities with
the world of Samuel Beckett (e.g. *Endgame*), in which figures
in extraordinarily reduced circumstances pluck human
warmth from the depths of despair. However, both the

surprising optimism and the formal innovativeness of
Stallerhof are partly cancelled out by the more social realist
plot and the pessimistic conclusion of its sequel *Ghost Train*,
in which Beppi fails in her attempt to create an independent
life for herself and her child, kills it and leaves it on a
fairground ghost train, closing the fatalistic circle by
returning the child's corpse to the place of its symbolic,
possibly actual conception.

Request Programme

Beneath the surface simplicity of *Request Programme*
(*Wunschkonzert*, 1971; sometimes translated as *Family
Favourites*), first performed in Stuttgart in 1973, lies a
fascinating formal ambivalence that (given that the play is
also very economical to produce!) has ensured it a lasting
place in the international repertoire. It is a one-woman play,
entirely without dialogue. Besides precise instructions about
the set, characters and duration, the play proper consists of
a half-dozen pages of detailed description of how Miss
Rasch, a 40–45 year old single office worker, returns home,
performs a multitude of everyday tasks such as eating,
washing, listening to a radio request programme, weaving a
tapestry and making her preparations for bed. Her pedantic
precision, a strategy to prevent her loneliness and despair
from surfacing, also serves to make them very clear to the
audience. Then, seemingly abruptly, she takes an overdose
of sleeping pills and the play ends, before it is certain
whether it was, in fact, a fatal dose.

The detailed instructions for the set, the call that 'stage
time should be real time' and the precise reconstruction of
Miss Rasch's activities on the evening which leads up to her
overdose, have led the play to be seen as an extreme
example of naturalism, reminiscent of the 'Sekundenstil' of
Naturalist writers Arno Holz and Johannes Schlaf, whose
The Selicke Family (1890) for example sought to copy the flow
of reality in minute detail.

If the replication of reality to which naturalism aspires is taken to extremes however, it begins to subvert itself, as in photo-realist painting. 'Sekundenstil', indeed, has been compared to slow-motion shots in film[24], an un-natural technique for drawing attention to the otherwise unnoticed, which is very much what Kroetz seeks to do in reconstructing Miss Rasch's evening. In the symbolically charged space of the stage, Miss Rasch's exactly re-enacted mundane activities become an artistic performance of the processes of repression manifested in them. Miss Rasch 'recognises (that is: acts out) the emptiness of her life'.[25] What we are seeing is not a slice of life, but its restatement as a compelling ritual and, in the silent but eloquent act of suicide, her verdict on it, like Beckett's *Krapp's Last Tape*.

Naturalism is, in the end, a literary style, its presence in a work not contingent on whether that work faithfully records real life at all. Kroetz presumably did not sit behind a peephole watching a woman's preparations for suicide, though he asks his audience to do so. His play is an imaginative feat, a speculative recreation of events, and Miss Rasch is no less a creation of her author than is the heroine of a melodrama.

From this perspective, even the set in *Request Programme* has a function beyond naturalist reproduction of reality, exemplifying Miss Rasch's intensive yet alienated relationship with her environment. Throughout, she interacts constantly with her room and its contents. The idyll of retreat and recuperation is also her antagonist, an agent in the drama, which perverts her behaviour into a neurotic subordination of self to an extreme norm of cleanliness and order.

There is a further inherent paradox in *Request Programme*: the more perfect the naturalistic replication of life on stage, the more one may forget to be moved emotionally or intellectually by the demonstrated states of affairs in favour of admiration for the tour-de-force of the performer. For without superb acting, this kind of play, with no dialogue, no obvious plot or interaction to carry one's interest, might be unwatchable. With superb acting, it transcends replication to become artistry. It has even been suggested that the play could become a famous 'Clownsnummer' in the tradition of the clown as grotesque mirror to the human condition.[26] At least once, *Request Programme* has been performed by an actress manipulating a puppet to act out Miss Rasch's story. Thus the seemingly straightforward naturalism of *Request Programme* can be seen to be complex: naturalistic and non-, even anti-naturalistic elements co-exist unresolved.

But, if not naturalistic, then surely *Request Programme* is, as many commentators have suggested, the logical extreme of the 'Sprachlosigkeit' supposedly suffered by the characters in Kroetz's plays of the early 1970s? The only words spoken are those of the radio disk jockey; Miss Rasch is silent throughout. But to call this the extreme of 'Sprachlosigkeit' is a misconception. Inarticulacy can only be represented by showing characters interacting in situations where communication might be expected to take place but does not. It is dialogue, not silence, in which we hear the death rattle of language.

Miss Rasch's problem is not linguistic poverty but the lack of anybody to talk to, not even the budgerigar which acts as a silent conversational partner in *Prospects...* or the dramaturgically equivalent gurgling baby in *Reise ins Glück* (*Journey to Happiness*, 1976). Her silence, in the isolation of her home, might be the fate of a perfectly articulate, educated person; on the linguistic level it has little to do with the fate of Willy and Martha in *Working at Home* or Sepp and Beppi in *Stallerhof*.

There is a link, nonetheless, between *Request Programme* and Kroetz's other plays of the period. It is established in Kroetz's own interpretative preface. Written in 1971, the year before he joined the German Communist Party, it confirms his hardening anti-capitalist stance, the desire for change to those social and political circumstances that his early plays describe but cannot escape. *Request Programme*, the preface states, is Kroetz's interpretation of police reports of the often 'incredible tidiness' of the environment in which suicides take place. In capitalist society, exploitation creates an explosive potential which, turned against the exploiters, would produce a situation 'ripe for revolution'. But instead, the exploited have been socialised to respond with obsessive orderliness and acquiescence. The explosive potential is thus turned inwards on the exploited themselves and their fellows, resulting in unobtrusive, senseless suicides and murders, after which the survivors deliver themselves up 'to the jurisdiction of their natural enemies'. They thus help to regulate and cleanse the society that, by their actions, they implicitly accuse.

This indictment is fired by a vague, if passionate, humanitarian anti-capitalism. Applied literally to *Request Programme*'s white-collar heroine, terms like 'the slavery of labour' and 'beasts of burden' sound anachronistic and comically out of proportion. But understood allegorically, Miss Rasch's pedantic precision, her silence and her moment of rebellion do represent the processes Kroetz's preface describes. The suicide attempt is accompanied by her first disorderly act, wiping away the spilt wine with the sleeve of her dressing gown. But this first act of rebellion, the suicide, is also its own suppression: she is the fourth piece of dirt, after those on her coat, her windowsill and her face, which she expunges from the sterile world whose order she has self-destructively internalised.

Though in its form a one-off experiment, *Request Programme* provides a link between the second and third phases of Kroetz's work. With considerable empathy for the plight of the lonely and the unwanted, Kroetz has written a moving, voyeuristically uncomfortable, for some critics overly deterministic reminder of the fate of yet another 'submerged' group in society, who are marginalised though not marginal. It is not just the outsiders who are oppressed. Miss Rasch is a respectable clerical worker whose standards of order and hygiene suggest bourgeois aspirations (not that any of Kroetz's characters drown in low-life squalor, in fact). She is an outsider not in a conventional sense but because she is isolated in a society which has no use for her outside the workplace. Like a disconnected machine – here too her silence has metaphoric significance – she is being restored, in common with millions of other workers, to full productive

capacity ready for the following day. As Kroetz asserts
rather clumsily in his preface, and shows in subsequent
plays, such as *Tom Fool*, where Otto Meier refers explicitly to
his own leisure time as that of a switched-off machine, the
process of alienation in industrial capitalism afflicts this
society's average, integrated members as much as it does the
marginal outsiders. This is the central theme of the
'Kleinbürger' plays that dominated his work in the middle
and latter 1970s.

The Nest

'Since roughly autumn 1971 I have been unhappy about the
extreme nature of my plays', remarked Kroetz in February
1973, arguing that precisely their shock effect had obscured
his criticism of more general social ills. As a newly fledged
Communist, he was eager to demonstrate that commitment
to the interests of the masses was more important than
radical formal experiment. He would thus concern himself
with the 'Durchschnitt', the average members of West
German society and their problems. (WA 586–7) The
results can be seen in his plays from roughly 1972–1980,
from *Upper Austria* through *The Nest*, *Tom Fool* and *Sturdy
Max*, to *Neither Fish nor Fowl*, with their relatively prosperous
working class figures, the increasingly articulate language
with which these figures engage with their problems, and
the construction of plots with broadly more positive
outcomes. By the end of this series of plays, Kroetz was
tiring of this 'Wohnküchen-Gasherd-Realismus' (best
translated as 'domestic realism', since 'kitchen-sink-drama'
suggests a milieu closer to that of his earlier plays), and
Neither Fish nor Fowl represents the moment of transition to a
phase of more experimental aesthetics in the 1980s.

Kroetz's is a cumulative theatre, his plays not just a
procession but a process. A given play will take issue with,
develop or contradict the positions of previous ones. Thus
Upper Austria waves a decisive goodbye to the inward-
turning, self-mutilating violence of the previous plays. Anni's

pregnancy and Heinz's loss of his licence for drunk driving
are twin threats to the couple's fragile prosperity. But they
are better able to articulate and so to overcome the
relationship crisis this provokes, and decide against an
abortion, even at the cost of a radical reduction in their
standard of living. In doing so, they take a first modest step
towards self-determination.

But *Upper Austria*, while a radical departure for Kroetz,
actually champions distinctly conservative values, pleading
for reduced consumption so as to make the contradictions of
capitalism more bearable. The 'Happy-End', with Heinz
picking out a waltz on his accordion, church-mouse-poor
but content, since his firm has found him another job while
he sits out his driving ban, propagates an odd moral for a
communist playwright: frugality and an understanding
employer as path to contentment.

As though taking up the debate at this very point, *The
Nest*, first performed at the Modernes Theater, Munich, in
1975, opens with another very similar couple, Kurt and his
pregnant wife Martha, watching the end of a television
broadcast of *Upper Austria*, and rejecting it as 'not like real
life'. Kurt, a lorry driver with an HGV licence a class better
than Heinz's, calls Heinz 'not normal' for even considering
an abortion. The nest of the title, the idyll Kurt has built for
his family, depends on the shaky basis of his extensive
overtime and therefore on Kurt's forelock-tugging attitude
to his employer, the latter's whim, and the state of the
economy. It is also defined by the self-satisfied isolation in
which Kurt and Martha live. Howling sirens outside do not
prompt concern for the welfare of others, but increase the
cosiness of their nest; they enjoy their allotment the more
because not everyone has one; their 'corner of paradise', the
lake where they sunbathe, is special because supposedly
secret: dangerous illusions which make them vulnerable to
events through which the wider world penetrates and
threatens to destroy the idyll.

The underlying socio-economic analysis has a somewhat
schematic Marxist basis: both Kurt, who fails to see the
connection between his sixty-three-hour weeks and his

boss's new luxury car, and Martha, who is exploited as a 'Heimarbeiterin' making neckties, create surplus value for the owners of the means of production. Consumer capitalism creates inherently destructive contradictions, and even those like Kurt who identify with its values cannot fulfil the expectations it awakes without dehumanising and endangering themselves and their families.

Kurt's breadwinner identity is founded on maximum fulfilment of the consumer values he and Martha have internalised. A key scene refers back to that one in *Upper Austria* where Heinz and Anni 'pass a verdict on the child' by calculating whether they can afford it. For Kurt and Martha this is never in doubt, but in a skilful extraction of dramatic interest from the banal minutiae of the prices of baby clothing and equipment, Kroetz shows them mortgaging their as yet unborn child's future. They calculate 'what we need for the little one to welcome it to the world, as they say', interpreting this welcome in terms of material goods. Martha's appended 'as they say' shows that the welcome is not hers but one constructed by marketing discourse. Increased articulacy, accompanied by relative prosperity, makes the figures of the 'Kleinbürger' plays more, not less, vulnerable to this particular loss of autonomy.

Thus Martha, unconscious of the mechanisms whereby she takes these needs to be her own, but conscious of how to fulfil them, manipulates Kurt into approving one expensive and unnecessary purchase after another, until the sum committed is one it will take months of overtime to pay off. This leads, inevitably, to the literal poisoning of the deceptive idyll Kurt and Martha have constructed: after the birth, Kurt is offered a 'special mission' by his boss, and dumps what is supposedly 'bad wine', in fact poisonous chemicals, in the lake. When Martha bathes baby Stefan in their 'corner of paradise' he is near-fatally burned.

This however sets the process in motion from which change and moral growth emerges. Martha, blind at this moment of maternal trauma to her own contribution to the pressures which led Kurt to the fateful act, bitterly rejects him as a creature of his employer, an 'organ grinder's monkey', a monster who would put money before his child's life. This stings Kurt into a painful process of self-recognition, and he comes to recognise how much he and Martha have been the unthinking objects of social forces. 'How far does it have to go, before something inside, for once, says "no"?' Kurt reports himself to the police and confronts his employer, who scorns him as a 'Würstl', a 'poor little sod'. The once self-satisfied Kurt now knows this to be true in capitalist society, but precisely at this point when his boss's affable mask drops, Kurt becomes less of a 'Würstl', because he is asserting himself. The human being degraded to object is thus here given the possibility of regaining capacity for action and so of becoming a self-determining subject.

The final scene returns to the allotment. Kurt's resolve is unbroken, and he has decided to convert an initially defensive white lie – telling his employer that he had support behind him – into truth by taking up contact with the trade union he had previously shunned: 'Kurt (quietly, hesitantly) In the union you are not alone.' [The stage direction, missing from the translation here, is crucial]. Of course, Kurt is drawn to the union more for reasons of self-preservation rather than political conviction or solidarity. But that would be consonant with Kroetz's goal in his 'Kleinbürger' plays of showing small, plausible steps from a wholly apolitical towards a political consciousness, rather than indulging in the pathos of grand political slogans or gestures.

In any case, the question of union membership is hardly the play's principal theme. The play's final words return to the idea of 'Ordnung', rule-bound orderliness, the other determinant of the false idyll in which Kurt and Martha live before the accident. In the first allotment scene in Act One, the thought of the as yet unborn child trampling the tiny and immaculate garden fills Kurt with anxiety. The garden is the social order in miniature, and Kurt's sincere desire to provide the child with a loving and supportive environment conflicts with the 'Ordnung' he has internalised. Martha objects to his suggestion that they build fences round the flowerbeds: 'a child should keep to the rules ['natürliche Ordnung', natural order, in the original], not just a fence. Then it will be easier for him later in life.' In precisely her appeal to the 'natural', Martha is pleading for early socialisation to obedient conformity and the internalisation of an unreflected social order (flower beds are hardly 'natural'). Mental fences, being invisible, are doubly effective. When, at the play's conclusion, Martha draws attention to Stefan trampling the flowerbeds, Kurt's response is now 'Let him be.' With his sense of self now secured by his newfound moral courage, he does not need to adhere blindly to the unnatural 'natural order'.

Alongside its plea for social solidarity, *The Nest* is thus an argument that individual moral fortitude, though it will not overthrow the system or usher in utopia, can at least produce a satisfyingly optimistic conclusion. This may seem a surprising verdict from a playwright who was a Communist at the time. But here as elsewhere Kroetz seems to combine a Christian moral concern for the individual and his moral integrity – his soul, indeed – with a Marxist analysis of social mechanisms and contradictions and their influence on individual behaviour.

A serious dramaturgical weakness of *The Nest* may seem to lie in the pivotal scene in which Kurt dumps the chemicals in the lake into which, immediately afterwards, Martha dunks the baby. Is it wise to tie a plot to such a mechanical coincidence? This is less fatal to the play if one understands it as an allegory. No man is an island, there can be no truly secure individualistic idyll in the midst of society, and the threat to such an idyll grows as the efforts to preserve it are intensified. The unthinking pursuit of material gain will have fateful results. Sins against the environment return to punish the sinners. Blind servility in the interests of material self-betterment will backfire on that self-betterment. Kroetz shows in parable form how humanity – here, specifically, and in a very conventional pattern, how man, with woman goading him on – produces his environment, ecologically, morally, politically.

However, Kurt and Martha must also be credible as psychologically real characters. Audience identification of some sort with Kurt is necessary for the learning process he undergoes to strike a chord in the observer. Can psychological realism and allegory co-exist unresolved in a single play? Indeed, can one send an actor repeatedly tottering across stage with an oil-drum, as *The Nest*'s stage directions require, without giving an audience the giggles? This certainly was the play's downfall at its British premiere at the Crucible Theatre, Sheffield, in 1980.

What is unquestionably the case is that *The Nest*, while extremely critical of the false consciousness of the average 'Kleinbürger', is also substantially optimistic about their capacity to change. In contrast to Kroetz's earlier plays, the catastrophe does not expose helplessness but catalyses improvement. The characters are still the product of their socio-political environment, but they do not have to be its victims. Is Kroetz's return, essentially, to a Kantian ideal, his handing back to the individual the capacity to regain moral integrity and the power of self-determined action, an unrealistic, anachronistic step, contradicted by the real developments of the contemporary world around him?

Tom Fool

The optimism of *The Nest* is virtually unique in Kroetz's work. His later plays do not, any more than the earlier ones, share its morality play character. After *The Nest*, Kroetz's humanism gains dialectic subtlety (before, as the 1980s progress, appearing to enter profound crisis): he now shows that the step out of object existence not only brings the awakening of consciousness and the beginning of self-determination, but also lays bare the painful conflicts between individual and social existence, conflicts which the progress from object to subject may intensify rather than dissolve. The first result of this development in his work was *Tom Fool* (*Mensch Meier*), given its German premiere at four theatres simultaneously in 1978, after the world premiere had taken place almost unannounced in a small Brazilian provincial town.

The German everyman Otto Meier is plagued by his dissatisfaction with his identity, or lack of it, as an assembly-line worker, exacerbated by rationalisation processes in which workers two or three stages down the line, familiar faces with whom he has rarely spoken, seem to disappear with barely a hiccup in the factory's rhythm. From this acute crisis of self-worth stem success fantasies (in which the romantic dream of flying is distorted by Otto's internalisation of hierarchic social values into a dream of owning a model plane factory) and his refusal to let his teenage son Ludwig take a manual job like himself. Instead, the unemployed Ludwig becomes the target for the aggressions and insecurities Otto accumulates at work, which also shape his sexual relationship to his wife Martha.

This eventually destroys the family in a series of scenes in which Otto humiliates first Ludwig, by making him strip naked in front of his parents, and then Martha, by treating her as his skivvy and the all-purpose receptacle and compensation mechanism for his emotional and physical needs. Martha leaves, echoing exactly another Martha's words on leaving her husband Willi in *Working at Home*. But whereas after Willi has murdered the child that is the cause of the rift between them, his wife returns, thus restoring, fundamentally unchanged, the fateful order of things, Martha Meier builds her own separate existence. Like Ludwig, who also leaves and becomes a bricklayer, Martha grows by asserting herself, and within her modest possibilities, begins to determine her own future. Kroetz does not romanticise this act of female self-assertion: Martha's life in a grim bed-sit on the wages of a shoe saleswoman, like Ludwig's in a labourers' hostel, is materially comparable to that lived by many of the figures in the early plays. But they represent first steps in and towards freedom.

Otto in contrast remains enmeshed in brooding fantasies, convinced that his real self is straitjacketed by his socio-economic status, yet unable to act to free it. A masturbation scene recalls Sepp's helpless isolation in *Stallerhof.* The diary entries Otto makes in the hope of winning Martha back with evidence of his reformed personality, unlike those of yet another Martha in *Through the Leaves,* reveal only his entrapment in further success fantasies. Life without the prospect of escape from a working-class identity he rejects seems senseless: 'Before you begin, it's all over.' This echoes the 'Born astride a grave' speech in *Waiting for Godot,* but Otto draws this conclusion from the alienation of his specific material existence as an assembly-line worker, the sensation of being little more than a human robot. In a fantasy version of the game show 'What's My Line?' he imagines himself to be first 'an arsehole' and then, since his work-created identity emanates from repetitively screwing sixteen screws into the same holes in a succession of cars he'll never be able to buy, 'a car-screw in-screwer, a screw-screwer – a screwologist', indeed a human screwdriver selectively bred with fingers fused and enlarged for optimum functioning.

Thus though the play ends with the appeal that Otto should 'learn' just as Martha and Ludwig have begun to do, with a glimpse of psychological and spiritual enlightenment via small but existentially significant steps, the potentially facile optimism of *Das Nest* is replaced by a much more ambivalent one, an unresolved tension between Martha's and Ludwig's small and painful acts of liberation and Otto's still much more helpless state. While the English title *Tom Fool* is more tendentiously critical than the more neutral German everyman label suggested by *Mensch Meier* and the many moments of audience identification offered by the Otto Meier figure, the title *Tom Fool* does encapsulate the accumulating sense in Kroetz's plays of his male characters' socio-economic, psychological and existential crises as crises of masculinity, in a world where both changing perceptions of gender roles and changing types and patterns of work are removing crucial props to male identity. This theme recurs in *Sturdy Max,* in *Neither Fish nor Fowl,* in *Fear and Hope in the FRG,* and becomes the central factor in the return to a radical, provocative dramaturgy in *Desire.*

Through the Leaves

Through the Leaves (*Wer durchs Laub geht . . .*, premiered in
Marburg in 1981) is Kroetz's third version, after *One Man,
one Dictionary* (*Ein Mann, ein Wörterbuch*, 1973) of his early play
Men's Business. In *Men's Business*, the factory worker Otto
compensates for his inferiority complex within his
relationship with Martha, the independent owner of a small
business (a pet-food butchers), by chauvinist strutting and
sometimes brutal insults. 'You're not much to look at, but
you're hot for it', he remarks during intercourse. He resists
Martha's attempts to translate the sexual relationship into
an emotional commitment by insisting on meeting at the
shop, not at her house, and by accusing her of having a
sexual relationship with her dog. This edgy mixture of
affection and aggression, lust and disgust culminates in a
black comic 'Metsch' in which Otto and Martha take pot
shots at each other at close range. Neither is willing to leave
the field to the other, and they pass the gun to and fro until
both topple to the ground.

Men's Business typifies the social realism with which the
early Kroetz was identified: grim milieu, sparse, aggressive
dialogue, and sordid acts of intercourse. But it also disrupts
expectations. Firstly, the shoot-out scene pushes social
realism over the edge into a surreal allegory of the battle of
the sexes. Secondly, if one looks more closely, one notes that
both Otto and Martha earn respectable incomes; it is not
straitened socio-economic circumstances, but Otto's
recourse, when defining and defending his masculinity, to
crude yardsticks of economic and sexual superiority as a
reaction to his deep sense of threat by Martha's
independence, which render any material or emotional
partnership impossible.

Where, though, in *Men's Business* this possibility never
even begins to materialise, *Through the Leaves* gives the
figures, especially Martha, much greater scope to
understand and engage with their world as active subjects.
The dialogue shows both Otto and Martha better able to
articulate their emotions, reflect on their experiences, and

understand their social situation. Yet there are huge and crucial differences in how the author has rewritten the female and the male roles.

Martha's increased capacity for self-awareness as a reflecting subject is demonstrated and expressed through the diary she keeps. This had featured briefly in the first scene of *Men's Business* but is now, in *Through the Leaves*, a central element in the dramatic structure, adding a completely new dimension to the way the characters are portrayed. Where in *Men's Business* and so many other of Kroetz's early plays, communication breakdown was characteristically marked and followed by a silence, in *Through the Leaves* it is often followed by a diary entry in which Martha historicises the event and interprets it for herself. The entries reveal the dignified patience with which she responds to and interprets Otto's helpless aggression. In dramaturgical terms, this is a two-edged sword: it enriches the figure of Martha and varies the rhythm and perspective of the drama, but also, arguably, sentimentalises it (especially, perhaps, the ending) and risks didacticism.

The Otto figure has changed significantly less. As in *Men's Business*, he still compensates for the insecurity Martha's independence awakes in him, by acting boorishly, sulking, or claiming superior worldliness, whether over the difference between German and Russian caviar or over sexual practices. His knowledge, though, is second-hand. When Martha settles down to write, practising the active development of her human subjectivity through recording and reflecting on her experience, Otto pulls a porn magazine from his briefcase. Thus he remains, as in *Men's Business*, a passive participant in the determination and perpetuation of his masculine self-image. Threatened by the discursive power of the diary, he rejects it nervously as 'rubbish'. He is as defensively aggressive as in *Men's Business*, though the brutal harshness of the language with which he tries to put Martha in her place has softened, and, perhaps more importantly, she fights back.

However, even though Otto still remains effectively trapped in his rigid defence of a masculinity under threat, the black comic shoot-out no longer takes place. The play now ends with Martha, alone, reading a series of diary entries over a three-month period during which Otto, finally frightened off by the threat the relationship poses to his self-image and his fear of emotional entanglement, has not reappeared. The final entry is 'Very alone. Longing Full stop.' For critics of Kroetz's move, in the latter 1970s, to the creation of characters whose situation is less extreme and whose ability to verbalise their feelings is more developed, the potential sentimentality of such an ending is symptomatic of fatal artistic compromises. For others, the greater insight into, and sympathy for, Martha's situation which the revisions in *Through the Leaves* bring, makes the failure of the relationship far more poignant and the play less cheaply sensational and much more complex. In the first British production, at the Traverse Theatre Edinburgh in 1985, Eileen Nicholas as Martha brought out the role's full potential for a demonstration of warmth, patience and dignity as acts of resistance to the truculent brutality of Otto.

Desire

Interwoven with the sometimes didactic, but more often tentative exploration of processes of emancipation and enlightenment, steps from passive object existence to active subjectivity, Kroetz's plays have also always reflected gender tensions, men's and women's disappointment, particularly sexual disappointment, with each other. Though muted in his 'Kleinbürger' plays, this has subsequently become both more explicit and more intense. As he has imbued his stage characters with greater powers of insight and expression, they have not only acted out, but also all the more powerfully vocalised their desire, their disillusion and their disgust. This reaches a peak in *Der Drang* (*Desire*, 1994), Kroetz's radical revision of his early drama *Dear Fritz*. He retains the setting, a florists' business, and the constellation of figures: the owners Otto and Martha, their assistant

Mitzi, and Martha's brother Fritz, recently released from a
prison sentence for exhibitionism. But Kroetz recombines
and distils these elements into a seething hell of desperation,
aggression and bitterness, that in its picture of the
interrelationships of sexuality, gender, power and emotional
needs is one of the densest and most subtle, yet also most
drastic and certainly most savagely comic of his works.

It is, emphatically, a sex comedy, based on the eternal
tensions between familiarity and novelty, age and youth,
freedom and constraint, attraction and repulsion, reason
and folly, the blinding power of sexual desire and the bitter
aftermath of its decline. Otto's sexual frustration, born of
boredom within his marriage to Hilde and of her lack of
sexual initiative or interest, boils over when Fritz's presence
continually reminds him that Fritz's transgression consisted
of doing what he desired. Ashamed to admit the banality of
his exhibitionist tendencies to Mitzi, Fritz pretends to be a
vicious sadist, but cannot respond accordingly to her
advances. Otto though throws himself at Mitzi, the thrill of
transgression multiplied by knowing that she had tried and
failed to live out her masochistic desires with Fritz. The
relationship is explosively carnal, and Mitzi, after herself
being angered and humiliated by Fritz's rejection (or rather,
his willingness to offer friendship but not desire), queens it
over the humiliated Hilde in turn. But Hilde fights for her
marriage despite every indignity, begs and then assaults
Mitzi, and wins Otto back by offering him the sexual
pleasures which, when previously refused had driven him
into Mitzi's arms. Moreover, being married to Otto, a
conformist for all he desires temporary transgression, Hilde
holds the stronger hand. 'Ordnung', that key value of the
'Kleinbürger', is reinstated. With the extramarital passion
spent, Mitzi is no longer a threat to Hilde nor a distraction
to Otto, and her economic value as an experienced (and
probably underpaid) worker outweighs her sexual currency.
The play closes with the three variously scarred survivors
saying goodbye to the departing Fritz and returning to
work.

Apart from Fritz, whose language is as cautious and

circumspect as the controlled way he tries to live his life, the
figures communicate with the directness of a blacksmith's
hammer. Sex, especially anal intercourse, is demanded and
offered to express, gain or confirm power. The verbal and
physical humiliations are more brutal than in any Kroetz
play hitherto: Otto, referring to his wife, in front of her,
Mitzi and Fritz, declares at one point, 'Even shitting's more
fun than fucking her. At least I've got the paper to read.' Yet
unlike the silent misery of the scene in *Stallerhof* where Sepp
masturbates in the toilet, they provoke the involuntary,
discomforted laughter that arises when comedy targets sites
of social unease. Moreover, repeatedly a verbal assault is
followed by a reconciliatory gesture or utterance, half
manipulative, half genuine. These rhythms in the dialogue
and the relationships are superbly controlled.

That Fritz, the one who has been least active in this
sexual maelstrom, is the one who has to leave, is the play's
central irony: the one figure who has learned, through bitter
experience in prison, to control his desires, is the sexual
catalyst who must be removed from the equation. In a key
scene (Act Three, Scene Eight), Otto reveals his envy for
what he believes is Fritz's self-control as a result of less
complicated sexual circumstances: 'You pick on some
woman, scare the shit out of her, jerk off in front of her,
then melt away on your trusty steed in a cloud of dust.' He
longs for a comparably clear link between desire and
fulfilment. Fritz insists that his sexual orientation does not
make him a raging furnace of lust; the criminal pervert turns
out to be a cool, rational being, rejecting Otto's fatalistic
nature metaphors by insisting that humans have a choice,
and do not, like plants, have roots. Instead, Fritz argues that
a human being can reconstruct himself: 'Even with plants
you can graft one thing on to another [. . .] /Otto: But it's
not in nature's scheme of things. /Fritz: Bugger that.
Nature's one thing, I'm something else.' This self-control
and autonomy have, though, been bought at the cost
of emotional relationships. Fritz is and will remain an
outsider. He thus leaves partly because his presence is a
sexual provocation, in that it unleashes the repressed sexual

fantasies of the other figures, partly because he himself
wishes to avoid the emotional ties that too long and too
close a contact would bring. The closing tableau thus
contrasts the crazed, humiliated, but living triangular
relationship of Otto, Hilde and Mitzi with Fritz, the
melancholy singleton: three's company, four's a crowd.

   Desire is a deceptive play. Some critics see it as a partial
return to 'the less critical, more entertaining "Volksstück"
tradition' with what Brecht called its 'vulgar japes, mixed
with sentimentality, its crude morality and cheap
sexuality'.[27] But *Desire* is surely much more than that, an
exploration of aspects of the human condition which distils
its author's skill for powerful dialogue crafted out of a
mixture of the everyday and the artistic, the banal and the
intense, into a single savage yet melancholy comedy.

'There was a time when I was not', writes Anton
Kreuzberger, wheelchair-bound narrator of Kroetz's novel
The Moonshine Lad. 'But I will have no more fear. I want to
have existed, before I lie like a lump of meat. I want to
gouge my story into their skin until the slate pencil is bloody.
I want.'[28] Crippled by polio, disinherited by his farmer
father as a consequence, Anton suffers all the prejudice,
rejection and social marginalisation disability often brings
along with its physical miseries. He battles to fulfil his
emotional and sexual needs and to make his way through
life as a typesetter and a trade union activist. He is fated
never to win, but will never give up. Almost daily, and both
intellectually and viscerally, he learns that identity is
constantly threatened, but can, through individual and
collective resistance, be constantly reasserted.

   The six plays in this volume make an important
representative selection of Kroetz's plays available to the
English-speaking reader. Taken collectively, they exemplify
how his work explores the tension between socially
grounded and existentially rooted suffering, between
resignation and resistance, between pessimism and optimism
about the human condition and its possible betterment.
Kroetz's remarkable and sustained achievement has been to

create a whole series of memorable figures, memorable stories out of sometimes marginalised, but more often ordinary lives, and, in his alter ego Anton Kreuzberger's characteristically drastic metaphor, to gouge these stories into the skin of his audience. That is what makes his work worth engaging with, on the page and on the stage.

Moray McGowan
Trinity College Dublin

References

1 Kroetz, quoted on the cover of his novel *Der Mondscheinknecht* (*The Moonshine Lad*), Frankfurt: Suhrkamp 1981.

2 In a conversation with the present author on 16.7.1976; quoted in Moray McGowan: 'Sprache, Gewalt und Gesellschaft. Franz Xaver Kroetz und die sozialrealistischen Dramatiker des englischen Theaters', *text+ kritik* 57 (1978), pp. 37–48; here p. 38.

3 References to Otto F.Riewoldt (ed.): *Franz Xaver Kroetz*, Frankfurt/Main 1985, will be identified by FXK and page number in the text.

4 Harald Burger and Peter von Matt 'Dramatischer Dialog und restringiertes Sprechen. Franz Xaver Kroetz in linguistischer und literaturwissenschaftlicher Sicht', *Zeitschrift für germanistische Linguistik* (1974), 2, pp. 269–298, here p. 270.

5 References to Franz Xaver Kroetz: *Gesammelte Stücke*, Frankfurt/Main: Suhrkamp 1975 will be identified by GS and page number in the text.

6 *Theater 1972* [yearbook of the journal *Theater heute*], Velber 1972, p. 65.

7 See Anne Betten: *Sprachrealismus im deutschen Drama der siebziger Jahre*, Heidelberg 1985, pp. 218–90; Ernst Hess-Lüttich: 'Neorealismus und sprachliche Wirklichkeit', in FXK 297–318.

8 C.D. Innes: *Modern German Drama*, Cambridge 1979, p. 232.

9 'Ich kann nur schreiben von dem, was ich sehe', Interview with Donna Hoffmeister, *Modern Language Studies* 11, 1 (1980/81), 45.

10 'Rede an den Wiener Literaturtagen', 1980, unpublished manuscript.

11 'Ich schreibe nicht über Dinge, die ich verachte', *Theater heute* 21 (1980), 7, pp. 18–19.

12 Quoted in John Willett: *Expressionism*, London 1970, p. 100.

13 Franz Xaver Kroetz: *Furcht und Hoffnung der BRD*, Frankfurt 1984, p. 260.

14 See Moray McGowan: ' "Die Stadt ist der Metzger": The Crisis of Bavarian Peasant Identity in Franz Xaver Kroetz's Bauern sterben', *German Studies Review* 19, 1 (February 1996), pp. 29–40.

15 References to Franz Xaver Kroetz: *Ende der Paarung. Neue Stücke 2*, Hamburg 2002, identified in the text by EdP and page number.

16 Ingeborg C. Walther: *The Theater of Franz Xaver Kroetz*, New York, Bern, Frankfurt/Main, Paris 1990, p. 213.

17 The most detailed study of Kroetz's biographical background is to be found in: Richard W. Blevins: *Franz Xaver Kroetz: The Emergence of a Political Playwright*, New York, Berne & Frankfurt 1983.

18 Quoted in Rolf-Peter Carl: *Franz Xaver Kroetz*, Munich 1978, p. 8.

19 'Subventionssauerei', *Neues Forum* 229 (February 1973), p. 58–59.

20 'Zur Diskussion: Beiträge vom Bonner Parteitag der DKP: Franz Xaver Kroetz', *kürbiskern* 1976, 3, pp. 163–6.

21 References to Franz Xaver Kroetz: *Weitere Aussichten . . . Ein Lesebuch*, Cologne 1977, will be identified in the text by WA and page number.

22 'Ich habe immer nur von mir geschrieben', *Theater 1985* [yearbook of the journal *Theater heute*], Velber 1985, pp. 72–87, here p. 78.

23 Martin Esslin: 'In the mouths of the speechless', *TLS* (7 October 1977), p. 1163.

24 Otto Best: *Handbuch literarischer Fachbegriffe*, Frankfurt 1973, p. 249.

25 Heinz Ludwig Arnold, 'Franz Xaver Kroetz' in H.L. Arnold (ed.): *Kritisches Lexikon zur deutschsprachigen Gegenwartsliteratur*, Munich 1978.

26 Gerd Jäger, 'Selbstmord?', *Theater heute* 14 (1973), 4, p. 56.

27 Michelle Mattson, in what is otherwise one of the very best books on Kroetz's work: *Franz Xaver Kroetz. The*

Construction of a Political Aesthetic, Oxford & Washington, DC: Berg 1996, p. 198.

29 *Der Mondscheinknecht*, Frankfurt/Main 1981, p. 7.

Stallerhof

Translated by
Katharina Hehn

Characters

Staller
Stallerin, *his wife*
Beppi
Sepp
A dog

Set

Sparse. Moveable props. Same set for each act. Bright light. Lights are dimmed only at the end of each act.

Note

A dog is an essential part of the action. This should be handled as follows: in Act One, Scene Six, the dog is alone on stage with Sepp. At other times, its presence is sometimes desirable but not essential. As the dog's behaviour cannot be built into the dialogue, the direction must allow some improvisation.

The dialect

The dialect spoken is Bavarian. Beyond South Germany, its tone and grammar above all can be imitated, but the language itself must then be regarded as an artificial one.

The pauses

The play is set in a rural milieu. Its clarity and intelligibility depend above all on strictly observing the indicated pauses.

Act One

Scene One

Room. **Stallerin** *is cooking.* **Beppi** *holds a picture postcard.*

Stallerin From your godmother, in Munich. Read it.

Beppi Auntie Hilda.

Stallerin Written to you as she's thinking of you.

Beppi Where is – ?

Stallerin Never mind, read.

Beppi (*reading*) My . . . my . . . dear Beppi. (*Smiles.*) Soon me'll come . . .

Stallerin (*strikes her*) What does it say?

Beppi Soon we . . . we'll come and visit you (*smiles*) . . . if me . . .

Stallerin (*as above*) Not again. Keep your eyes open.

Beppi . . . we . . . (*Uncertain.*)

Stallerin What letter is that? (*Writes in the air.*)

Beppi t-t-t –

Stallerin All right then.

Beppi . . . if me . . . we have t – time. (*Short pause, then quickly.*) Your godmother Auntie Hilda.

Stallerin Right. Now you know. (*Turns to her work again.*)

Beppi (*looks for a long time at the picture on the card, then turns it over, reads it again, slowly, without mistakes*) Dear Beppi. Soon we'll come and visit you, if we have time. Your godmother Auntie Hilda!

Stallerin Dry the dishes.

Scene Two

Beppi *and* **Sepp** *work in the stable.*

Sepp   And then they welcomed the Captain and said
(*pause*) he should pick out a woman. (*Pause.*) And he didn't
want to. – And then the Indian he was friendly with, the one
who understood the Indians' language said (*Pause.*) if he
didn't choose one, the Chief would be insulted, so he went
to their camp (*Pause.*) and they showed him all the women.
None of them pleased him (*Pause.*) as they all had such
strange faces, but finally he saw one he did like. – But the
Indian Chief told him (*Pause.*) she was expelled from the
tribe and no one could touch her, because he would fall sick.
(*Pause.*) But he said, it's her or no one and went up and
embraced her. (*Pause.*) The Indians ran off in all directions
and said he'd now die immediately as he'd touched her.
(*Long pause.*) But that was rubbish, just a superstition, and of
course he didn't die but went on to marry her. (*Pause.*) And
when the wedding night was over and they were both still
alive, the Indians realised (*Pause.*), that's to say, they thought
the 'white man' had supernatural powers and had broken
the evil spell. (*Pause.*) Then they all came and wanted him to
be their medicine man. But as he really was a doctor, he
became the first white man the Indians trusted and they let
him treat them. And then the woman he'd married told him
(*Pause.*) that the tribe planned revenge for an attack by the
whites (*Pause.*) and he talked to them and they made him
their envoy and he arranged a truce. That's what happened.

Pause.

Beppi   And then!

Scene Three

Sepp *Sitting on the loo, shitting – while masturbating.*

Scene Four

Room. Evening. **Sepp** *and* **Staller** *are at the table.* **Stallerin** *is cooking.* **Beppi** *plays with firewood.*

Sepp   I've never had any luck in life, that's what it is. Without luck, there's nothing you can do.

Pause.

Staller   They say you make your own luck.

Sepp   Not everyone.

Staller   Excuses.

Stallerin   If he says it, that's the way it is.

Sepp   Right – I know. I retire in six years, then my troubles are over. With any luck, I'll go sooner.

Staller   If I were you, I'd find a steady job.

Stallerin   But he says it's not that easy.

Pause.

Staller   We've got a boom economy.

Stallerin   Still . . .

Staller   You want work, you'll find it. Once harvest is over, he'll go and sign on till they find something for him. That's how it is.

Sepp   They say it's not easy to find me something permanent as I'm not young any more. That's how it is.

Staller   Just like the gypsies.

Sepp   I used to have a steady job.

Pause.

Or if I was in town, that would be better. But I'm not.

Staller   Still.

Sepp   Once I was on a farm ten times as big as yours. Freehold.

Staller   Then it was an estate.

Sepp   Exactly.

Pause.

Staller   And why'd you leave?

Sepp   I wanted to go into town.

Staller   Munich.

Sepp *nods.*

Staller   And how come you're here now?

Sepp   Hm, that's hard to say.

Staller (*to* **Beppi**)   Stop messing about with the firewood, it's for the fire.

Pause.

Staller   She's too old for dolls now.

Stallerin   Such a shame.

Sepp   She only wants to play.

Stallerin   No more playing, should do something useful.

Staller   She's backward.

Stallerin   You hear what your father says, you're backward. You don't make us happy.

Staller   Others at your age are already at college.

Stallerin   At your age, I was up on the mountain.

Sepp   That was then.

Stallerin   Alone on the mountain. Working all day, frightened at night. Once I nearly ran down again but I didn't dare.

Staller   Listen to that.

Stallerin   Give me the wood . . . the fire needs stoking. (*Takes the wood from* **Beppi**, *puts it on the fire.*)

Beppi   Not burn dolls.

Stallerin   Lay the table. Food's nearly ready.

Pause.

Sepp   If she can't see, that's terrible.

Stallerin   She can see, she's got glasses.

Staller   Her fourth pair – we get them free.

Stallerin   She could have anything, if she wasn't backward.

Sepp   I can still see without glasses. And read the paper.

Staller   None of us here has bad eyes, except her.

Pause. They start eating.

Beppi   There's a funfair.

Stallerin   Eat, don't prattle.

Scene Five

Evening in the stable. **Sepp** *and* **Beppi** *are watching cats play.*

Sepp   At night all cats are grey. (*Long pause.*) You see them, those two?

Beppi *nods.*

Sepp   Which is which?

Beppi *looks.* **Sepp** *smiles. Pause.*

Sepp   The one on the left is ginger and on the right is the other.

Beppi *nods.*

Sepp   You see. (*Pause.*) Everyone sees what the Lord God wants them to see. (*Pause.*) Now they're fighting, see?

Beppi *nods.*

Sepp   You see everything.

Pause.

Beppi   Not now.

Sepp   It's over. Now it starts. Now he goes after her, see? (*Pause.*) Watch. If she lets him, it's her own fault. It's only a year old, that cat, isn't it?

Beppi *nods.*

Pause.

Sepp   To be young is to be wanted. – I can't stand the young. (*Laughs.*)

Pause.

Scene Six

Evening. **Sepp** *in his room with his dog, which is feeding.*

Sepp (*watches it*)   Now eat up. (*Pause.*) You don't like it? (*Pause.*) Got nothing else. (*Pause.*) If I had, you wouldn't get it. Beggars can't be choosers. (*Pause.*) If you don't eat it, the cat'll get it. Then you'll see what going hungry is. A good dog eats what's put in front of him, didn't you know that? (*Pause.*) You're choosy, that's the problem.

Act Two

Scene One

A very small country funfair. After lunchtime, a dead time. **Beppi** *and* **Sepp**. **Beppi** *completely fascinated.* **Sepp** *slightly drunk.*

Sepp   Anything you want?

Beppi *does not react.*

Sepp   Want a go on the merry-go-round? (*It is a ghost train.*) Scared? Look at the spooks.

Beppi *is frightened but fascinated.*

Sepp   Let's go on it.

He takes her by the hand to the cashier.

One adult, one child.

They go on the ghost train, then return. **Beppi** *is upset.*

Sepp   That was good, wasn't it?

Beppi *is uncertain.*

Sepp   What's the matter?

Beppi *walks stiffly.*

Sepp   Hurt yourself?

Beppi *shakes her head.*

Sepp   Have you wet yourself? – Wet your pants, come with me. – Were you scared?

Beppi *is totally confused.*

Sepp   Or was it the drink? Come on, we'll take care of it.

They go behind a tent.

Wipe yourself with leaves.

Beppi *cleans herself: diarrhoea runs down her legs.*

Sepp   Oh great. Shitting in your pants. – Let me do it.

Cleans her up.

Take them off. – You can't go on like this.

Beppi *does as she is told.*

Sepp   Wipe yourself with them. – Let me.

He wipes her, takes out his handkerchief, wipes her with it.

Okay now. Come here.

Takes her, deflowers her.

Scene Two

Sepp'*s room.* **Sepp** *and* **Beppi**.

Sepp (*gives* **Beppi** *a purse*)   Here, I brought this from town for you.

Beppi *looks.*

Sepp   If you don't like it, just say and I'll take it back.

Beppi   No.

Sepp   Okay then. Do you say 'Thank you' or not?

Beppi   Thank you.

Sepp   So you see someone is thinking about you.

Looks at the purse himself.

Believe you me, it wasn't cheap. Genuine leather.

Puts one mark into it.

There, that's a start.

Beppi *takes the purse.*

Sepp   If you ever have any money, you won't lose it.

Beppi *smiles.*

Scene Three

A pub with a garden. **Sepp** *and* **Beppi** *arrive on a moped.* **Beppi** *is riding pillion. They dismount, enter the garden, etc.*

Sepp (*as he dismounts*)   Was it too fast?

Beppi *shakes her head.*

Sepp   Slower on the way home?

Beppi   No. (*Pause.*) I'll ride with you.

They move into the garden, sit down at a table.

Sepp   We won't eat anything, it costs too much.

Beppi *nods.*

Sepp   Or do you want a sausage?

Beppi *shakes her head. Pause.*

Sepp   Nice here, isn't it?

Beppi *nods.*

Sepp   You like it?

Beppi   Yes.

Pause.

Sepp   You can have a sausage, if you want.

Beppi   A lemonade.

Sepp   Not hungry?

Beppi   No, lemonade.

Sepp (*looks around; no one comes*)   I'll have a beer. I'll go inside, as no one's coming.

Beppi *nods.* **Sepp** *goes inside.*

Beppi *unsure of herself. Pulls down her dress, adjusts her neckerchief, pulls up her knee-socks, etc. Clasps her hands, puts them on the table.*

Sepp (*returns*)   On its way. (*Sits down. Long pause.*) In five years, with any luck, I'll retire. (*Pause.*) Then I'm a free man. No one can tell me what to do. (*Long pause.*) I'll move into town and get a flat. Then you can come if you want. (*Pause.*) The flat will be in town.

Beppi   Munich.

Sepp   Right. In Munich. On the outskirts, where it's cheaper. (*Pause.*) Lots of possibilities in town. They're always looking for people. Everywhere. They don't bother much about finding out who you are, they're just happy to find anybody. (*Pause.*) You're still too young at the moment. But in a year or two, it will be fine. (*Pause.*) You'll see what I'm telling you. Time passes more quickly than you think. Turn round and another year's gone.

Beppi *stares.*

Scene Four

In a barn. **Sepp** *and* **Beppi** *together, after intercourse.*

Sepp   I don't mean to hurt you, it can't be helped.

Beppi *shakes her head.*

Sepp   Right.

Beppi   Why?

Sepp   That's the way it is, you wouldn't understand.

Pause.

Beppi   Do unto others as you would have them do unto you.

Sepp *is silent. Pause.*

Sepp   That's a different matter. (*Pause.*) What are you looking for?

Beppi   Glasses.

Sepp   Can't you find them?

Beppi *nods.*

Sepp   They're where you left them.

Beppi   Where?

Sepp   I can see them.

Beppi *looks.*

Sepp   Very close.

Beppi   Where?

Sepp   Say please.

Beppi   Please.

Sepp   Hot-or-cold.

Beppi (*smiles*)   Game.

Sepp   Cold. Cold. Cold. Getting warmer. Cold. Warmer. Warm. Very warm. Hot, hot enough to burn you.

Beppi   Where?

Sepp   Very hot. You don't look so nice with your glasses on.

Beppi   See.

Sepp   You don't need to see now.

Beppi   Red.

Sepp   That's normal. Doesn't matter. You see, it'll stop, like I say.

Beppi   When?

Sepp   When it stops. (*Pause.*) Tomorrow.

Beppi *nods.*

Sepp *is uncertain. Pause.*

Sepp   I'll go outside again now, so no one notices I've been gone.

Beppi   Stay.

Sepp   You stay a while, if you want. I'll keep an eye out. Then you come too. (*Stands up, leaves.*)

Beppi   Glasses. (*Searches for them.*)

Scene Five

Room. **Stallerin** *and* **Beppi**. **Beppi** *smartly dressed.*

Stallerin   Let's have a look at you.

Beppi *lets her.*

Stallerin   Yes, you look nice. You just need your ribbon, then you can go.

Beppi *nods.*

Stallerin (*ties her hair ribbon*)   Now be off. Come straight home after confession to help me make jam.

Beppi   Yes.

Stallerin   Now see you get a move on.

Beppi   God bless.

Stallerin   You won't be gone for ever.

Beppi *leaves.* **Stallerin** *gets things ready for jam-making.*

Scene Six

In the field. **Beppi** *and* **Sepp**.

Beppi   Confessed.

Sepp   Of course. But don't tell who with.

Beppi   'I have been unchaste.'

Sepp   Exactly. And that's enough. No one's business but ours. And we won't be questioned.

Pause.

Let's do it.

Beppi   Later.

Sepp   Don't feel like it? Try, with a bit of goodwill, it'll work.

Beppi   Tell me something.

Sepp   If you're good, I'll tell you a story afterwards.

Beppi *undresses.*

Sepp   Soon be over. Over before you even notice.

Pause.

Beppi   Confessed already.

Pause.

Sepp   And what did the priest say?

Beppi   Six Our Fathers, two Hail Marys.

Sepp   You confessed everything?

Beppi (*nods*)   Mortal sin otherwise.

Sepp   Exactly. How did you say it?

Beppi   First commandment: Honour and love the Lord your God. Second commandment: Love and honour your father and mother. I made Father and Mother angry. Third commandment: Sundays and holidays. Fourth commandment: I have never cursed, never. Fifth commandment. Sixth commandment: that I have been unchaste.

Sepp   How did you say it?

Beppi   Sixth commandment: I have been unchaste.

Sepp   Nothing else?

Beppi   That I told a lie.

Sepp   Did the priest ask anything?

Beppi   Nothing.

Sepp   Penance?

Beppi   Six Our Fathers, two Hail Marys.

Sepp   Have you said your prayers?

Beppi   Ten Our Fathers, three Hail Marys.

Sepp   Good girl.

Beppi *smiles.*

Sepp   You've done well.

He strokes her. **Beppi** *smiles.*

Sepp   Now everything's been forgiven and forgotten. You'll see.

Beppi *nods.* **Sepp** *begins coitus.* **Beppi** *lets it happen without aversion.*

Sepp   Good girl.

Pause. **Beppi** *utters some cries. She reaches orgasm.*

Sepp   Quiet, so no one hears. You hear?

Beppi *is not listening.*

Sepp *(uncertain, stops)*   Did I hurt you? I didn't mean to. Quiet now and I'll tell you a story.

Pause.

A lovely one!

Scene Seven

Staller *and* **Sepp** *in* **Sepp**'s *room.*

Pause.

Staller   That'll cost you ten years and me my good name.

Sepp   But it wasn't on purpose.

Staller   Fat lot of use.

Long pause.

I'm speechless.

Pause.

I trusted you.

Sepp   That's the way it is.

Staller   Three months.

Sepp   Wasn't counting the days.

Pause.

Staller   Want to hear a secret: she's pregnant.

Sepp   Why?

Staller   She is.

Sepp   It's not true. All lies.

Staller   We've got proof.

Sepp   That's not possible.

Staller   It is.

Sepp   There's nothing.

Staller   They do a test. It costs ten marks.

Sepp   Why?

Staller   It's done using urine.

Sepp Whose?

Staller Hers.

Sepp At the doctor's?

Staller At the doctor's! What do you know? At the chemist's. They do it with a frog. You inject the urine into a frog and it changes colour. That's it.

Sepp I never knew that.

Staller Now you do. If it changes colour, she's pregnant.

Sepp And it did.

Staller Exactly. Confirming she's pregnant.

Pause.

Sepp But it wasn't intended.

Staller You're a swine, no getting round it.

Sepp Right.

Staller We'll tell the priest too. We'll tell everyone.

Sepp I'll leave.

Staller Where will you go?

Sepp Into town.

Pause.

Staller If we'd known, we'd never have taken you on.

Sepp I'm still going.

Staller You stay. There's a penalty to be paid, you'll see.

Sepp What?

Staller Rely on it.

Pause.

You're the worst swine I've ever known.

Pause.

An underage girl, and backward too. I'm speechless.

Sepp   I didn't want this, I swear.

Staller   Couldn't you find someone else? You don't shit on your own doorstep – and just a child too.

Sepp   Didn't dare try anywhere else.

Staller   How come?

Sepp   I'm not saying.

Scene Eight

In the stable. Kittens in one corner. **Sepp** *and* **Beppi**.

Sepp   It's a nice litter but we can only keep one.

Beppi *watches the kittens.*

Sepp   That's the way kittens are. You can choose one. You'll see what you get for giving me away.

Beppi *looks.*

Sepp   Which one?

Beppi   None.

Sepp   They're all the same. But one will catch it.

Beppi   Eeny meeny miney, mo . . . that one.

Sepp   As you like. They know everything, your mother and father.

Beppi *looks.*

Sepp   Betrayed.

Beppi   No. My mother knew.

Sepp   Did you tell her?

Beppi *shakes her head.*

Sepp   I believe you.

Scene Nine

Farmyard. **Sepp** *and* **Staller**.

Staller   What you looking for? Run out of work?

Sepp   My dog.

Staller   Your dog's not on my farm.

Sepp   Where else?

Staller   It'll turn up somewhere.

Sepp   I'm allowed to look.

Staller   You've nothing more to look for on my farm.

Sepp   Right.

Staller   You know that.

Pause.

Sepp   I'm only looking for my dog.

Staller   Then look. 'Seek and ye shall find.'

Sepp   Right.

Staller   He was here.

Sepp   Where?

Staller   By the stable.

Sepp   Why?

Staller   Ask him yourself. Dog doesn't bother me, especially if it's not mine.

Sepp   He does wander off.

Staller   You'll find him.

Pause.

And if I catch you on my farm again, I'll shoot you. Just so you know.

Sepp   You haven't got a gun.

Staller   What do you know?

Pause.

Sepp   I'm only looking for my dog.

Staller   Right.

Sepp (*by the barn*)   There he is. Here, boy! (*Whistles.*) Heel!
Aren't you listening? I'll give you a belt.

The dog is dead.

Staller   You found him?

Sepp   He's here.

Staller   Then see that you push off, the two of you.

Sepp   Murderer.

Staller   Rat poison must have got him. It was put down in
the barn.

Sepp (*picks up the dead dog*)   Let's go home. (*Leaves with the
dog.*)

Staller   Quits.

Scene Ten

Sepp's *room.* **Sepp** *is packing a small suitcase.* **Beppi**.

Sepp   Don't look, there's nothing for you.

Beppi   Yes there is.

Sepp   He's in there.

Beppi   I know. (*Looks into the case.*)

Sepp (*stops packing*)   You see him?

Beppi *nods.*

Sepp Nothing more to do?

Beppi (*shakes her head*) Nothing.

Sepp (*crying*) Now go, don't need you any more.

Beppi (*smiles*) Nice dog. (*Nods.*)

Sepp All done. Just go.

Beppi *shakes and nods her head, stands up, goes round the table, looks, uncertain, takes the prepared things and continues packing the case.*

Sepp What are you doing?

Beppi Nothing. (*Stops.*)

Pause.

Sepp All over. Now comes the crunch.

Beppi Why?

Sepp It's over.

Beppi Stick with you, me.

Sepp A lot of use.

Beppi *nods.*

Sepp You have no rights, you're nothing, that's it.

Beppi *nods.*

Sepp Now I'll go into town and report what's happened.

Beppi Stay.

Sepp You'll make it on your own. Don't need me.

Beppi Yes I do.

Sepp Nothing to keep me here now the dog's dead.

Beppi I say 'Please'.

Sepp Nothing doing.

Pause. **Sepp** *continues packing.*

Beppi   You come back?

Sepp   When the baby's there, I'll see how it's turned out.

Beppi   Not go, stay.

Sepp   Over for us.

Beppi   Why?

Pause.

Sepp   Here's some chocolate I bought for you.

Beppi *takes it, cries.*

Sepp   No need to cry.

Beppi   No need.

Interval.

Act Three

Scene One

Staller *and* **Stallerin** *on the way to church in bad weather.*
Beppi *is slightly ahead of them.*

Staller   Does it show yet?

Pause.

Stallerin   Nothing yet.

Long pause.

Staller   I can see something.

Stallerin   You're imagining it. There's nothing to see.

Pause.

Staller   No one should ever see anything.

Stallerin   Of course not.

Long pause.

They say if you're slightly crazy, you don't feel death like the rest of us.

Staller   Right, just as a fly feels nothing.

Pause.

Stallerin   Fifth: 'Thou shalt not kill.'

Staller   Sixth: 'Thou shalt not commit adultery.'

Pause.

I'll keep that between me and my God.

Pause.

Stallerin   They say a child lives on for hours in the mother's womb.

Staller   Not this one.

Long pause.

Stallerin   Anyway, I wouldn't forget that for the rest of my life. That I know.

Staller   If you don't know which way to turn, 'cause it's all useless, you have to find a way out.

Stallerin   Yes.

Pause.

'Blessed are the poor in spirit, for theirs is the Kingdom of Heaven.'

Staller   Don't believe a word.

Stallerin   The thoughts one has, they don't bear thinking about.

Staller   Just talk.

Stallerin   But to hurtle towards destruction with your eyes open, that's not on either.

Staller   So?

Stallerin   Just thinking about it.

Staller   One thing I know, my daughter, who's under age and backward, has no business getting pregnant by a good-for-nothing. What would people take me for? No.

Stallerin   Why a good-for-nothing?

Staller   That's what people say.

Scene Two

Daytime, in the kitchen. The churn is fixed to the bench. **Beppi** *is turning it.* **Stallerin** *cleans the floor with a wet cloth.*

Stallerin   You won't get butter but sauce.

Beppi *churns. Long pause.*

Stallerin Get on with it.

Beppi It's hard work.

Stallerin It wasn't so hard before. You've made your bed, now you must lie in it.

Scene Three

Room, evening. **Staller** *at the table with a newspaper.* **Stallerin**. **Beppi** *writes in an exercise book.*

Staller (*to* **Stallerin**) What are you doing? (*Pause. To* **Beppi**.) What's up? (*To* **Stallerin**.) She should be in bed.

Stallerin Leave her, she's doing her homework.

Staller At night!

Beppi Handwriting.

Stallerin Good girl.

Pause.

Staller (*to* **Stallerin**) What are *you* doing?

Stallerin Soapy water.

Staller What for?

Pause.

Stallerin You'll see.

Pause.

Staller You'll do it?

Stallerin You're just talk, nothing else.

Pause.

Staller And if she refuses?

Stallerin She must do as she is told.

Staller   That won't work.

Stallerin   Got a better idea?

Beppi *listens.*

Stallerin   Do your work and don't bother about things that don't concern you.

Pause.

Staller   If there were anything in it, everyone would be doing it.

Stallerin   You don't often need it.

Pause.

Staller *carries on reading the paper.*

Right.

Pause.

Stallerin (*to* **Staller**)   You go outside, we'll do this among ourselves, and no peeping.

Staller (*stands up*)   I'm off, this is your business. (*Leaves.*)

Stallerin   Now we'll soon get this over and done with.

Beppi *watches.*

Stallerin   Come here now. Take your knickers off and lie down there.

Beppi   No.

Stallerin   We've got to wash you to get the dirt off. Take them off.

Beppi *obeys.*

Stallerin   Been so filthy the dirt must come out the same way it went in. It hurts a bit, but that's nothing, just the soap washing everything away. Pull your skirt up, legs apart!

Beppi *has undressed completely, stands there naked.*

Stallerin   You're freezing, you idiot.

Pause.

Stallerin *takes the cleaning rag and floor brush from the stove, wets them in the soapy water and starts scrubbing the floor.*

Pause.

Well, didn't you hear what I said? Go and wash in the tub outside, then get to bed. You've got to be up tomorrow. I've got work to do.

Scene Four

Night. **Staller** *and* **Stallerin** *in bed.*

Stallerin   I tried my best, that's for sure. I don't need to reproach myself, that's for sure too.

Staller   Did I say anything?

Long pause.

Stallerin   That's how it is. Nothing you can do.

Staller   Well, we can't. We need people here who understand these things. They can help themselves.

Stallerin   If there's nothing you can do, there's nothing you can do.

Staller   That's what I thought straightaway, that there was no point.

Stallerin   Right.

Pause.

Staller   If at least we'd had another child, a boy, that would be a glimmer of hope.

Stallerin   How come?

Staller   It's obvious.

Stallerin   If I couldn't have a second when I was young,
I'm not going to have one now, everyone knows that.

Pause.

Staller   But I can still speak and imagine something that
gives me pleasure.

Stallerin   Of course.

Scene Five

Hillside with cranberries. **Stallerin** *and* **Beppi** *are picking fruit.*
Beppi *is very pregnant.*

Long pause.

Beppi (*has found a good spot*)   Lot here.

Stallerin (*smiles, then quietly*)   Then pick, don't talk.

Pause.

Scene Six

Room, evening. **Staller**, **Stallerin** *and* **Beppi** *eating.*

Long pause.

Beppi *stops eating, looks at* **Staller** *and* **Stallerin**, *her labour
pains begin.*

Pause.

Beppi   Daddymummy.

Request Programme

translated by

Katharina Hehn

Introduction

The play is the possible visualisation of facts in police reports that have often struck me.

In many instances suicide takes place with incredible tidiness. The preparations proceed as one part of a daily, and therefore normal, routine, and the act is undertaken with the same love of order, as cleanly, stolidly and dumbly despairingly as the life which led to it.

This can say a great deal about the life of some among us, about their unfulfilled expectations, their hopeless hopes, their little dreams; it can illustrate their inability to free themselves from the slavery of labour, it can show that the aimlessness of their lives is not unlike that of beasts of burden.

Such people express their desperation like animals, in uncomplaining composure that contains a strong element of order, of endurance, of 'unquestioning acceptance', of exploitation and limitation to the point of weakness and collapse.

If the explosive force of this enormous exploitation and suppression did not target, alas, the suppressed and exploited themselves, the situation would be ripe for revolution. As it is, we have only a collection of small, foolish suicides and murders, which in turn underlines only that those who have reached the point of summoning up the strength and courage to 'throw their own life on to the scale' deliver themselves up to the jurisdiction of their natural enemies. In so doing, they unwittingly purge the society they are accusing. Now they become the accused and disappear into prisons or graves, which are the same thing.

Only in this way is it possible for the inhuman order in which we live to be sustained.

Character

Miss Rasch is about forty to forty-five years old, has dark
hair and is about five feet five inches tall; she still has a good
figure, except for her legs, which are quite swollen, possibly
because of dropsy. Her complexion is brownish, not in the
beautiful and desirable sense of being tanned, but smudgy
and spotty. Miss Rasch gives the impression of being
exceptionally well groomed which softens, though without
quite concealing, her obvious unattractiveness.

Above all, her clothes – restrained in style and of good
quality – show variety. It is evident that she spends a lot of
money on them. Miss Rasch is employed at a paper
manufacturer. In the stationery department she is
responsible for envelopes. That aside, the action takes place
in a small town and Miss Rasch's take-home pay is DM
615,50 a month.

Because she is a spinster (not by choice), or rather (and it
is more or less the same thing) because of her long-standing,
involuntary sexual abstinence – the result of a one-off,
distant, embarrassing and sad case of love – she is
particularly susceptible to advertising and therefore
consumerism; within the limits of her finances, this is
apparent from her furnishings, her clothes and her body
care.

Set

The set is a realistic, furnished bedsit. It should give the
impression that the neighbouring rooms are also bedsits, as
is common with many converted flats. At the end of a long
corridor is a lavatory.

In contrast to the other rooms, which are only hinted at,
the room itself is particularly clean, petit bourgeois, tidy,
lovingly, welcomingly and cosily furnished.

It is apparent to the audience that in a sea of back-to-
back housing – which does not make for agreeable living –

someone, with love, effort and taste, has created a space which sets itself apart from its surroundings.

Neckermann and *Kunstgewerbe* (roughly equivalent to BHS and The Pier) are very much present.

Duration of the play

Since the aim is not to provoke the audience, but to give them insight into the wretchedness of Miss Rasch's life, care should be taken to ensure that none of her chosen tasks take too long, as this might bore the audience and therefore provoke them. If a certain task is no longer meaningful but just becomes constant tedious repetition, it should be broken off, even if this means breaking the rhythm of the play. Stage time should be real time. For this reason, I imagine the play lasting no longer than one hour.

Translator's Note

Wunschkonzert was written in 1971. Details which reflect the time and place of its composition have been retained but any modern production will need to update them as appropriate. Whatever external details are changed, however, the sense of despair and loneliness implicit in the lifestyle of the central character must remain. And the request programme must be a constant accompaniment.

Part One

On any working day, at about 6.30 p.m., Miss Rasch
returns home after work, having done her shopping. She
enters the house, looks for her mail, finds only junk mail,
picks it up, goes to her door, unlocks it and enters. She puts
her shopping bag containing food items and a newspaper
down on the table, puts her handbag down on a chair,
leaves the junk mail on the sideboard and closes her door.

Taking off her coat, she puts it on a hanger which she hangs
on a hook on the door. She removes a mark from the back
of her coat. Then she goes to the window, touches the
radiator to check that it has come on. She draws the net
curtains carefully and opens the window slightly.

Noticing something on the window sill which has to be
removed instantly, she picks up a cloth by the sink and
proceeds to clean the whole window sill. She puts the cloth
back and starts to unpack her shopping, storing it away in
the fridge, the sideboard and the bread bin. Then she hangs
the shopping bag on a hook next to the gas cooker. She
takes off her high-heeled shoes and puts them away in the
wardrobe. Then she puts on the slippers standing next to
the wardrobe.

She takes off the jacket of the smart tailored suit she is
wearing and hangs it on a hanger inside the wardrobe. She
takes out a well-worn cardigan to wear.

Then she goes to the mirror next to the cooker by the sink
and takes off her earrings, necklace and a ring. She places
this jewellery in a dish on top of the chest of drawers.

Returning to the mirror, she studies her face for a long time,
then arranges her hair with brush and comb. A blemish on
her skin, which has grown worse since morning, is examined
at length, and after she has washed her hands, she applies
some cream to the spot.

She lights the cooker, puts on some water for her washing-up. There are only a few dishes. She has quite a big sink, but only a single cold-water tap. She uses the sink for all her washing and therefore cleans it meticulously after each procedure.

She goes to the television in the corner of the room and switches it on. She sits down at the table, picks up the junk mail from the sideboard and opens it. She reads it attentively and puts it aside. From her handbag on the chair she takes a packet of *Lord Extra* cigarettes and a lighter. She lights up. In the meantime, the TV has warmed up. It is a home-shopping programme or some other early-evening show and she watches it while smoking slowly and pensively. She puts the cigarette down in the ashtray on the sideboard, goes to the chest of drawers and picks up the TV guide. Returning to the table, she puts down the guide, fetches the ashtray with the smoking cigarette from the sideboard, picks up her handbag from the chair and puts it down to one side of the sideboard.

She sits down again and browses through the TV guide to see what's on this evening. She takes a last puff and carefully stubs out the cigarette.

She gets up again, goes to the cooker and switches off the gas. She returns to the table, remains standing, turns the page to the radio programmes. She studies it, finally goes to the TV and turns it off. She looks at her wristwatch, takes it off and puts it with the other jewellery. She picks up the TV guide, closes it and returns it to its original place.

[*Author's Note: In Bavaria, Fred Rauch introduces at 7.15 on Wednesday evenings* Your request?, *an especially popular programme featuring alternating popular hits and light music, operetta and opera. It comes as no surprise that Miss Rasch should prefer a popular radio broadcast to a tedious evening in front of the TV. Beyond Bavaria, a similar radio programme must be found.*]

She puts on an apron, first runs cold water into the sink then pours in hot from the kettle. She picks up her stacked dishes from the kitchen dresser and washes up quickly and efficiently. She dries the dishes and puts them away inside the sideboard. She then lays the table for her evening meal – a plate and cutlery. She drains the water from the sink and cleans it meticulously. Then she washes her hands, and applies hand cream. She takes a selection of things from the fridge and places them on the table. As she can get a cooked lunch at the works canteen, her evening meal will be light and only something cold.

Part Two

She walks across to the radio and turns it on. She returns to the prepared table and sits down. She makes a sandwich. With a movement of her fingers she indicates that she has forgotten something.

She gets up again and fetches a bottle of fruit juice from the fridge. From the sideboard she gets a glass, pours in some fruit juice, and tops it up with water. She puts the glass with the other things on the table. The fruit juice she returns immediately to the fridge. Then she sits down and begins to eat.

She eats deep in thought. She prepares each sandwich lovingly and garnishes it. It is evident that she is listening to the request programme and she laughs when Fred Rauch makes a joke. She sips her juice.

When she has finished eating, she tidies away, wrapping up the butter and cold meat and closing the pickle jars. She lights up and smokes the cigarette without doing anything else.

Then she gets up, clears the table and returns everything on it to its original place. Her dishes, the plate, fork and knife she puts on the kitchen dresser.

She leaves the room to go to the lavatory. It takes some time before she is done and can wipe her bottom. The cleaning process is done as pedantically and hygienically as possible. She pulls the chain and cleans out the bowl with the brush standing next to it. She opens the lavatory window slightly.

She returns to her room and washes her hands, then she goes to the radio to correct some static which has given her poor reception in the meantime. She fiddles around with the knobs until she gets just the right sound.

Returning to the mirror, she examines the blemish she had applied cream to earlier on. She touches it up and then applies cream again.

From the cooker she picks up the kettle and pours the remainder of the hot water into the sink. She adds some cold water from the tap. She goes to her wardrobe and takes out a pair of silk stockings, which she puts into the sink and washes.

She drapes a towel, which she has taken from the rail by the sink, over the back of the second chair and very carefully lays the stockings over it to dry.

As the water drains away, she cleans the sink. The music from the radio animates her and she dances a few steps. Then she leaves the room to close the lavatory window and returns.

Part Three

From the top of her wardrobe she brings down a handmade rug that is nearly finished. She spreads it over the back of the other chair and looks at it. She tweaks it here and there. Then she clears the table completely. She returns the ashtray to the sideboard, and puts the cigarettes and the lighter next to it. She finishes the fruit juice and puts the glass on the kitchen dresser.

She spreads the rug over the table. From beneath the sofa she pulls out an iron bar which she lays across the top end of the rug, so that it cannot slip. She returns to the wardrobe and takes down a wooden box, puts it on the table, goes to the sideboard, opens a drawer and takes out the pattern. Another drawer contains the scissors, which she also fetches. She arranges everything and switches on the standard lamp. She checks the lighting and decides to switch on the overhead light as well. The switch is near the door.

She sits down on the other chair, moves it about a bit and, after she has arranged everything to her satisfaction, starts to take wool and needles out of the box. She studies the pattern without spreading the sheet completely, counts the knots, threads the needle and begins.

She works very carefully, very accurately and skilfully. Whenever she has completed a particular colour in the pattern, she puts the needle aside, cuts the loop and cuts off the loose ends. [*Author's Note: During rehearsal one should get precise instructions on home rug-making!*]

Some time later she gets up and puts water on again. She returns to her work. When the water comes to the boil, she takes a tea bag and a teapot from the dresser and makes tea. She puts it on the dresser, gets a cup and stands it next to the teapot. She resumes her work.

After a few minutes the tea is ready and she pours herself a cup, takes sugar from the sideboard, stirs the sugar into the tea and carries the cup to the table. From the chest of drawers she gets a packet of biscuits, which she puts down on the table next to the rug. She continues her work, eats two or three biscuits, drinks her cup of tea and fetches a second cup when the first is finished.

Part Four

Gradually her interest in her work begins to wane. More often than not she looks up and compares her work with the pattern for longer than is necessary. She stops working, gets the cigarettes, lighter and ashtray from the sideboard, puts everything down on the table. She sits down and smokes a whole cigarette without doing a stitch.

She now appears tired, exhausted and irritated. She gets up, takes her wristwatch from the dish and looks at the time. She goes to the radio and turns it down. Then she sits down again and continues her work, more slowly than before, but still skilfully. She gets up again, picks up the empty teacup and carries it to the dresser. She rinses out the teapot, throws the used tea bag into the waste bin under the dresser.

She fetches the ashtray, empties it into the bin, wipes it with a cloth and puts it down on the sideboard. Then she returns to the mirror, looks at herself. She seems to be content with her appearance.

Again she returns to the table and sits down. She studies the pattern carefully, counts the knots and continues efficiently and quickly until the rug is finished. But nothing should indicate that the rug is completed. She locks the needles in the small wooden box, folds up the pattern and puts the scissors next to it, then she gets up to view the rug from a distance. [*Author's Note: If one works on a 45 cm by 70 cm tapestry for an hour daily the work should be completed within one and a half to two months.*] She smiles, takes up the rug and spreads it temporarily across the back of the sofa along the wall. She looks at it critically for a long time from as far away as possible. She is pleased with her work. She picks up the rug lovingly and, without folding it, drapes it over the other chair. She then starts clearing away all the items on the table, returning them to their respective places in the same order as she originally took them out.

When she has finished this, she again studies the finished rug, is pleased, pulls and tweaks it a little. But she seems almost frightened as if the tweaking might have spoiled something.

Part Five

Fred Rauch takes his leave, the request programme is over.
It is evident that Miss Rasch is pensive. She switches off the
radio before the next programme is announced.

She goes to the window and again opens the net curtains
carefully, then she looks out of the window. Eventually she
closes it, pulls the curtains so closely that no one can look in.

Finally she lays the table for her breakfast in the morning.
From the eggcup and other items, one can discern that she
likes to take her time over breakfast.

Then she converts her sofa into a bed. [*Author's note: Best use a
sofa bed with a drawer for storing bedding underneath.*]

The ritual of body care begins. This ranges from putting
curlers into her hair, pedicure, vaginal spray to brushing her
teeth. All this is carried out as thoroughly as possible. She
examines each item of underwear carefully. She decides to
put her knickers with the dirty washing in the laundry bag
inside her wardrobe and to take out a fresh pair for the next
morning. She also chooses a different suit for the next day.
She hangs it on the outside of her wardrobe, her fresh
underwear is laid out on the free seat of the chair. The
clothes she has worn that day are hung up and returned to
the wardrobe, to hang out, till she next wears them.

From among her bedding she takes a pretty thermal
nightdress and puts it on, then a dressing gown. She then
goes to the lavatory. This time she only has to urinate;
despite this she dries herself meticulously with loo paper and
again opens the window slightly. She returns to her room
and washes her hands again.

Then she starts her evening rounds: she double-locks her
door, checks carefully that the gas is turned off, that the
waste-bin lid is closed and the tap is not dripping. Then she
carefully opens the window again, taking a long time to get

it just wide enough to let fresh air in, although she closes the curtains again.

Then she prepares her makeshift bedside table. She pulls an upholstered stool from near the top end of the couch close to her bed. On it are an alarm clock, a book, an empty glass and a copy of *Stern* magazine. She picks up the empty glass and rinses it, fills it with fresh water and returns it to its place.

Then she sits on the edge of the bed, picks up the alarm clock, winds it up and sets it for six in the morning. She tests that the alarm is still working and when it is, is satisfied and returns the clock to its place.

It is not long before she gets up again. She turns off the overhead light, checks the gas cooker again, takes off her dressing gown and puts it at the foot of her bed. Then she lies down in bed. She does this very carefully and cannot get comfortable because of her curlers.

She picks up the book, looks for her bookmark, finds it, does not read but stares into space. This lasts for some time. Then she lays the book aside, glances once more around the room and switches the light off.

At first she lies quite still, then she turns on her side, carefully because of her curlers, and attempts to sleep.

Finally she stirs impatiently in bed and then switches the light on. She gets up, puts on her dressing gown again, unlocks her door and goes to the lavatory. All extremely quietly. Inside the lavatory she closes the window. She returns to her room, locks the door behind her, washes her hands, dries them. Then she goes to her rug, studies it again. A few minutes later she goes to the sideboard, opens the top part and takes out a packet of tablets. She returns to the table and puts them down, picks up the glass of water from the stool and puts it down next to the tablets. She sits down on the chair with the stockings, carefully avoiding leaning on them and rumpling them. She takes a tablet from the packet, takes it with a sip of water. She takes out the instructions for use and reads them through.

She opens the tube again, empties it and arranges the tablets in pairs; there are nine left from a packet of twenty. Slowly she takes one after the other until the water that she sips with each tablet is finished. She gets up, moves towards the sink, changes her mind, goes to the fridge and takes out a half-filled piccolo of *Sekt*, returns to the table, opens the bottle, pours a little into her glass and takes the remainder of the tablets. Then she waits a while.

She pours the rest of the *Sekt* into her glass, it fizzes up and spills on to the tablecloth. She lifts the glass and wipes the stain with the sleeve of her dressing gown, she takes a sip of *Sekt*.

Then she waits, calm and collected, but her face shows a sudden interest.

Pause. End.

The Nest

translated by

Katharina Hehn

Characters

Kurt
Martha
Stefan

Kurt is thirty-something, short, stocky and quite ordinary.
Martha is about the same age. They are not quite suited to
each other. It is evident that Martha has worked for fifteen
years, but she is a little more attractive than Kurt and,
seeing them, you would not necessarily assume that they
were a married couple. That should be evident but not
exaggerated.

Time

The present, in a small village in Upper Bavaria.

Translator's Note

The players can speak their lines in an English regional
dialect if they can master it with ease, otherwise standard
English. (Kroetz directed players to 'speak the Bavarian
dialect, though High German is preferable to silly imitations
of dialect.')

German brand names can be Anglicised if and where
appropriate. Other details specific to the time and place of
the play's composition (1974) can be updated according to
the setting chosen for the production.

Act One

Scene One

Inside the flat, late evening. The TV is on. **Martha** *is heavily pregnant; she is sewing ties as home work.* **Kurt** *is dozing.*

Announcer   You have just seen the Heidelberg Theatre production of *Upper Austria*, a play by the Bavarian playwright Franz Xaver Kroetz. We now continue our programme with the late edition of the news.

Kurt *wakes up.*

Martha   Shall we turn it off?

Kurt   Yes, we've seen the news already.

Martha *laughs.*

Kurt (*switches the TV off*)   What's so funny?

Martha   Because it happened in the play, just the same.

Kurt   What?

Martha   Except that you fell asleep, the one in the play didn't.

Kurt   He should work as much overtime as I do and stop talking so much, then he'll see and fall asleep too.

Long pause.

Martha   No, it wasn't like real life.

Kurt   Not in the least, and I should know.

Martha   But you did watch a bit. As I said: it hit the nail on the head, Kurti-Wurti. You remember?

Kurt   It was a surprise.

Pause.

Martha   I'd have fought for the child if you hadn't wanted it, like the man in the play.

Kurt   He didn't know what he wanted at all. A man's got to know what he wants, then he's on his way. And it's not normal for a man to be scared of his own child.

Martha   He had an inferiority complex.

Kurt   Why? I'm a lorry driver too, and *I* don't have one.

Martha   No, not us.

Kurt   Exactly.

Pause.

Martha   Besides, there is a difference. You can't compare it. You're a lorry driver and he was just a van driver.

Kurt   A heavy-goods licence is a job, true enough, and they always said so when I was passing my test. The ordinary licence isn't.

Pause.

Let's go to bed. Tomorrow is another day.

Martha (*nods*)   Yes.

Pause. She looks at her work.

I'm not getting much done here.

Kurt   You shouldn't be working at all, not now!

Martha   Practice makes perfect. (*Smiles.*) But it doesn't amount to much yet. How long did the play last?

Kurt   A good hour.

Martha   Three ties! (*Short pause.*) That's not much.

Kurt   One mark fifty.

Martha   It's bound to get better. You can make up to ten ties an hour it says on the instruction sheet. That would be five marks; not bad.

Kurt It'll come.

Martha Yes.

Scene Two

In the bedroom. **Kurt** *is already in bed.* **Martha** *is getting ready for bed. Outside a police car with its siren turned on drives past.*

Pause.

Kurt It's nice, isn't it, when they drive past like the devil, and you know very well they can't be after us, because it wasn't us. Whatever it is.

Martha A good conscience sleeps through thunder.

Kurt True.

Pause.

Are you satisfied with me?

Martha Why not, you're a good, hard-working man.

Kurt After all, you didn't really want me at all, in the beginning. Do you remember?

Martha Here he goes again!

Kurt Because it's true.

Martha You have your illusions when you're young, nobody should knock that.

Kurt And I wasn't an illusion?

Martha Thank heavens, no. – Illusions get blown away.

Short pause.

Kurt You were my illusion all right.

Martha *smiles.*

Pause.

Martha *gets into bed as well.*

Martha   Now it's moving – want to listen?

Kurt (*nods, lays his head, ear down, on her stomach*)   Can't hear a thing.

Martha   It's stopped. (*Smiles.*) Whenever you listen it always stops immediately. Usually he kicks away, the little rascal.

Kurt   He just senses that it's his dad.

Martha   Yes.

Pause.

Kurt   I still feel like it sometimes.

Martha   We must control ourselves.

Kurt   Of course. (*Pause.*) But I read in the papers that you can go on doing it until just before the birth. At least that's what they say.

Martha   What paper?

Kurt   In *Stern*.

Martha   Right. – Well, we ought to stick to what the doctor says and not *Stern*. Three months before, two months after.

Kurt   I was just talking.

Pause.

Martha   You'd better go to sleep.

Scene Three

Inside the flat. Saturday afternoon.

Kurt   Let's start.

Martha   I was really surprised.

Kurt   I wasn't.

Martha   Just you wait. I've researched all the prices down to the last detail.

Kurt   Get going.

Martha   I thought Adele would know about these things, since they've got three children. And she is a friend.

Kurt   Right.

Pause.

Martha   Listen. (*She reads from a long list.*) First: a pram! A pram is difficult, because you have to decide one way or the other. You should have looked at them yourself.

Kurt   Which then?

Martha   I'd like a supermodern one, they have the edge on the older models.

Kurt   Which?

Martha   You can open the hood like a window, so the baby can look out, and the sun can shine in and it isn't dark. An important development for baby, it calls it.

Kurt   Windows are always good.

Martha   But expensive: two hundred and seventy-nine marks it costs.

Kurt (*proudly*)   Approved!

Martha   If that's what you want. – Mattress seventeen marks eighty, that's normal.

Kurt *nods.*

Martha   You can't do without a Varietta carrycot, anyone who's anyone has got one.

Kurt   Varietta (*Nods.*), that really means something.

Martha   Right. Varietta one hundred and ninety-five marks.

Kurt   Dear.

Martha   But very beautiful.

Kurt (*laughs*)   Approved!

Martha   And we've got to have a mattress, seventy-five marks, a cover fifteen marks and a duvet fifty-nine marks.

Kurt   Approved!

Martha   One good thing is that Adele can lend us a wicker cot and some scales.

Kurt   We don't need handouts.

Martha   Don't be silly – everybody does it, because they're things you only need for a few months. Everyone with close friends borrows from them, even if they don't have to.

Kurt   Right.

Martha   There is more. What we need for the little one to welcome it to the world, as they say.

Kurt   Go on!

Martha   First layette; shirts, cardies, rompers, nappies, there's a special offer for mothers-to-be, ready selected: two hundred and thirty-five marks seventy.

Kurt   Approved!

Martha   Two small under-blankets at fifteen marks ninety comes to thirty-one marks eighty. Rompers, shorts and two woollies I've already bought: fifty-four marks sixty. You also need a large under-blanket: nineteen marks eighty.

Kurt   Haven't you had two already?

Martha   You need a large one as well.

Kurt   Why?

Martha   I'll explain it all later, first the reckoning up.

Kurt   Right.

Martha   Sleeping bag forty-one marks, four sheets for the pram at ten marks ninety each comes to forty-three marks sixty, a basket for under the pram, three sheets, two small duvets, pillows, child's towel, two bath mats – no, wait, that comes under a different heading. Linen depending on the quality, roughly eighty marks for the ordinary stuff, one hundred marks for the best.

Kurt   Twenty marks more or less?! The best.

Martha   That's what I thought too. To continue: bath mats, a pair at nine marks ninety, comes to nineteen marks eighty, soap dish, three marks twenty-five, baby hairbrush and comb ten twenty-five, water thermometer three marks eighty, a changing table forty-eight marks fifty, a baby bath fifteen marks thirty, a bath rack, which is practical, thirty-two marks fifty, a bottle holder seven marks fifty. Question: should we buy an electric bottle warmer, which costs twenty-six marks eighty? It's not essential, but does save a lot of time.

Kurt   You'll have plenty of time, if you stop working for good.

Martha   What about my home work?

Kurt   Is it usual, a bottle warmer?

Martha   Not usual, only if you can afford it.

Kurt (*thinks*) Approved!

Martha   It's better! Six Alete wide-neck bottles with screw tops at two marks ninety-five makes seventeen marks seventy. Economy-size Milton steriliser eleven marks eighty (*Breaks off.*) – no, that belongs with the chemist's things! I'll need a maternity dress for best, one hundred and sixty marks eighty, and one for everyday, fifty-eight marks ten, as well as a maternity suit, which is practical and costs a hundred and twenty-five marks. Once I'm back home after the birth, I'll want a nursing bra – twenty marks ninety. So . . .

Kurt   Approved!

Martha   Now come the problems. Adele would give us the used cot duvet, mattress and baby blanket.

Kurt   No child of mine needs seconds.

Martha   I thought so too, though the things are still nice.

Kurt   No.

Martha   Very well. Duvet roughly forty marks, mattress twenty-two marks eighty and an extra blanket for forty-five marks. Now here's something: 'Frei-Oel' for stretch marks! This is recognised as a good oil, but it's very expensive.

Kurt   Stretch marks?

Martha   Otherwise the skin gets red stripes across the legs and on the stomach, the Frei-Oel prevents this from happening, but each jar costs nine marks ninety.

Kurt   That's not too bad.

Martha   But it's only enough for about ten days, and I should have started using it already. It's high time.

Kurt   You'd better start, so you don't get any marks; if you're economical, one jar might last two weeks.

Martha   Right, so that I am beautiful again after the birth.

Kurt   You're beautiful now. But marks would not be good.

Martha   Right.

Kurt   Because you're my pride and joy.

Martha   Have no fear, I'll take care. A birth, they say, is a cleansing process for the woman, especially if it's a boy.

Kurt   It's a boy, you can tell.

Martha   Yes. – Let's carry on, because it's important. A changing box is not an essential, but there are some very pretty ones around, though they all look much the same. Should we?

Kurt   How much?

Martha   Depends on what catches my eye. They don't come cheap.

Kurt   Because you have taste, over and above what's normal. Remember that time when you chose a tie for me to go with my new suit and how you just picked that particular one from the lot?

Martha *nods.*

Kurt   And how the sales assistant said: 'Your wife has a nose for quality, which not everyone has! This one is more expensive than average, but exquisite', that's what he said.

Martha   It's a beautiful one.

Kurt   Yes.

Martha   Should I buy the changing box that I like? It does cost two hundred and forty-five marks though.

Kurt (*looks up, smiles, nods*)   Approved!

Martha   Right, now comes a question of conscience.

Pause.

(*Deep breath.*) Should our baby have disposable nappies or the normal ones you can wash and reuse?

Kurt *looks uncertain.*

Martha   As I said, it's a problem! The modem household uses the disposable ones, because they save time and are more hygienic. They're called 'Pampers' and are very well known.

Kurt   If they're better?!

Martha   I am not sure, because the old sort have their advantages, and they are not cheap either, those Pampers. A pack of thirty costs six marks sixty, and a baby might need changing six or seven times a day. But buying nappies, the ones that need washing, is not cheap either. And if I don't have that much to do, I can make more ties.

Kurt   I can see to everything that's essential and desirable. I'll take care of it, even without your ties.

Martha   I would prefer the modem nappies, they are recommended too.

Kurt   Then you shall have them. Approved!

Martha   Right. (*Writes.*) Nappy holders are required too and liners, that's normal. (*Writes.*)

Kurt   Right.

Martha   That's the essentials to start with.

Kurt   Nothing else?

Martha (*laughs*)   For the time being I shan't count the chemist's costs, but we can expect about one hundred and fifty marks. And I've already bought knitting wool for seventy-five marks and I'll be knitting about twenty-five marks' worth, not more, because for now I still have the home work. I'll buy a book about 'the child in the womb' and another one for after the birth.

Kurt   So we're well informed.

Martha   Right, as recommended by the doctor! (*Deep breath.*) That's it – unless, I think of something else.

Kurt   You can add some things for me: a flashgun for seventy marks ninety, five films at five marks fifty each plus developing costs of nine marks eighty. (*Laughs.*) Record everything from day one!

Martha (*laughs as well*)   I'd've forgotten that!

Kurt   But I wouldn't! (*Looks up.*) Let me add it up, I'm good at that.

Martha   There.

Kurt *enjoys adding up.*

Martha (*looks on with pleasure*)   It's a lot, you'll see!

Kurt   It's all agreed. (*Adds up.*) Two thousand, seven hundred and twelve marks, fifty pfennigs.

Martha   I would have guessed about three thousand marks, if you add in the things we've forgotten.

Kurt   Three thousand. (*Pause.*) I told my co-driver, a baby costs four thousand for starters.

Martha   Once it's here, there will be more, that's clear.

Kurt   I'll get it. (*Nods.*) No problem.

Scene Four

On the allotment. Quite small, but very neat. Kurt and Martha planting small plants.

Kurt (*holding up one plant*)   Its head's dropped off. Shame!

Martha   But otherwise they're lovely.

Kurt   Thank heaven. They were expensive.

Martha   But lovely. (*She straightens up.*)

Kurt   Tired?

Martha (*nods, smiles*)   Yes. (*Short pause.*) You've never seen me like this, have you? Getting tired so quickly?

Kurt   Do you think I'm dumb and don't understand your condition? Sit down and have a rest. I'll carry on on my own.

Martha   For a little while.

Kurt   No, for longer.

Martha *moves away from the flower beds to the small terrace and sits down in a garden chair.*

Long pause. **Kurt** *works,* **Martha** *watches him.* **Kurt** *plants the flowers with great precision and care; lovingly.*

Martha (*smiles*)   A real love of nature.

Kurt   I've always had it.

Martha   Yes.

Kurt   Do you remember the day Dad came and said: 'We're giving up the allotment, we're too old. Do you want it? I'll give it to you, then I know it's in good hands!' And I didn't need to think about it and said 'Yes' straight away.

Martha   A good move.

Pause.

You know what I'm thinking?

Kurt (*looks up*)   No.

Martha   Something in particular.

Kurt   I'm no mind-reader.

Short pause.

But I have an idea! (*Laughs.*)

Martha   You're a crafty one. (*Laughs.*)

Kurt (*points to her stomach*)   About *it*?

Martha   Yes.

Kurt   And what were you thinking?

Martha   I was thinking, there will come a time when it'll run about in the garden and we'll sit here watching and be happy.

Kurt   I've thought of that myself. (*Short pause.*) We'll have to teach him right from the word go, everything has its place. No getting round it. We'll have to start right at the beginning, explaining things, where the flower beds are, that you must walk on the planks between the beds, and where you can move about freely. It would be a shame if everything got trampled.

Martha   There'll be no trampling; it's our child after all, don't worry.

Kurt   The apple won't fall far from the tree! (*Short pause.*) This is what I thought: I'll make a sandbox. I'm not sure where. Sand really isn't much good and if it's thrown about, a small garden like ours will be ruined before you can blink!

Martha   But there must be a sandbox.

Kurt   I'll make one, but where? First I thought: just next to the terrace, so that we can keep an eye on things in case something happens.

Martha   And why not?

Kurt   It's right next to the flower bed. That bothers me and if we've got to scold all the time, that's no good either.

Martha   Only if we've got to, when something is not allowed.

Kurt   True. Then I thought: perhaps I'd put a little fence round the flower bed. It needn't be very high, then there would be peace and quiet.

Martha   A fence wouldn't look nice and besides a child should keep to the rules, not just a fence. Then it will be easier for him later in life and he won't put his foot in it.

Kurt   True enough.

Pause. **Kurt** *continues to work.* **Martha** *sits and watches. Pause.*

Kurt   Not everyone has a garden. We must appreciate it!

Martha   Yes.

Pause.

Scene Five

Kurt and Martha's flat. Martha prepares dinner. Kurt looks through a thick car catalogue. Kurt wears a jumper.

Martha   Can you feel anything?

Kurt   What?

Martha   Do you feel anything?

Pause.

Perhaps a little discomfort?

Kurt   Why?

Martha   Nothing bothering you?

Kurt   No.

Martha (*smiles*)   I'd better come clean. Since we started saving a bit because of the baby, I'm saving on the housekeeping as well.

Kurt   Look after the pennies . . .

Martha   True. I'm no longer using any Lenor for the woollies. (*Short pause.*) Well, you know 'the woman with the bad conscience'.

Kurt   In the ad.

Martha   Yes. But now that we're saving, I thought, forget 'baby soft' as they say, and see what happens to the woollies. Is the jumper scratching?

Kurt   Not at all.

Martha   I'm glad. (*Laughs a little.*) My conscience is clear then.

Kurt   Yes.

Martha   There're a few other things I managed to save on. I worked it out carefully, you'll see.

Kurt   Like I said before, I'll earn enough for everything that's needed, and there's no need to save on washing powder.

Martha   Be kind to me, I'm pregnant!

Kurt   Everything is for you and the baby! (*Short pause.*) The boss is considerate and understanding, you must give him that. This week it'll be – can you guess?

Martha   A lot?

Kurt   Right. This week it'll be thirty-six hours, that's something, and next week too I'll be top of the list for overtime. Thank God!

Martha   They know we need it.

Kurt   The boss says, 'Not to worry!' (*Smiles.*) Look here, I want to show you something!

Martha   What?

Kurt   He's finally got it, having waited for months on end.

Martha *goes over to him and looks into the catalogue.*

Kurt   The new car. Iso Rivolta Fidia 300. Eight-cylinder engine up front. Five thousand, three hundred and fifty-nine cc, three hundred horsepower, overhead valves, gravity feed dual carburettor, fully synchronised four-speed transmission, manual optional, individual front suspension, De Dion rear axle, hydraulic springs, self-locking differential, top speed two hundred and twenty kilometres an hour! (*Looks up, smiles, nods.*) The boss knows his cars – none of your Mercedes – common as muck. An Iso Rivolta, they'll all look and turn green with envy!

Martha   What's it cost?

Kurt (*reads*)   'Price: sixty thousand marks.'

Martha   No, I mean the catalogue!

Kurt   All the cars you can dream of are in here! Six marks.

Martha　Expensive, considering we're saving.

Kurt　You've got to have some fun.

Martha　I'd rather we eat.

Kurt　One day we'll get a car too, won't we? Some time in the future.

Martha　The baby comes first.

Kurt　Who else? But one day, later, when we can breathe again.

Martha　Then, yes, but first . . . (*Smiles.*) Three weeks to go, if it's on the dot! (*Breathes hard, laughs.*) Eat up!

Scene Six

In hospital. **Martha** *with baby in her arms,* **Kurt** *standing next to the bed with a bunch of flowers.*

Long pause. **Martha** *beams,* **Kurt** *looks on.*

Martha (*quietly*)　There he is.

Kurt *nods.*

Martha　Your son.

Pause.

Can you see him?

Kurt *nods.*

Pause.

Martha　You like him?

Kurt *nods.*

Martha *laughs.*

Kurt　Yes. (*He smiles, stops, looks, starts crying.*) Yes.

Act Two

Scene One

In the kitchen. **Kurt** *has* **Stefan** *on his lap and plays 'church bells' with him.* **Martha** *is occupied with her tie-sewing; she is quite competent now.*

Kurt (*to* **Stefan**, *in a high voice*) And now come the small bells: bim-bim-bim-bim-bim-bim-bim-bim-bim-bim. And now the big bells (*Deeper voice.*): bum-bum-bum-bum-bum-bum-bum-bum-bum. (*He rocks* **Stefan** *gently and hums.*) And now the very, very, very big bells (*Very deep voice.*): bumbam-bumbam-bumbam-bumbam-bumbam-bumbam. (*He rocks* **Stefan** *very gently.*) And now the teeny-weeny bells (*High-pitched voice.*): bimel-bimel-bimel-bimel-bimel-bimel. (*He rocks the child quickly from side to side. Then he gives* **Stefan** *a kiss.*) You're Daddy's boy, aren't you? You're my sunshine, as they say.

Martha (*smiles*) And how about me?

Kurt You too.

Scene Two

A lovely day. **Martha** *and* **Kurt** *arrive on bikes.* **Kurt** *with* **Stefan** *in a child's seat.*

Kurt You must know your way about, mustn't you?

Martha Such a beautiful day.

Kurt True.

They get off their bikes, spread out a blanket, make a place for **Stefan**, *put out and arrange various things. They take off their clothes and are already wearing their swimming costumes. They lie down in the sun.*

Martha How is my figure coming along? The swimming costume fits perfectly, just like before. Not all women are like that.

Kurt (*looks at her proudly*)   But you are.

Martha   And you can't see a single mark.

Kurt   No, nothing, just as it always was.

Martha   You wouldn't want another woman, would you?

Kurt   Never.

Martha   That's all right then! (*Lies down next to him. Pause.*) A corner of paradise.

Kurt   You've got to know your way about.

Martha   You don't need a car when the nicest places are right on your doorstep.

Kurt   Only if you know your way about.

Martha   And we do. You do.

Pause.

Kurt   I'll build him a sandcastle with a moat around it in a minute.

Martha   He's much too small.

Kurt   Then he can watch and learn. (*Turns to the child.*) Can't you? (**Stefan** *happy as a sandboy.*)

Pause.

Kurt (*quietly*)   I'd rather be working now. (*Smiles.*) But if there isn't any work there's nothing to be done about it.

Martha   You can take a Saturday off. It's been going on for a year.

Kurt   Did we need it or didn't we?

Martha   As I said then, after the birth there will be a lot more.

Kurt   A baby is expensive, that's true.

Martha   Be glad. Not everyone can afford what we can.

Kurt   If there was more work again, that would be better.

Martha   Enjoy the day. There might not be another like this for a long time.

Kurt   True.

Scene Three

Middle of the night. Bedroom. Separate beds, carrycot, etc.

Kurt *pants and talks incomprehensibly in his sleep.* **Martha** *wakes up.*

Martha   Kurti-Wurti. (*Shakes him.*) What's the matter, Kurti-Wurti?!

Kurt *is startled.*

Martha   What's the matter?

Kurt   What is it?

Martha   You're acting like a wild man in your sleep.

Kurt   Why?

Martha   How should I know?

Pause.

Kurt (*collects himself*)   I was dreaming, I'm driving along and notice the load slipping forward, you know, slipping downwards over the cab, and I can't stop, on the motorway, or wherever. (*Short pause.*) What rubbish, the load slipping, that sometimes happens to other firms, right, but not us – impossible. (*Laughs.*)

Martha   Yes.

Kurt   Did I wake you up?

Martha (*lies*)   I was awake.

Kurt   Right. (*Short pause.*) We probably had too much to eat. Mayonnaise lies heavy on the stomach, that's common knowledge.

Martha   I made the salad like I always do. My salads are always digestible.

Kurt   Then it must have been the pie.

Martha   You don't take care of yourself, Kurti-Wurti, that's the problem. Never pass up any mark that's going.

Kurt   Certainly not!

Pause.

Everything's there. Are you going short?

Martha   Of what?

Kurt   There are a lot of things you can offer a woman.

Martha   You do what you can.

Short pause.

Kurt   Others earn more than I do.

Martha   I'm happy.

Kurt   Or they get the same, but without doing the overtime. More time at home! (*Smiles.*)

Martha   How a man gets it is his own business. Main thing is that it's there.

Kurt (*laughs, nods*) And it is!

Pause.

Nearly one thousand four hundred net every month! (*Nods.*) A chief inspector probably doesn't get much more, given you were married to one.

Martha   No.

Kurt   Yes.

Pause.

'Course if the economic situation, as they say, means they cut back on overtime, that would be bad.

Martha   I'm sure you'll manage.

Kurt   You bet!

Pause.

A civil servant, of course, has no such worries, is not susceptible to crises, it's always the same, no matter what happens, it makes no difference.

Martha   Not everyone can be a civil servant.

Kurt   No.

Pause.

The boss says that the migrant workers are getting the push now, one after the other. (*Short pause.*) You understand? Being made redundant.

Martha   You're not a migrant!

Kurt   Thank God, no.

Pause.

First the migrant workers, then the rest of us, some are saying at work.

Martha   Nonsense. – And even if they sack everyone, the boss will hang on to you.

Kurt   Because he likes me, right. (*Short pause.*) Because I keep myself to myself and only think of work. He says he appreciates that. He'd like everyone to be like me, he says.

Pause.

(*Smiles.*) No, we have nothing to fear, because long before I get to feel the pinch, the others will be made redundant first.

Martha   Because the boss likes you, because you are reliable and don't make trouble.

Kurt   Certainly not.

Pause.

Martha   You're sweating!

Kurt   I'm hot.

Scene Four

The garden. Beautiful late afternoon. **Kurt**, **Martha** *and* **Stefan**.

Kurt *builds a sandbox next to the terrace.* **Martha** *works in the flower beds.* **Stefan** *plays. Long pause. They work.*

Martha   I'll lie down in the deckchair for a bit, and catch the sun.

Kurt   Right. I'll just finish the enclosure here, then do the flower beds.

Martha   You have a rest too. You should enjoy this weather too.

Kurt   I enjoy myself when I'm doing something. Tomorrow is the first Saturday for four weeks that I can work overtime again. (*Laughs.*) Only me, the boss said!

Martha   What is it?

Kurt   A special mission! (*Laughs.*)

Martha *lies down in the deckchair.*

Kurt   Thank God! (*Continues to work.*)

Pause.

Scene Five

Concealed clearing by a small lake. A beautiful day. Noise of an approaching lorry. The engine is turned off. Pause.

Kurt *enters, looks around, smiles, goes off again. He returns with a barrel, opens it, empties its contents, a reddish-brown liquid, into the lake. He shows no signs of anxiety, but is rather triumphant and self-assured. He takes the empty barrel back and returns with a full one.*

This process is repeated eight times. With the last barrel **Kurt** *stands still by the lake, and looks around. Then he sees the sandcastle, which he had built previously for* **Stefan**.

Kurt   Out of sight, out of mind. Right. (*Smiles.*)

Pause. He takes the last barrel and leaves the stage. Noise of a heavy lorry starting up, revving up, driving away and disappearing into the distance. Silence . . . Long pause.

Martha *arrives on her bike,* **Stefan** *in a child's seat. She gets off the bike, secures it, lifts* **Stefan** *out, takes a blanket, etc., arranges everything, sits down on the blanket, remains dressed,* **Stefan** *close to her.*

Martha   Dad would be surprised, wouldn't he, if he could see us now through a telescope, how independent we've become. He's a good dad. Works from morning till night for his family, so we go without nothing. (*Looks at the child.*) A good dad, our Dad! Are you hot? Shall Mummy play splash-splash with you? Hm? Swim-swim like a big fish? (*Laughs, takes off her clothes, already in her swimming costume, undresses* **Stefan** *completely, they play, then she carries the child to the water.*) Look at the sandcastle Dad built specially for you, still all in one piece because nobody knows our spot!

With the child in her arms she goes into the water, finally she is in the water up to her waist, she puts **Stefan** *a little into the water, splashes him a bit, dips him some more into the water, then more. Splashes about with him. Pause. Suddenly the child starts yelling terribly.* **Martha** *is startled.*

Martha   Silly boy, scared of water – it won't bite you!
Little fish spend day and night in the water, even when they
are babies. They can swim right away, slow coach! (*She dips
him more carefully into the water – the child yells louder, and even more
terribly.*) What's up? My little darling? If you don't feel like a
swim today, we'll go now. (*She carries* **Stefan** *out of the water to
the blanket and lays him down. The child's yells increase.*) It's all
over, it's all over. No more water, only the sun. Now listen,
there's no need to cry, just because of a little water! (*She tries
to calm down the child, takes it in her arms, rocks it.*) And the big
bells, listen: bum-bum-bum-bum – and now the medium-
size bells: bimbum-bimbum-bimbum-bimbum-bimbum –
and now the teeny-weeny bells: bimmel-bimmel-bimmel-
bimmel-bimmel-bimmel-bimmel-bimmel-bimmel-bimmel –
and now the very, very, very big bells: bummelbum-
bummelbum-bummelbum-bummelbum. For Christ's sake,
what is it? (**Stefan** *turns a bluish colour all over his body.*) Why
are you turning blue? This is too silly for words. (*Quietly.*) Oh
God, a child that turns blue is in danger, that's what it says
in the book. It's heavily underlined too. Because of
suffocation or something,

*She jumps up, puts on her dress, leaving everything else, dresses the
child hastily, puts him on the bike and cycles away quickly.*

Scene Six

Inside the flat. **Kurt** *sits and stares at* **Martha**. **Martha**'s *face is
puffy from crying. She wears thin cotton bandages around her legs. It is
afternoon.*

Pause.

Martha   They said at the hospital, you've got to wait to
see how bad the burns are.

She breaks out crying.

Kurt *sits and stares.*

Martha   For me – because I'm grown up – it's not so serious.

Pause.

They're criminals polluting the water with poison. And our place was a secret; even the sandcastle you built – untouched.

Pause.

Kurt   Why did you go there, without me?

Martha   What?

Kurt   Without me. You need me to look after you. I know my way about.

Martha   Why?

Pause.

Kurt (*quietly*)   Because it was me. The poison. (*Short pause.*) This morning.

Martha *looks. Pause.*

Scene Seven

It is evening. Same situation. **Martha** *by the cooker. Long silence.*

Kurt   I don't feel human any longer. Me!

Martha   Shut up, murderer!

Pause.

Kurt   You don't want to know me any more, do you?

Long pause.

If it was possible I'd swap places. I'd be in hospital now. But it isn't possible.

Smiles, embarrassed.

Martha   How can a man like you still laugh?

Kurt   I didn't laugh.

Martha   You did.

Kurt   You're wrong.

Long pause.

Martha   I told you to shut up.

Kurt (*although he has not said anything*)   Yes.

Pause.

We're finished, aren't we?

Martha   Finished.

Kurt   Yes.

Pause.

You can't live with the murderer of your child.

Martha   No.

Kurt   But if he pulls through?

Martha   Please God.

Long pause.

Kurt (*quietly*)   Martha?

Martha *is silent. Long pause.*

Kurt   Have you cooked anything?

Martha   Not for you.

Kurt   No.

Martha   We'll never share a table again.

Kurt   I'll sit somewhere else.

Martha   I shan't sit down otherwise.

Kurt   I'm gone already. (*Sits down in a corner.*)

Pause.

Martha *starts eating.*

Kurt   Enjoy your dinner.

Martha (*looks up*) A *man* like *you* can *still* think about food?

Kurt   Sorry.

Pause.

Makes your stomach turn, doesn't it, just looking at me?

Martha   Yes.

Kurt   I feel the same.

Long pause. **Martha** *eats.* **Kurt** *looks on. Suddenly and without any particular reason he starts yelling.*

Kurt   Wine, wine, wine – *bad wine.* That's what the boss said. Harmless, he said. The fish will get tipsy, he said, and get merry, nothing else! (*Yells even louder.*) Drive somewhere remote, he said, because of the law. Bad wine is against the law, but it's harmless. Because of that – the spot – which only we know – just for the boss – dead certain – I am reliable – just a hint from the boss is enough. – No bother! (*Beats his chest with his fist.*) A hard worker – special mission – carried out with the boss's approval. (*Reaches into the side pocket of his jacket.*) One hundred marks bonus. There! (*He cries. Pause.*) The boss said –

Martha (*raised voice*)   The boss said! – (*Yells.*) The boss said! – And if the boss said: Bring me the head of your child, it wouldn't hurt the child, but I'll give you a hundred marks, then you'd have done it, because the boss said so. Right! (*Short pause, then quietly:*) You're not human, I must have missed that. Just an . . . organ grinder's monkey! Believe you me, your boss is no more than a criminal. But I'm not married to him but to you. And it's terrible for a woman to realise she's given her best years to something like you.

Kurt   An organ grinder's monkey?

Martha   Right. Ugh! I'm off to the hospital to see how Stefan is. You do as you please. (*Goes off.*)

Kurt *looks after her.*

Long pause.

Scene Eight

The clearing. The bathing things are still there as Martha had left them. It is early evening. **Kurt** *arrives on his bike. He cycles as far as the bathing things. Gets off and secures the bike.*

Pause.

Kurt *looks, embarrassed, uncertain. Slowly he moves his head, and looks to the left and the right, nods sometimes for no reason. Then he picks up all the things which Martha had left. He rolls them all neatly together, the blanket as well. He picks up a small teddy bear which belongs to Stefan, looks at it, puts it down carefully on top of the pile. He packs everything away on the rack of his bicycle. He takes the briefcase hanging on the handlebars, a large cardboard box, a pair of scissors and a pen. From the box he cuts out a piece, the size of a poster, puts it on the ground, and writes on it with the pen: NO SWIMMING! BEWARE OF POISON! DANGER! He must frequently redo the individual letters, to make the lines very thick.*

Then he goes back to the bike, takes a broomstick, which he had fastened to the crossbar, and gets more tools from his briefcase. He nails the warning to the broomstick. He digs a hole in the ground by the shore and then pushes the broomstick with the warning into it. He fills it up with earth, and treads the earth down, etc.

This work lasts for a very long time, it is carried out thoroughly, almost pedantically. Not until everything is finished, and he is certain that the warning cannot be missed, does he take his bike again, mount it and cycle off.

Pause.

Kurt *returns. He remains seated on the bike by the shore. Looks into the water.*

Long pause.

Kurt *nods to himself. He gets off the bike, and starts slowly undressing himself down to his underpants. He puts his things neatly by his bike. Then he moves very slowly towards the water, goes into it.*

Pause.

Kurt *looks. Then he dips under, first up to his neck, then his head as well, so that one can no longer see him. He remains under water for some time. Then he straightens up, waits and returns to the shore.*

Pause.

He looks down at himself. Searches for any changes on his body. There are none. He goes back again into the water, dips under again, returns to the shore. Meanwhile, he is shivering because it is cool. He waits, examines his skin, nothing. He dries himself with a towel that Martha has left behind. He gets dressed again. Looks. He makes a forlorn gesture.

Pause.

Act Three

Scene One

Darkness. The front door is being opened. The light is switched on.
Kurt *enters. Very slowly, quietly. He closes the door behind him. His face and hands are slightly pink, the skin around his eyes is bright red. He stands still. Looks around.*

Pause.

He goes into the living room, turns the light on. Looks. Waits. He goes into the bedroom. Looks. Waits. He is startled, although there is no cause. He goes into the kitchen again. Stands still by the door.

Long pause.

He goes to the sideboard, opens a drawer and takes out pieces of string. He inspects them with expertise and puts them back again.

Pause.

He has an idea. He goes into the hall and gets an old-fashioned washing line. Takes it into the kitchen. Sits down by the table and starts to unwind the washing line. He is economical with the line, and tries to imagine the required length. He gets up, goes to the sideboard, takes from it a pair of scissors, cuts part of the line off. He inspects it, pulls at it. He takes the cut part of the line and measures it against the roll. Measures the same length again. Cuts it off again. He ties the two lengths together at both ends, so that they are double. He puts the rope on the table. He returns the washing line to its place in the hall. Comes back, returns the scissors to the sideboard.

Pause.

He takes the doubled rope and just stands. Looks around. He doesn't know what to do next. He walks through the flat. Searches for something secure to hang it on. Finds nothing. Comes back into the kitchen. Goes to the kitchen window, takes the curtain rail with the closed curtains down. He is seized with fright, when he realises that he can be seen from outside. He quickly puts up the curtains again, and closes them carefully.

Pause.

He goes to the loo. It is a modern one without a cistern above it. He comes back.

Long pause.

(This scene should last for some time.)

Kurt gives up the idea of hanging. He puts the rope on the kitchen table. He goes to the sideboard, takes out several kinds of medicine, puts them on the table. There is nothing there that would kill him.

Pause.

He goes into the bathroom and takes his shaving gear out to the kitchen, puts it on the table. He sits down. From the safety razor he takes the used blade. Examines it. Puts it back again.

Pause.

He takes out a pack of new razor blades. Holds them in his hand. Looks. Starts perspiring.

Pause.

He looks around. He gets up and switches off all the lights. Darkness. One can hear him coming back into the kitchen, sitting down.

Very long pause.

One can hear **Kurt** *getting up. He switches the light on again. There are tears in his eyes. He is quite exhausted. He starts putting back the medicine.*

Pause.

He take his shaving gear, is about to put it back as well. Front door opens. **Martha** *comes in.*

Martha (*calling out*)   Kurti-Wurti, he's over the worst! Kurt? (*She comes into the kitchen.*) Kurti-Wurti?

Kurt (*startled, smiles, quietly, quickly*)   Just shaving!

Martha (*looks, is unsure*)   But look at you.

Kurt   I've just been into the water. To see how it is!

Martha   I see.

Pause.

Goes to the table sees the medicine and the rope; unsure.

Messy habits.

Long pause.

Kurt   I make my flesh creep, Martha. That's why.

Long pause.

Martha   Stefan, he's over the worst, Kurti-Wurti!

Kurt   Yes.

Martha   In two or three days he'll be allowed home again. Made it by the skin of his teeth.

Kurt   Yes.

Pause.

Martha   Aren't you glad? That your son is on the road to recovery?

Kurt   Yes, I am.

Long pause.

Martha   A decent man doesn't kill himself; there's no need.

Kurt   Yes.

Pause.

Martha   You've been had, because you're a good man! You trust others! – The boss is to blame. Not you.

Kurt   Yes.

Martha   He lied to you – you weren't to know, as he's always been good to us. And then this! You couldn't expect that.

Kurt   No.

Long pause.

Martha   It'd be difficult to find a better man than you. Look around you, what you've made possible.

Kurt   Yes.

Martha   Because you work hard!

Pause.

Martha   Stefan needs a dad!

Pause.

(*Quietly.*) Suicide is wrong. (*Short pause.*) Kurti-Wurti!

Pause.

Kurt   I couldn't do it. I've been mucking around for an hour.

Pause.

An organ grinder's monkey doesn't commit suicide.

Martha   That hurt you, didn't it? That I said that. I'm sorry.

Kurt (*quietly*)   But it's true.

Martha   Nonsense!

Kurt (*calm*)   Don't lie!

Pause.

Unsuitable for personal use, that's me. (*Smiles.*)

Pause.

Martha   Most men are like you!

Kurt   If someone had told me that a few days ago, I wouldn't have believed it. Laughed at him.

Pause.

That's it. (*Short pause.*) A revelation, as they say.

Pause.

You don't like living with yourself, when you know all that. When you look in the mirror, you think: that can't be me. That one there.

Martha   We need you, Kurti-Wurti!

Kurt   Killer of his own children.

Martha   I'm sorry I said that.

Kurt   You did.

Martha   I know. I'm sorry. Forget it.

Kurt   And if it's the truth?

Martha   It's not.

Kurt   Because the child lived.

Martha   And it wasn't deliberate . . . it was a mistake.

Pause.

Kurt   That was no mistake, Martha. That's just it. You can send off someone like me in the morning, like a little boy to run errands. How far does it have to go, before something inside, for once, says 'no'? What can't I be ordered to do? No, it wasn't a mistake. I'm like that.

Pause.

There are more things you could have, Martha! And those (*Points at himself.*) who would get them for you.

Martha   Not you, I know you better. You're a good man, and I won't let anyone say different, not even you. You've had it hard, that's the trouble. – I'd rather you looked around for once, to see what you've made possible, because you're a decent man – working your fingers to the bone. Then you'll think differently! – Right from the start! You remember? (*Smiles.*) The latest pram available, a Varietta,

linen fit for a king, hospital – private (*Nods.*), for the birth, a
Persian lamb coat with a mink collar; recently the new
washing machine and it won't be long till the colour TV is
here . . .

Kurt (*yells*)   No! (*Matter-of-fact.*) Tomorrow morning I'm
going to the police to report us: the boss and me.

Martha *looks.*

Scene Two

During the night in the bedroom. **Kurt** *and* **Martha** *in their beds. It
is dark.*

Martha (*quietly*)   Couldn't you pretend it was a mistake
that never happened? And take care next time?

Kurt   Do you still really like me though, Martha?

Short pause.

Martha   You should live. Not drive us to despair.

Kurt   But you would like me to be different?

Martha   If I had the choice, a bit perhaps.

Kurt   Right, me too. Because I'm not a man, or at best
only in the lowest sense.

Pause.

I'm not turning back, Martha. (*Shakes his head.*) I'd rather be
dead, and, sooner or later, I'd get it right.

Martha   You only think of yourself!

Kurt   How could I face the child again as things stand? 'It
was a mistake, Stefan, but now that the boss won't ask me to
do a similar job, it won't happen again!'

Pause.

No, Martha, it can't go on like this. I want to come clean, all the dirt must come out and you must help me, please!

Martha   I'm frightened.

Kurt   Me too. If I go and blow everything and land the boss in it then I'll get my cards tomorrow and it won't be easy to find a new job here. The boss will see to that. That's for sure.

Martha   We could move away, Kurt, where no one knows us! But then we're finished here. Remember that.

Pause.

Kurt   Martha, no one can blame us because we behaved the way we did – you and I. The ones higher up than us, they will see to it that the likes of you and me will never wake up to reality. We can prove that any time. But, Martha, if now, at this point, we don't change, if we stick our heads in the sand again, then this time it's our own fault, and there's no one else to blame. That's it.

Martha   Being brave is supposed to be difficult, Kurti-Wurti.

Kurt   That's true. – Would you help me anyway?

Martha   I don't know that I can.

Pause.

Kurt   Please, Martha. Look: I can't live as an illusion any more. But as a man you can at least respect – that must still be possible.

Martha   True enough. I don't think the illusion was any more beautiful or richer, but –

Kurt   – but not an organ grinder's monkey.

Martha *is silent.*

Kurt   With you, it would be possible, I am certain of it.

Martha   I am your wife. What do I get from a man who enjoys life as opposed to one who wants to die? Think about that. Although it's hard, I can see that.

Pause.

But who knows, the proof of the pudding is in the eating. How does the ugly duckling know that it's a swan? (*Short pause.*) Go to sleep. You need all your strength tomorrow.

Kurt   Yes.

Scene Three

Early morning in the kitchen. During breakfast. **Kurt** *wears his best suit.* **Martha** *in her dressing gown.*

Martha   Dig in; that'll calm you down.

Kurt   I hope I don't have to throw up, I don't feel well.

Martha   Want a schnapps?

Kurt   The boss will say right away that I'm drunk and should sober up. (*Smiles.*) I'm a coward all right, aren't I?

Martha   No. (*Short pause.*) I remember something now! In school, as a kid, I had a teacher who frightened everyone. Art. (*Laughs.*) Once I had to stand up and somehow I knocked over an ink pot. Just an accident, right. He gave me such a hiding in front of the class that I wet my pants. Everything was wet, even the skirt, and I had to sit like that till school was over. (*Short pause.*) I was so embarrassed I can't tell you! (*Shakes her head.*) At home I told Mum and Dad, and Dad give me another slap in the face. I'll never forget it.

Pause.

Kurt   And?

Martha   Nothing, I just remembered.

Kurt   Memories.

Martha   Yes.

Pause.

Kurt   I'm off.

Martha   Right.

Kurt *gets up, puts his coat on, looks.*

Martha *nods.*

Kurt *leaves.*

Scene Four

In the kitchen. **Martha** *and* **Kurt**. *Lunchtime.*

Kurt   First he called me names, for dumping it in a bathing spot. You're useless, he said. He said that the poison was an *oversight*. Now, he said, everything will have dissolved and it's harmless.

Martha   And you said?

Kurt   I said I was going to the police to report both of us.

Pause.

Then he started yelling, acted like a wild man! He shouted that I was drunk, although I didn't even have *one* drink. When he really yelled I was scared at first, but then not. (*Smiles.*) We're used to being yelled at. I said, I admit my part in the affair, for which I'm responsible, and that he should come to the police and own up. He turned quite pale, right! And said: Who are you to talk of responsibility. A man like you can't take on any responsibility whatever. You are on your own, he said. You're just a poor little sod, nothing else. To take on responsibility for things like this, you need a real man. – And not an organ grinder's monkey, I said? (*Laughs.*) When I'd said that, he stopped and thought – and then asked: Who is behind you?

Pause.

And then I lied (*Smiles.*) and I said: A lot of people.

Pause.

I didn't want to be alone, that's why. Desperation can make you lie. (*Short pause.*) That had its effect. You'd hardly believe it. He stopped yelling right away and was quite polite. Before I left he suggested a compromise: he would arrange for the hospital, that's no problem – he knows the consultant. He'll pay any bills and some compensation to us. If I stood by him, I wouldn't be sorry. But if I went to the police he would see to it that I would not only be made redundant, but would never get another job. Anywhere! Because he's got connections. Then I could go and hang myself. But he said that in such a way, Martha, that I could feel that he was frightened and didn't believe it himself. (*Nods. Pause.*) I've already been to the police.

Martha   And?

Kurt   They took a statement with all the details, just as it happened, which I signed. Today is Sunday and the people in charge weren't there, but I'll hear from them. (*Nods.*) The inspector who took down the details said they wouldn't be locking me up. At least, not yet. (*Looks.*)

Martha *is silent.*

Kurt   A police car drove to the lake, to examine everything and take samples of the water. They'll drive to the hospital as well, because of Stefan.

Pause.

That's it.

Pause.

Scene Five

Martha *in the kitchen.* **Kurt** *returns from work.*

Kurt (*comes in*)　Survived the first day!

Martha　Do they know in the firm already?

Kurt　I don't think so. It was like it always was. And the boss wasn't there.

Martha　He'll have plenty on his plate.

Kurt　Right.

Pause.

Martha　Go and have a look in the bedroom.

Kurt　Is he back?

Martha　Have a look.

Kurt (*goes to the bedroom, to the cot*)　Yes. (*Smiles.*)

Scene Six

In the allotment. A lovely evening. It is warm. **Martha**, **Kurt** *and* **Stefan**, *who is playing. The parents sit on the small terrace.*

Pause.

Martha　It's lovely, isn't it?

Kurt　Yes.

Pause.

Martha *suddenly starts crying.*

Kurt　What's the matter?

Martha　Nothing.

Pause.

I'm afraid for us.

Short pause.

Kurt   We have made our bed, now we must lie in it.

Martha   If it comes out, and the boss realises you were lying, and we're on our own, he'll eat us alive, believe you me. He'll see to it that you go to prison and he'll get a medal. Lies won't get us far.

Kurt   It isn't a lie any more.

Martha   Why?

Kurt   I don't know that it will do any good but the shop steward from the union, you know, he came to see me yesterday morning, as I was about to drive off, and said someone had let on.

Martha   Who?

Kurt   They keep their eyes open.

Martha   But you're not in the union!

Kurt   The boss always said he wasn't too keen on the idea.

Martha   And what does he want?

Kurt   He said he'd been tipped off, and if it's true what I said to the police, they'll help us, that's what he said.

Pause.

He'll come Saturday afternoon with someone else to talk about it.

Martha   And what did you say?

Kurt   Yes, I said, he should come.

Martha   Will that do any good?

Kurt   In the union you are not alone!

Pause.

Martha   There now, he's right inside the flower bed.

Kurt   Let him be.

End.

Tom Fool

translated by

Estella Schmid and Anthony Vivis

Characters

Martha, *the wife, normal and about forty – rather plump but quite pretty, very honest and practical.*
Otto, *the husband, also normal and about forty – quite tall, lean, likes to smoke and drink, rather nervous, erratic, in his best moments he appears almost elegant.*
Ludwig, *their son, a nice fellow of about fifteen, looks more like his father than his mother, tall but shy and silent, listens a lot but says little.*

Setting

The play is set in Munich – on the outskirts, perhaps in one of the housing estates which were built in Neuhausen in 1950.

Time

The play takes place in spring/summer 1976.

Act One

Scene One: Lie-Abed

In the sitting room is a sofa bed. **Ludwig** *sleeps in it, but you cannot see him, as he is covered up with a blanket. From the bed you hear sentimental pop music. Around the bed, in a circle of about one metre, there is built up a small 'diaspora': a few cassettes, two or three posters on the wall, personal belongings like a wallet, sunglasses, a comb, a beautiful lighter, cigarettes, rocker boots, jeans and jacket, watch, etc.*

Martha (*from the kitchen*) Get up!

Ludwig *does not hear her.*

Martha It's the early bird that catches the worm!

Pause.

(*Enters.*) How many more times! Nearly eight and you're still in bed. Get up now and don't waste God-given time.

Ludwig (*from underneath the blanket*) Just ten more minutes.

Martha Not a minute more. Up, I said, and let's have the place tidy. I don't want it looking like a doss-house.

Ludwig (*pops his head out*) Why should I get up?

Martha Because I say so and because a young man should not be lying in bed till this hour of the day. Your dad went to work an hour ago. Come on, up you get. You get on my nerves. (*She goes out of the room.*) You're such a worry.

Pause.

Ludwig *listens to the music a bit longer, then switches it off. Puts the cassette player carefully to one side. He gets up and dresses himself slowly. He starts to tidy up. He does this every day – like a routine. He puts all his things together in one spot, then takes them to 'his drawer' and puts everything in. He goes on tidying up, he takes the two or three posters off the wall, very carefully, so that no plaster comes off, rolls them up fussily, and puts them behind the cupboard. Everything is*

*clinically tidy – he leaves the bed as it is. Then he goes into the
bathroom – you hear him turning the water on, etc.*

Pause.

Martha *comes busily into the room, goes to the sofa bed, shakes the
covers and pillows, takes everything off and makes a bundle, puts the
sofa together, and puts the sheets, etc., into the sofa drawer – then
finally it's become a 'sitting-room sofa'; she tidies up a few other things,
puts a cover on it and a few cushions, puts everything in its right place
and is happy – all traces of the night are wiped out, everything is
clinically tidy again; she goes into the kitchen, calls:*

Martha   Hurry up, the coffee won't stay hot for ever!

Ludwig *(from the bathroom)*   Yeah, just a minute.

Scene Two: With Guests

*Saturday lunchtime. They are all in the living room watching TV.
Original sound.*

Ludwig   They say he can't even write his name. *(Laughs.)*

Martha *(angry)*   Who says? Honestly, some people are just
trash but he's a king!

Pause.

Otto   I'd love to have a tenth of his money, that's all – I'd
gladly do without being able to write my name.

Martha *(nods)*   It's only envy speaking.

Pause.

Otto   Is she as chaste as a future queen ought to be, I
wonder?

Martha *(emphatically)*   At her age – 'course not. Even a
commoner can get away with it these days.

Ludwig   It's all mush.

Otto   Still, she's German! (*Nods.*) Our German girls – even the King of Sweden's hooked! (*Nods.*)

Pause.

Martha   Ours was a lovely wedding, wasn't it?

Pause.

Now he's said it (*with relish*): Sylvia Renate Sommerblatt – What's she feeling now, I wonder?

Pause.

Now they've said 'I do'. (*Smiles and nods.*) Now they exchange rings!

Otto   What do you think the whole circus costs?

Martha   She can hardly speak. She's all choked up. (*Short pause. With certainty.*) Lovely!

Otto   She's got fat hands!

Martha   That's just typical. You would say that – now they're singing. Male voices! Lovely!

Otto   No they aren't.

Martha   They're cardinals – not a proper choir. We had a harmonium player, remember?

Otto *looks, can't remember.*

Martha   What was that tune? 'Land of Smiles' by Franz Lehar. (*Nods.*) See, I remember, you don't.

Otto   Dead right.

Pause.

Martha   They're all there, you know, all the big nobs.

Ludwig   Boring.

Martha   You've no sense of beauty, that's why. How many kings are left in the world? You can count them on the fingers of one hand. Be grateful we can still experience such an event.

Otto (*standard English*)   Epoch-making. Though they have no say any more, the 'crowned heads'!

Martha   She's supposed to be very intelligent, Sylvia.

Otto   But *he* isn't, he's right there. (*Referring to* **Ludwig**.) But get yourself a career first and make his money, then you can talk.

Martha   Shh: quiet – now they're husband and wife. (*Laughs.*) She keeps winking at him. See her?

Otto (*laughs*)   Bitch! She's got him in her grip. 'Well, well, now you're mine – my little man,' she's thinking.

Martha (*joins in the laughter*)   Men!

Otto   Snap – the trap! (*Laughs, nods.*)

Pause.

Martha   There, what is happiness? You listen to them: forget about yourself, just be there for others.

Otto   Easy for them.

Martha   What's so lovely is it's a real love match! He met her at the Olympics and said: 'I'll take her, never mind who she is.' – That's royalty for you!

Otto *laughs.*

Ludwig   I'm starving!

Martha   It's all ready.

Otto (*looks at his son, out of the blue*)   I wish I had your life!

Martha   Nobody works Saturdays – well, most people don't.

Otto   And what did he do yesterday?

Ludwig (*looks, nervous*)   Nothing.

Otto   Exactly. Follow their example! On the box!

Martha   Exactly. It is lovely! (*Emphasises it.*) Really, really lovely! (*Nods.*)

Pause.

Recognise her?

Otto   Who?

Martha   He's so ignorant. Fabiola and Baudouin. Our President is there too, look, and his missus.

Otto   She looks like a hippopotamus.

Martha (*apologetically*)   Well, she is nearly six foot tall.

Pause.

Hear that, she speaks six languages. I respect that! That's more than wealth and possessions. And he's got four sisters, the King. They keep at it, don't they!

Otto (*he gives his son a friendly shove*)   Now, you get her and you got no more problems.

Ludwig *thanks him by laughing excessively.*

Pause.

Martha   'Man proposes, God disposes!' (*Means the wedding.*) Well, that's the main bit over. Now they're moving out of the church. – So dignified! – Imagine if you tripped up – I'd die on the spot. (*Laughs.*)

Pause.

He's nice, the King. Look at him, laughs the whole time! That's not easy, you know.

Otto   Shhhh!

Pause.

They don't seem to go in for red flags. (*Nods.*)

Martha That wouldn't be right – at a wedding! Think of the politics.

Otto Sweden.

Martha Exactly.

Ludwig I'm starving.

Martha Listen to him. He behaves as if he was the breadwinner. I want to watch this.

Otto Earn some money, then you can give the orders. Right!

Ludwig Right.

Pause.

Martha What's so nice is she's German.

Ludwig Supposing he married a black?

Martha (*quick*) Royalty would never do a thing like that.

Otto Dead right.

Pause.

Martha The whole population's come out to cheer them! (*Short pause.*) A 'fairy tale-marriage'. That's what it is. (*Nods and smiles.*)

Ludwig (*provocatively*) Won't we be eating today?

Martha (*equally provocative*) Work-shy loafers don't need to eat.

Otto I'm hungry myself.

Martha (*angry*) Can't you just wait ten minutes! Ruin your whole life, their lordships!

Ludwig It's boring.

Pause.

Otto (*slightly stupid*)   He'll never get anywhere, always swimming against the tide.

Martha   He's young yet.

Otto   Not for much longer.

Martha   Young and foolish.

They continue to watch TV. **Ludwig** *gets up, takes something out of his drawer and goes out – we hear a door slamming but* **Otto** *and* **Martha** *do not hear it.*

Martha   Juan Carlos – Murderer! – Franco the Second! – was written on that wall.

Otto   Pigs.

Martha   I hope he never read it – he's a king as well. It would have spoilt the most beautiful day of his life.

Otto   No, they won't have.

Martha   Let's hope not. It'd be a shame when she's so happy.

Otto   Live and let live.

Martha   Sylvia Sommerblatt, Queen of Sweden.

Otto   I'm starving.

Martha   Earn some money, then you can eat at the Hilton.

Otto (*thinks that she means him*)   Silly cow!

Martha   What?

Otto   I'm asking you.

Martha   Where is he?

Otto   He's gone.

Martha   I'm watching this right to the end. And that's that!

Pause.

Martha She's never stopped waving that bouquet. White orchids – lovely flowers, but wrong, you know. They should've told her, she's making a fool of herself.

Otto Not in Sweden it isn't.

Martha Really?

Scene Three: Coitus Interruptus

In the Neckermann Popular Store Bedroom. **Martha** *and* **Otto** *at work.*

Martha What are you thinking?

Otto Nothing.

Pause. They do it.

Martha Your mind's not on it.

Otto Mmmm.

Martha No, it's not.

Pause. They do it.

What is he thinking of, I'd like to know?

Otto Not telling you.

Martha If you're thinking of something else – when you're with me – a woman sticks up for herself, it's her bloody right. (*Pushes him away.*) Smut!

Otto No, not at all. No, no.

Martha What then? (*Has torn herself away from him.*)

Otto Can't tell you.

Martha There you are.

Otto No 'cause I feel shy about it.

Martha   Smut, any woman can tell.

Otto   You're on the wrong track. It's a fortnight now since he borrowed my pen, the one that cost twenty-eight marks. (*Short pause.*) He's forgotten to give it me back. (*Turns away finally.*)

Pause.

For two weeks I can think of nothing else all day, but how to go about asking him to return my pen without getting offended. Suppose I go: 'Excuse me, boss, but you borrowed my pen. Please can I have it back.' Or drop the 'please' – just: 'I'd like to have it back.' So he'd laugh and go: 'Of course, I'm so sorry.' (*Laughs.*) And he'd put his hand in his pocket (*Short pause. With emphasis.*) – if he'd still got it, that is.

Pause.

Martha *has hardly listened; after all she's just been used as a woman, she is trying to regain control of herself more than listening to him; she also doesn't quite understand, because she expected something different.*

Otto   But what if he hasn't got it any more? – 'Oh, really? What did it look like?' Then I'd describe it in detail, right, so then he'd send somebody to look on his desk, and if it's not there then, of course, the whole thing would be quite embarrassing. 'Are you sure that I borrowed it?' – 'Oh, yes.' – 'When?' – 'Well, a fortnight ago.' – 'Why didn't you ask me sooner?' – (*Short pause.*) And what do I say then?

Pause.

I have a strong suspicion, you know. (*Short pause.*) A very strong suspicion that he hasn't got it any more! (*Nods, looks at* **Martha**, *who understands nothing.*) He mislaid it the same day on the tour of inspection.

Long pause.

Martha *nods.*

Otto   It's hopeless!

Pause.

He smiles and nods.

Martha (*looks up*)   It's true, you borrow a pen and pop it in your own pocket automatic.

Otto (*quick*)   Even though you know it cost money?

Martha *looks.*

Otto   Whether he'd notice it, that's the question, he's used to having expensive things, right? So I thought: should I pin a notice up on the board? 'Lost, one pen.' Diplomatic, you know! – 'Metallic grey with revolving cartridge and red top. Original article, not cheap copy, genuine Parker 51. Please return. Reward.' (*Looks at his wife.*) Five marks maybe? It cost twenty-eight marks seventy. (*Looks.*)

Martha   Not much use, if your boss's got it.

Otto   There's the rub, the boss won't look at the board of course, that's obvious. And if it's anybody else, he'll see straight away what a fine specimen he's got there. He puts it in his pocket and confiscates it as his own private property. (*Nods.*) That's only human, it nestles so nicely to your grip and it glides so smoothly across the page.

Pause. **Martha** *starts to think.*

Martha   You should've gone to see your boss immediately and wangled the pen out of him.

Otto (*hooks at* **Martha**, *angrily*)   The way she talks!

Pause.

The boss arrives with a delegation, maybe twenty people, each one of them at least some head of department, most of them from the supervisory boards, and the boss gives them a tour of inspection, personally, which is an honour in itself as we know – and he explains something which he needs a pen for.

Nods. Pause. A difficult problem.

He borrows it off of me, me of all people – which you can say is also an honour. He explains the problem and then moves on with the (standard English) gentlemen forgetting, of course, that it's my pen. Shall I stop them all now, the whole delegation, restrain the boss – so to speak – and ask him to give me my pen back?

Pause.

No way! (*Looks at his wife.*)

Martha   You should've gone to him immediately after the tour.

Otto   Immediately afterwards they had a big dinner at the Casino – after all, they had to celebrate a thirty-million deal. (*Emphatic.*) No way!

Martha   The next day?

Otto   He was in Brussels.

Martha   How do you know?

Otto (*low*)   'Cause I'm not that stupid, I wanted to go and see him, so I checked beforehand if he was there. Negative!

Pause.

Martha   Well, why didn't you go and see him the day after?

Pause.

Otto   I didn't dare to any more.

Martha (*wheezes*)   Oh God, a good start is half the battle, that's true.

Otto   Exactly, I'd lost the impetus.

Pause.

Martha   Nothing you can do, that's fate.

Otto   Yes, I'll forget it – my Parker 51.

Pause.

But I won't be in a hurry to buy such an expensive one again, a cheap one's good enough and no worries either.

Martha (*laughs*)   In the end you'll get one just as expensive!

Otto *laughs, happily caught.*

Martha   But when the boss or somebody like that comes along again you've either got to put it away smartly or have a cheap one ready in your pocket, so you can swap them if necessary.

Otto   If I bought myself another Parker, I wouldn't take it to work, I'd keep it at home – safe.

Martha (*nods*)   Out of home, out of sight!

Otto   Though I must say I do take care of my things, don't I? It's a long time since I lost anything. I've had that gold lighter six years now.

Martha   I haven't seen that expensive silver tie pin I bought you for some time.

Otto   Because I don't wear it – because it's too good, and it doesn't suit me. But it's in the bedside table. One move and I've got it.

Martha   That's all right then.

Otto   I've still got all my 'portable assets'.

Pause.

Martha (*nods*)   And you just couldn't have known the boss would suddenly come along and borrow your pen.

Otto   I had a funny feeling soon as he said: 'Have you anything to write with for a second?' – and away he went with my Parker.

Pause.

Martha (*looks at her husband from the side*)   Go to sleep now and forget about it.

Pause.

Martha   Sleep well.

Otto   Same to you. I'll forget about the pen.

Martha   Dead right.

Scene Four: World Champion

Otto *sits in a tiny room without windows. It is probably a storeroom which* **Otto** *has arranged as his hobby room. He is building a model plane which is made very difficult by the fact that the room is so small and the wingspan of the plane is so large – around two to four metres.*

Otto *works for a long time, and suddenly begins to talk.*

Otto   I understand it's not the done thing to bother a pilot just before take-off – (*Laughs artificially.*) – but perhaps, Otto, you'll allow us to put a few questions to you. – Please, please go ahead. – This is a genuine vertical take-off plane you're flying, if one can use that expression? I believe you became a model glider pilot only two years ago. So it's quite amazing that in this short time you've already become both long- and middle-distance German champion. And you're now preparing yourself for the world championship by competing in the European championship, so to speak. Do you think you'll win today? – (*Laughs artificially.*) – Thinking back over the victories Herr Meier has already scored, specially his most recent ones, it certainly wouldn't be surprising, ladies and gentlemen, if our own Otto Meier became European champion. Otto, how does one actually become such an important pilot? – Well, I think you've got to have a certain thermic mind, besides a real love of flying and, of course, luck. – How long have you actually been involved in the sport? – I started, if you can call it that, fifteen years ago. But then techniques were, of course, quite different from what they are now. – Incidentally: you only fly models you've built yourself? – Yes, this is true. – And therein lies the secret of your success, according to the experts. You are – and I quote the top gliding periodicals – 'a technical flying genius'. Is that how you see yourself? – Well, one shouldn't praise oneself; but you've got to have some talent, of course, because the current models are naturally equipped with all the latest technical subtleties and the big manufacturers have all the resources at their disposal. Whereas I, for instance, have no wind tunnel. – You were a worker before, if I may say so? – Yes, I was. (*Laughs artificially.*) – But I understand now, if you don't mind me mentioning it, you have – a kind of small factory which you've built up into a profitable business out of your hobby. That's right! – Well, Herr Meier, all of us here – and the viewers – wish you good luck for the start of the European championship in Rome and hope that the European champion for long-distance model gliding will be Otto Meier, Germany. – Thank you. – Now, ladies and gentlemen, I hand you back to our sports studio. (*Pants.*)

Otto *looks up, he almost turns round to check that he can't be caught, then he goes on working in the tiny room with grotesque devotion on the big plane for the big wide world . . .*

Scene Five: A Stone's Throw to Freedom

In a department store. **Martha** *and* **Otto**. **Otto** *is trying on a 'leisure suit'.* **Martha** *examines the result.*

Martha   I don't know. (*Shakes her head – she doesn't like it.*)

Otto   Point taken.

Martha (*nods*)   Just looks cheap.

Otto   It is cheap.

Martha   Exactly. The other one's better.

Otto   I know, but '*quanta costa*'?

Martha   This one looks really cheap.

Otto   You shouldn't be able to tell straight away I'm just a worker on an outing.

Martha   Like you can in this one. The other one has more (*Smiles.*) 'the aroma of the big wide world . . .'

Otto   Gentleman of leisure. (*Laughs.*)

Martha   It should be a proper leisure suit. In that one you see straight away you haven't got much leisure time. In the other one less so. It's more casual.

Otto   But it costs nearly twice as much.

Martha .   'Beauty has its price.'

Otto   Bring the other one! (*Nods.*)

Scene Six: Stroke of Luck

Otto *and* **Martha** *at home in the small kitchen, having supper.*

Otto *laughs, looks to see if* **Martha** *is reacting to his laughter. She isn't.*

Pause.

Otto (*takes something out of his pocket*)   Recognise this?

Martha (*looks*)   Yes. It's a ballpoint, isn't it.

Otto (*shakes his head*)   What a memory the woman has! My Parker 51, that's what it is! (*Laughs.*)

Martha   What, the one you lost?

Otto   The very same. So you can stop looking! Right now!

Martha (*looks*)   Trust you – you're always looking on the black side.

Otto   Like we was saying, I'd already given it up for dead (*laughs*), hadn't I, but like I said, I put a note about it on the 'Missing' board.

Martha   And the boss read it?

Otto   Bollocks. It was just as we thought: he'd put it down somewhere and then a colleague had nicked it.

Martha   But given it back now?

Otto (*nods*)   And do you know who it was? (*Looks.*) It was one of those buggers I'd have sworn blind would never have given it back.

Martha   To err is human.

Otto (*laughs*)   What a stroke of luck!

Scene Seven: Living

In a beer garden. **Martha**, **Otto** *and* **Ludwig**. *Nice day. It's hot.*

Otto   This is living for once.

Martha   A beautiful Sunday. An outing was a really good idea.

Otto   How about our Ludwig, then. Happy?

Ludwig   If I get another beer.

Otto   Have one. (*Laughs.*)

Ludwig   A pint.

Otto   Half; don't be cheeky.

Scene Eight: A Winter's Tale

In the morning. Kitchen. **Ludwig** *and* **Martha**.

Martha   Look at him sitting there all morning as if he had nothing to do.

Ludwig   What is there to do?

Martha   A responsible person's always got something to do.

Ludwig   Shall I do the shopping?

Martha   That's my job.

Pause.

Ludwig   They said they'd notify me when to go to the DHSS. Besides, I was there last week anyway and I'm going back next week, even if they don't notify me.

Martha   You just have to keep on the ball.

Ludwig   I do. But if I keep going down there without them notifying me then the man at the DHSS gets uptight. I can tell. That doesn't do my prospects any good.

Martha   Other lads have got positions, only you haven't.

Ludwig   What can I do about it, Mum? You know what it's like.

Martha   What do I know, I don't know anything about it. You've got to be on the move and have initiative, that's what. Look around, keep your ear to the ground and be there wherever they need somebody.

Ludwig   Well, I'll go down the post office, get a Yellow Pages and call all the firms up – the big ones, anyway.

Martha   Phoning costs a fortune!

Ludwig   I know, but . . .

Pause.

Martha   You got to cut your suit according to your cloth.

Ludwig   Not me, I haven't.

Martha (*quickly*)   No, so we notice!

Ludwig *smiles and nods.*

Martha   There's a good boy. But when you're sat there the whole day I get nervous, see, then I get all narked.

Ludwig   But I don't know what to do, mum, honest. (*A short pause.*) I can't just go for endless walks like some pensioner.

Pause.

(*Looks and laughs.*) If you want I'll hang myself; then I won't be cluttering up the place any more.

Martha   Trust you to do that to your mum and dad – that's all we need!

Pause.

(*Decisive, obstinate.*) Dental technician, merchant banker, tax clerk.

Pause.

Clean your dad's shoes, that's your best bet – it'll chuff him to see you're really trying and not just sitting on your bum till it gets dark.

Ludwig *goes into the hall and starts cleaning the shoes . . . Pause.*

Ludwig   If the truth be known, it don't matter a fuck how you earn your money – long as you do one way or another.

Martha (*from the kitchen*)   What?

Ludwig   If the truth be known, it don't matter a fuck how you earn your money – long as you got a decent job.

Martha   That'll do.

Pause.

Ludwig   But an apprenticeship like what you both got in mind – I'll never find one of them. That's just wishful thinking.

Martha (*loudly*)   That is not wishful thinking, that's your right, what the state owes you, when you pay your taxes on time so your son don't have to be a unskilled labourer.

Ludwig   I'm not talking about being no unskilled labourer. Bricklaying's more my line.

Martha (*quickly*)   Bricklayers always have the worst of it.

Ludwig   What?

Martha   Just look at your dad – that's no life at all.

Ludwig   But he's not a bricklayer.

Martha   What's the difference? A worker's a worker.

Ludwig   Yes, but . . . if there wasn't any workers, then –

Martha   That'll do, I said. Where he gets that rubbish from I'd love to know. Not from home, that's for sure.

Pause.

The difference is staring you in the face – anybody can be a worker, there's no skill in that.

Ludwig   But for building labourers there's apprenticeships on offer – so they say down the DHSS.

Martha   Of course there are, because they can't find people stupid enough. You have to get on in life. And in the family. Your dad's just a worker – though he isn't doing too badly. That can't be changed. But you have (*Standard language.*) got to climb on the next rung, otherwise all we've done for you makes no sense.

Ludwig *says nothing.*

Martha (*comes out to him in the corridor*)   Look, when you have a son of your own –

Ludwig　– he's got to be Chancellor at least.

Martha　Dope.

Pause.

Time's slipping away.

Ludwig　That's what I mean. In July there'll be another lot of school-leavers and they'll be wanting apprenticeships and some of them will have better reports than me.

Martha　Because you didn't work hard enough. It wasn't due to your intelligence, no one will make me believe that.

Ludwig　I got my certificates anyway.

Martha　By the skin of your teeth.

Ludwig　Lots haven't.

Martha　Exactly, and that's why you won't become a labourer but a dentist.

Ludwig　Faith can move mountains.

Martha　Don't be cheeky. I only want the best for you.

Ludwig　Eight months hanging about.

Martha (*infuriated*)　He behaves as if it was all his parents' fault.

Ludwig　If I'd started as an apprentice bricklayer I'd be nearly in my second year now.

Martha　And if somebody asks: 'What's your son doing now?' – 'He's an apprentice bricklayer on a building site –'

Ludwig　Where else?

Martha　– 'It's me's got to tell them! But I'd sooner say –

Ludwig　– he's dead.

Martha　Don't sin against us.

Pause.

You've just got no understanding of what your parents are thinking. That's what it is.

Ludwig   Nor have you, either.

Martha   That's what you have to listen to while he sits there, does nothing, and stuffs his face.

Ludwig   Right. Because in this house we don't live in the real world. That's why.

Martha   We're too soft on you. We should change our tune, then you'd get a shock.

Pause.

It's easy enough to say: come on, earn your money! Go in the factory or on the building site, or wherever else you want to go, but bring some money home! – But we say to ourselves: he mustn't get into that kind of life to start with, 'cause he'll never get out of it.

Pause.

You are our only child, why don't you understand?

Ludwig *looks.*

Scene Nine: Remembering

At supper. **Martha** *and* **Otto.**

Otto   It suddenly struck me – you know, I've been done.

Martha   Who's done you?

Otto   Last week in the Löwenbräukeller, or have you forgotten?

Martha   'Course not, it was lovely.

Otto   I paid sixty-six marks twenty, and said: take sixty-seven to include the tip.

Martha   Dear. Still, it was lovely.

Otto   Monday morning I'm standing at work thinking about how enjoyable it was – you know what suddenly struck me?

Martha   Couldn't have been anything good.

Otto   It suddenly struck me the waiter's done me, because I couldn't make it tally up, the sixty-six marks twenty.

Martha   Yes, but we had that leg of pork.

Otto   Twenty-six marks.

Martha   But three of us were tucking in, it looked a lot – we all got a share.

Otto   Yes, though it was a bit stringy.

Martha   You had three pints.

Otto   Four marks twenty. I've already counted them. Twelve marks sixty.

Martha   And I –

Otto   I remember: you had two quarters of wine and some white-beer before that.

Martha   I'd forgotten the white-beer.

Otto   Well, I hadn't. The quarters of wine cost nine marks twenty-five. And there's something wrong: you can't divide five into two.

Martha   The waiter made a mistake.

Otto   In whose favour?

Martha   It can't be much, because I remember I didn't like the Bernkastler wine, even though it was only three marks sixty, and then there were only two others, one of them was too expensive, more than five marks for a quarter –

Otto   Daylight robbery.

Martha   – and that one in the middle, that Josefs wine for four marks fifty, I think it was.

Otto   Never mind that. Sixty-six marks the lot, three pints – twelve marks sixty, plus the wine –

Martha   The white-beer first.

Otto   How much was that?

Martha   I don't know.

Otto   Why not?

Martha   You don't look at the price of white-beer – it's the same wherever.

Otto   I remember everything I ordered for the boy and myself – you always check the prices before you order!

Pause.

At the Red Swan a white-beer's one mark seventy.

Martha *looks.*

Otto   Just in comparison: let's say one mark more, 'cause the Löwenbräukeller is popular and well known.

Martha *nods.*

Otto   Thirty-eight marks sixty plus two marks seventy is forty-one marks thirty plus wine – nine marks – (*With emphasis.*) makes twenty-five, so, altogether: fifty marks fifty-five.

Martha   Call it fifty marks.

Otto   Get it right! Ludwig had a *Spezi* to start, and then half a –

Martha   He wanted a whole pint.

Otto   Let him earn the money first, then he can buy himself a gallon for all I care. When I was his age I didn't get any beer at all. – Now it's getting exciting: I know for sure the *Spezi* was two marks ninety and the half-pint was two marks thirty. Interesting, a pint is four marks twenty and you get double – when you take less you get penalised!

Martha   Never mind.

Otto   Right. Let's add it up. Fifty marks fifty-five and two marks ninety is fifty-three marks forty-five, plus two marks thirty makes fifty-five marks seventy-five.

Pause.

And that was my problem: where did the rest come from? Fraud? Did the waiter make a mistake accidentally on purpose when he added it all up? That would be the solution to the problem. Well, that really annoyed me, I can't tell you how much that annoyed me. I was miserable for the rest of the day.

Martha   Well, that's a really dirty trick, if they diddled us out of ten marks.

Otto   Would've been, would've been – but I twigged! (*Laughs.*)

Pause.

One clue. Radish: side order!

Martha   That's right.

Otto (*nods*)   That's what it was. We had a dispute, remember? The radish-seller comes to the table with the radishes and we took three of them – we all like them and, anyway, what does it matter, we were going out for once. Then I wanted to pay with the hundred-mark note and the radish-seller said: I can't change that, pay me later. But she didn't come back. So when we were paying the bill I told the waiter: Look, we had three radishes as well, but they aren't paid for, I'll give you the money and you settle up between yourselves.

Martha   You think he did?

Otto   One colleague to another? – That's the missing ten marks fifty. One radish: three marks fifty. Dead right, it was.

Pause.

(*Laughs, relieved.*) When I twigged it took a weight off my mind.

Martha   Yes, normally they do you, whenever they can.

Otto   We was lucky.

Pause.

Well, that was the root of the mystery, then. (*Nods, a bit exhausted.*) I'm exhausted.

Martha   Well, it is late now.

Scene Ten: Record-Breaker

Otto *by himself on a hill in his leisure suit. He has a device in his hand and looks up into the air at his glider.*

Otto   Fear's one thing you mustn't have in this profession. (*Laughs.*) 'Course, it's no life-insurance policy being a test pilot, but (*Laughs.*) you can just as easy die in bed.

Pause.

Shhh! What if somebody's listening!

Looks around and smiles – there is no one about.

Well, up there you're free!

Laughs and nods.

Act Two

Scene One: Shadow Play

It is evening. In the living room/kitchen. **Otto** *is sitting there with a beer. It's after supper. He is smoking, staring out front.* **Ludwig** *is reading the magazine* Auto, Motor and Sport. **Martha** *is laboriously mending* **Ludwig**'s *leather jacket.*

Pause.

Otto *looks up, suppresses what he wants to say.*

Pause.

Otto   What're you doing there (*Standard English.*) until all hours of the night?

Martha   You've got eyes.

Otto   Why can't he mend his rags himself? He's got time enough.

Martha (*calm, but one can tell something's wrong*)   Mending leather's one of the trickiest things in sewing. He can't do it himself.

Otto   And I'm running around with holes in my socks.

Martha   You're doing what?

Otto *clams up.*

Martha (*looks at him angrily*)   What's bitten you that we've got to suffer for?

Otto   Nothing.

Martha   Well then, keep quiet.

Pause.

Otto (*means the magazine*)   He's got the money to spend on that, I see.

Martha   He can buy what he likes with his own pocket money.

Ludwig *looks, wants to say something, but doesn't.*

Otto   As long as I earn his pocket money. (*Short pause.*) Any propects of work, sir?

Ludwig *shakes his head.*

Otto (*laughs*)   The whole world's working and his lordship sits here reading his magazine. That's a state of affairs that'd take some beating.

Martha   Leave him alone.

Otto   She's always defending His Lordship.

Ludwig *reaches into his shirt pocket, takes out a packet of fags and lights one, because he is nervous. Smokes.*

Otto (*looks at him*)   A fine end you'll come to.

Pause.

Martha   What has bitten you?

Pause.

Otto?

Otto   Stupid question – nothing. Just looking at him sitting there makes me furious.

Ludwig   You give me fifty marks for the rock festival and you won't see me for three days.

Otto   Earn something, then you can take a trip to Paris for all I care.

Martha *looks, goes on sewing.*

Ludwig   An advance on my pocket money.

Otto   An advance on his pocket money – you hear His Lordship. I love that. His Lordship behaves as if he was employed by me as idler and loafer and demands wages in advance.

Ludwig   Well then, don't.

Pause.

Martha   I can't give it to him, the budget won't stretch to that. But if he was away over the holidays, we wouldn't see him. Out of sight, out of mind.

Otto   I don't earn my money doing nothing.

Ludwig   Nobody says you do!

Otto   Gruschke Kuno's got the boot.

Martha   What?

Otto   Forty-seven redundancies. Fourteen Italians, eight Turks, one Persian, fifteen women and nine (*Standard English.*) older employees. Including Gruschke.

Martha (*looks*)   Be thankful it's not you.

Otto   He was my mate, was Gruschke. The only one I really had.

Martha   Shocking.

Otto   Things go on at the same speed as if he'd never been there – Gruschke, just gone. He's not even missed either. Readjustments. I do two screws more, like some of the others – and just up the line from me they've given us a youngster – he does the locks. On our line five of the nine have gone – but they're further down, they don't affect me. The foreman's already been round with the new 'schedules'. Five men just swallowed up by the earth.

Martha   Just have to grin and bear it. They're sifting out the older ones. You're not among them.

Otto   You think forty-two's not really old, don't you?

Martha   You're in the prime of your life.

Otto   If only it hadn't been Gruschke. The shop stewards had okayed it. Orders is orders. Well, you can't close your eyes to facts. 'Cut back,' they say. Got to be flexible while there's still time, haven't you? At fifty-eight he won't find any more work, things being what they are. (*Under his breath.*) Premature pensioner!

Martha   Now he's got time for living.

Otto (*loud*)   I don't need time for living, I want to work. (*Quietly, pointing at* **Ludwig**.) Just look at him.

Martha   That's no reason to pick on him. They're not the first redundancies anyway, you've learned to live with them before now.

Otto   Yes, like TB. Twenty-five, thirty-one, thirty-one again and now forty-seven men. That's the limit, you understand. Forty-eight and upwards amounts to mass redundancies, and it's legal.

Martha   And what does it actually mean?

Otto   It means the situation is such they can't give any consideration to 'quality' any more – they have no time, they've got to go through the 'sound barrier'. It means they weren't the last to go; it means this is only the beginning.

Pause.

I've nothing to fear, I'm in the prime of my life, I'm skilled. There were some, you know, they said 'No!' when the foreman came round with the new rationalisation for the redundant bloke's job. He just gave everybody a look. I knew what he was trying to say.

Martha   What did you do?

Otto   I said yes, yes, I'd like to, that's easy, and he tapped me on the shoulder and said 'Good lad.' – I know what that means. (*Short pause.*) It means security. Thank God. (*He is sweating.*)

Martha   Is it easy, what you got to do now?

Otto   I'm screwing another side panel into the left-hand window and I'm doing one more screw at the front, which

Gruschke used to do. Somebody twenty metres up the line used to do the side panel. I didn't know him. (*Nods.*) All part of the new arrangements.

Pause.

The line runs a bit slower, know what I mean? Just for a few days, until each new operation becomes second nature to you and gets up to the new speed. (*He pants.*) It's still running, right, and when it gets up to speed, you got to be on the ball, see, and not be thinking about nothing else – like the foreman says.

Martha   When you do your best – it can be done.

Otto *nods. He sits there as if after some great effort, sweating, panting – he smokes and drinks at the same time.*

Pause.

Ludwig *looks at his father.*

Otto   What're you looking so hard for?

Ludwig   I'm not looking at all. (*Goes on reading, i.e. he buries himself in his magazine.*)

Otto   No, you'd better not either. I won't have it, I tell you. Just pick somebody else.

Ludwig   You give me the fifty marks.

Otto   No way.

Ludwig *looks.*

Pause.

Scene Two: Worldly Wisdom

Saturday morning. In the hallway. The shoes business.

Otto   With so much time on your hands you should be able to do it perfectly.

Ludwig Right.

Otto If you make yourself useful you won't be noticed.
See here. (*He picks up a shoe between the sole and the upper.*) This
is the critical point – here, see – you can't get in with the
brush, the dirt lies undisturbed and just collects.

Ludwig Right.

Otto But now comes the trick. (*Takes a piece of string out of
his pocket.*) You tackle the problem with that string. (*Laughs.*)
You can get right in amongst it – see, and get the last bit of
muck out.

*He takes the shoe between his knees, holds it tight and cleans the
troublesome welt with the string, which he gets hold of in both hands
and pulls to and fro. Looks.*

Here's the proof. (*Holds the string up.*) Completely changed
colour, see that dirt gone? Be grateful somebody teaches you
something.

Ludwig *follows the same process and cleans one of the shoes.*

Otto When you're finished, call me, I'll come and check
'em.

Ludwig Sure.

Otto Will you come gliding with me this afternoon?

Ludwig I've got something on.

Otto What?

Ludwig *looks.*

Otto Oh, great, when I'm inviting you along to the
inauguration of the new model. The test flight!

Ludwig Your test flight doesn't interest me.

Otto Well, it does me, the test flight interests me very
much.

Ludwig Right.

Otto   Dominating the forces of nature.

Ludwig   Sure.

Otto   When you're not right in the middle of the action, just steering it from down below, it can be more difficult than sitting in it yourself. Even the specialists say so. (*Pause.*) It's all in the eye, you got to be able to see the wind. (*Laughs.*)

Ludwig *nods.*

Otto   You'll never learn gliding.

Looks at him for a while, then goes into the kitchen, meeting **Martha** *coming out.*

Martha   Come on, let's go off and do the shopping. The supermarket'll be full to bursting.

Ludwig   Will you get me a packet of fags?

Martha   A little reward. Right.

Ludwig *cleans the shoes.*

Martha *and* **Otto** *dress themselves and go out.*

Scene Three: The Reckoning

At the supermarket checkout. **Martha** *and* **Otto** *have bought a lot of groceries. They – especially* **Otto** *– are observing the baskets of other shoppers standing in a long row waiting at the checkout . . .*

Otto (*under his breath, to* **Martha**)   See that?

Martha   What?

Otto   Them, over there! (*Nods, discreet.*)

Martha *looks.*

Otto   Look what they've got in there!

Martha *nods.*

Otto   And it's Sunday tomorrow. Two packets of Knorr beef soup, one cucumber, two cans of beer and a loaf. Can you believe it? That's a family, the two kids are theirs.

Martha   Maybe they did their main shopping yesterday and just forgot a few things!

Otto   Rubbish, two packets of Knorr beef soup, one cucumber, one loaf and two cans of beer! (*Nods, laughs knowingly.*) He's unemployed, simple as that.

Martha   How can you tell?

Otto   If you've got eyes in your head you can tell!

Martha *and* **Otto** (*look*)   We're next.

Martha *puts the items on the moving belt, the cashier rings everything up, and puts it all into another self-service trolley.*

Cashier   Seventy-three marks ninety-four.

Martha (*nods and blushes*)   You got any money? I haven't got enough. (*She is searching desperately in her purse.*)

Otto (*blushes also, turns to see if other people are watching. Very loud, to direct any suspicion away from himself*)   Nothing to do with me, if a woman will go out shopping without her money!

Martha   There was a hundred marks in there, I know, and now there's only fifty!

Cashier   Well? Seventy-three marks ninety-four.

Martha (*totally confused*)   Everything over fifty-four marks will have to go back.

Cashier   That's all I need. I've rung it up already.

Martha   I'm sorry.

Otto (*loud*)   And I'm married to somebody like that! Let me through, Fräulein. (*To the Cashier.*) It's nothing to do with me. She gets eight hundred and fifty marks for the housekeeping.

Martha   That'll do!

Otto *pushes his way past the checkout, runs off . . .*

Martha (*to the* **Cashier**)   I'm Frau Meier, you know me, don't you?

Scene Four: The Night Watch

In the kitchen. **Martha** *is crying.* **Otto** *is staring at his son.*

Otto   You'll pay for this.

Martha *just looks.*

Otto *nods.*

Martha   You made us look like fools. It was so embarrassing.

Otto (*nods*)   You'd dare to do that to us! (*Gives him a slap in the face.*)

Ludwig *takes it, stares out front, does not react.*

Otto   I want an answer. Where've you hidden the fifty marks you stole?

Ludwig *looks, says nothing.*

Otto   If you don't give back what's stolen, it makes it worse.

Ludwig *looks.*

Otto   And he calls himself my son; I've got a different idea what my son should be.

Ludwig *looks, does not react.*

Otto   Won't take a second to 'convict the delinquent'. (*Runs into the living room, goes to the sofa bed, lifts the top off; throws everything about, searches, doesn't find anything, comes back.*) Give me back the fifty marks, or there'll be big trouble.

Martha   Otto!

Otto   He's a prat, your son, once you see the light. (*Nods.*) It's obvious why nobody wants him, it's written all over his face. Personnel managers have a trained eye, they can spot it immediately: he's a thief, this gentleman! I'm going to count to three and that fifty marks had better be on the table! One, two, three. (*Looks.*)

Ludwig *doesn't react.*

Otto *jumps up again, runs into the living room, pulls the drawer out, throws it on to the floor, rummages about in it, tears the posters up, searches, finds nothing, comes back, looks at his son.*

Martha   Give us the fifty marks back, Ludwig, don't provoke your dad.

Ludwig *just looks.*

Otto   Can't you hear what you mum tells you? – Hopeless. Stubborn. But not with me. I can handle you any time if you push me.

Ludwig *looks.*

Martha *cries.*

Otto   Put the money on the table.

Ludwig *looks, doesn't react.*

Otto (*looks*)   Trousers down.

Ludwig *looks.*

Otto   Trousers down, I said, or do I have to help you.

Pause. **Ludwig** *doesn't react – then he takes his jeans off.*

Otto (*picks them up and searches through them, doesn't find anything*) Right, next!

Ludwig *looks, then he takes the leather jacket off.*

Otto *searches, doesn't find anything.*

Ludwig *looks.*

Otto (*raging*)   Give me the fifty marks. Don't drive me to extremities, I'm warning you. (*Screams.*) Give me my money back!

Ludwig *looks.*

Otto   Where've you got it hidden? – Own up!

Ludwig *says nothing.*

Otto   Right, sir, clothes off! At the double, that's an order!

Ludwig *suddenly starts to cry, the tears are running down his cheeks, totally uncontrolled; at the same time, he goes on undressing; finally he stands there naked.*

Otto *stands staring, he can't do any more; he stares at his son as he is standing there, there is no sign of the fifty marks.*

Long pause.

(*Suddenly light, apologetically.*) You needn't feel ashamed in front of your parents, they've seen little boys before. (*Nods.*)

Pause.

Martha *covers her face – she doesn't want to see* **Ludwig** *naked.*

Otto   All right, you've got your pride, you don't give away your secret 'cause you're clever. (*Nods.*) We know that! (*Short pause.*) I can guarantee you one thing: nothing will ever become of you, you can bet your life on that. I know the world, they don't want people like you, sure as eggs is eggs. You don't take after me.

Ludwig (*looks at his father, calm and crying*)   I'd rather be dead than be like you.

Otto (*almost bursts, as he looks at his son, to* **Martha**)   You hear that?

Martha   What? (*Cries.*)

A long pause.

Otto   That's just what I thought. Right. (*He looks, then suddenly he gets up, turns in on himself and, feeling insecure, disappears into his little room.*)

Martha   Put something on, you'll get cold.

Ludwig *quickly gathers up his things, goes out of the room, puts his clothes on again in the living room.*

Martha (*to herself*)   It's not as bad as all that, much worse things than this happen. (*Tries to give herself courage.*)

Ludwig, *having dressed himself, clears his things away, mourns for his torn posters, etc. Then he takes his travelling bag, puts some of his things in it: what he needs and what he likes, goes to the bathroom and collects his things. Now he has packed and comes back into the kitchen.*

Martha *looks.*

Ludwig *takes out the fifty marks from underneath a pile of plates in the kitchen cupboard.*

Martha (*looks*)   You be careful now, won't you, and don't come back too soon.

Ludwig *nods, puts the fifty marks in his pocket and leaves the flat.*

Martha *watches him go.*

A very long pause.

Otto (*comes out of his little room into the kitchen*)   Has he gone?

Martha *nods.*

Pause.

Otto *sits down at the table awkwardly, looks at* **Martha**.

A long pause.

Martha (*very calm*)   Otto, I'll never forgive you for that – ever.

Otto   Why?

A long pause.

Scene Five: Countdown

Late at night. **Martha** *and* **Otto** *watching TV in the living room.*

Otto *is drinking beer.*

Martha *looks at him reproachfully.*

Otto *does not react.*

Pause. They watch TV.

Otto *pours himself some more beer, drinks.*

Martha *gets up, goes into kitchen, checks that she has switched the electric stove off; waits in the kitchen, comes back, sits down again.*

Pause.

Martha *looks at* **Otto**.

Otto *drinks again.*

A western is now on TV.

Pause.

Otto *pours himself some more beer, accidentally spilling some on the carpet.*

Martha *notices. Jumps up, runs into kitchen, takes a cloth, wets it with hot water from the tap, runs back into the living room kneels down and cleans the spot thoroughly.* **Otto** *is bothered by this, has to put his feet somewhere else.* **Martha** *looks at him reproachfully and goes on cleaning.*

Pause.

Otto *looks down at* **Martha** *cleaning at his feet, then he takes the beer bottle and deliberately pours a few drops on the carpet, just next to where* **Martha** *is working on her knees.*

Martha *notices this – looks at* **Otto**.

Otto *puts the beer bottle down again.*

Martha *deliberately sighs loudly, then she fussily cleans the new spots.*

Otto *finishes his glass, looks.*

Martha *looks into* **Otto***'s face reproachfully, then she goes on cleaning.*

Otto *looks, sighs, picks up the bottle to pour himself another glass.*

Martha *looks at him reproachfully.*

Otto*, without warning, smashes the bottle on the living-room table.*

Martha *jumps up, screaming.*

Otto *gets up.*

Martha *takes this as a threat, screams even more loudly.*

Otto *goes to the television and, with one push, dislodges it from its table.*

Martha*, terrified, stifles her screaming, stares at* **Otto***.*

Otto *smashes everything he can get hold of; throws vases at the wall, knocks cupboards down, throws chairs at the wall, overturns the carpet – all this takes a very long time . . .*

Martha *runs from one corner of the room to the other – she's got to watch out that she doesn't get hurt.*

Otto *runs into his little room and smashes everything to pieces except the glider which is almost finished, then he picks it up and throws it several times at the wall until it is in pieces; then he starts to go into the kitchen.*

Martha (*suddenly rages as if hunted by hell cats, gets ahead of him, stands in the kitchen door – determined she is ready to do anything*) You'll only get in that kitchen over my dead body, I'm telling you!

Otto *looks at his wife, then he turns away again, stands there like a passenger on a railway station, waiting for a connection; looks round, sees the mess, which suddenly shocks him; he charges towards a wall*

*and, with all his force, knocks his head against it. He howls but does it
again, trying to knock his head through the wall.*

Pause.

Otto *suddenly goes into the bathroom and carefully washes his hands
with soap . . . stares into the mirror.*

Martha (*quickly*)   A broken mirror's seven years' bad luck
– that's a well-known fact. (*Nods.*)

Otto *looks at himself very attentively in the mirror.*

Pause.

Scene Six: Peace and Quiet

Sunday. Daytime. **Martha** *and* **Otto**.

*An agonising and very long scene. It consists of the two of them
'clearing up'.* **Otto** *tries to rescue what is still salvageable – like
repairing a chair, etc.* **Martha** *is mainly cleaning up. This all takes
a very long time . . .*

Scene Seven: On the Moon

It is evening. **Otto** *and* **Martha** *are sitting in the rearranged room.*

Pause.

Martha   Well, that's a job that needed doing. (*Nods.*) If the
tube's cracked we'll have to throw the TV away. I put the
damage at a thousand marks at least. (*With emphasis.*) Not
counting the telly, that is.

Otto *looks.*

Pause.

Martha (*encouraging herself*)   My God, what do other
people do at times like this! Do in the whole family? (*Looks at*

her husband.) I'd like a film of it to show you what you've done, you wouldn't half be surprised.

Otto *nods.*

Martha   A leopard can't change its spots.

Otto (*nods*)   Dive down, deep inside yourself, down in the deep sea and don't be afraid of the 'killer whale', follow my meaning?

Pause.

Wonder if he'll be back?

Martha   As long as he's got money he'll stay at the rock festival. Once he's skint, he'll soon get hungry and come back.

Otto *looks at* **Martha** *incredulously.*

Pause.

Martha   He'll be back, why shouldn't he be back? (*Pause.*) This is his home.

Otto   When I was little, my mum and me once met a rider, a real one on a horse – he was just riding along – and as he drew level he slowed down, maybe in case it kicked us, and he looked at us and said: 'Good day to you', rode on by and laughed. Then my mum said to me: 'That was a prince', took my hand and went on. (*Short pause.*) Before you even start, that's all I got to say. (*Short pause.*) Sometimes I feel as if they're switching me off.

Martha *looks.*

Otto (*nods*)   Only work's still going. 'Cause the assembly line's still running. But when there's a stoppage, they switch us off. At seven o'clock in the morning they switch us on, so we work from seven till quarter to nine. From a quarter to till nine they don't switch us off, they let us stand about and talk to our workmates, eat a snack and make plans. At nine o'clock work starts again and goes on till quarter past twelve. From quarter past twelve till one we're allowed to go to the canteen because it's on the works' premises.

Martha   His mind's going.

Otto   Then it goes on till five, or seven, if there's a special shift. Come going-home time they switch us off altogether like the electric typewriters – they put a cover over us so we won't get dusty. And then we're sitting there in the works. Three hundred and fifty men. Some on a chair, those lucky enough to find one, otherwise where they can – or they just sleep on their feet, like horses. Then somebody in the central office switches on our brain power. Then we see ourselves in our minds driving home in our own car to our family and the kids in the nice flats that have everything. And we get leisure time – just as you imagine it – but even then it goes on because there's a TV, which is switched on in the switched-on head. (*He laughs at this thought.*) And then on the telly somebody's switching on the telly – (*Laughs.*) – know this one?

Martha   What one?

Otto   Once upon a time there was a man, a wife and a little child who made a journey to St Giles – and when in sight of old St Giles, who did they meet? – A man, a wife and a little child –

Martha   – on a journey to St Giles. (*Laughs.*) You silly fool!

Otto   And the next day at seven, things liven up in the works again – the covers come off. And nobody notices anything. (*Looks at* **Martha**.) Know what I mean?

Martha   No, because you're talking rubbish.

Otto (*nods*)   'Cause you don't go to work like I do.

Martha (*angrily*)   I've got enough housework, thank you.

Otto (*nods*)   It's all fiction. No interference by anything human.

Martha   You're not round the bend.

Otto Are they using some kind of trick? When does recognition of yourself come into it? My fourteen screws in the windscreen and two new ones in the door. A few days' excitement in the works because them up top – the big nobs – have to give you a certain freedom to relearn.

Pause.

When we reach retirement we're all packed into an old empty warehouse, the lid's put on and they show us a two-hour-long film of our ten years' happy life as pensioners. And that's that. (*Short pause.*) Work that lot out . . .

Martha You certainly worked it all off, anyway. It was all real enough, what you smashed up.

Otto Are you trying to deliberately misunderstand me? Can't be done, because we're both wired into the same circuit.

Martha Right.

Otto I always thought I'd be free when I grew up. But then we met and got married.

Martha Doesn't mean you have to run me down, does it?

Otto (*low*) I sometimes buy myself a magazine and toss myself off instead of coming to you.

Martha (*looks*) I'm not a masturbatory sex object.

Otto Point taken.

Martha (*looks at* **Otto**) Do I put you off? Just tell me.

Otto (*denying it*) I put myself off.

Martha You don't put me off.

Otto Sometimes when I (*Very quietly.*) hold him in my hand, I think: he's shrinking. I feel like a little lad, and that makes me do it even more.

Pause.

Martha   He's not shrinking, you can depend on it. It's you who's shrinking, not him.

Otto (*looks at* **Martha**)   Everything's wrapped up. Whatever I reach for's all parcelled up. Inside myself everything's too big – it all falls through!

Martha   You're prone to diarrhoea, that's for sure.

Otto   Through-traffic.

Martha   What about me?

Otto   Yes, you as well.

A short pause.

Martha   I've tried so hard.

Otto   It's not your fault. Like you when you're washing up, I've got rubber gloves on.

Martha   You've got to take them off.

Otto   When I was little, I loved to sleep with a woollen cap on, even in summer 'cause it covered my ears, 'cause I always used to think somebody would come during the night and cut them off with a pair of scissors. My mum took it off if she ever caught me with it on.

Three-minute pause.

Martha   Finished your confessions?

Otto *looks.*

Martha *goes out of the room, gets a suitcase.*

Otto   What's up?

Martha   I'm going, Otto, I'm leaving you.

Otto   Why?

Martha   You treat me as if I was an animal, not a human being.

Otto *just looks.*

Scene Eight: Rebellion

Martha *alone in a small room. She has just arrived. Her things are lying around all over the place. She is busy tidying them away. In between she makes herself some coffee, but it takes a very long time, because she can't manage the cooker. You can see that she's annoyed at her awkwardness. She's at the end of her tether, fights with herself and her composure. Drinks coffee, sits there, looks around, snivels.*

Pause.

Act Three

Scene One: Demolition Order

In a very basically furnished rented room. Wearing his overcoat, **Otto** *is sitting on the only chair,* **Martha** *is sitting on the bed.*

Martha *looks at* **Otto**.

Pause.

Otto   Won't you come home, if I take you with me?

Martha *shakes her head.*

Otto   I wouldn't take you home with me anyway, not now.

Martha   No.

Pause.

Are you okay?

Otto   Yes.

Martha   And Ludwig?

Otto   Him as well.

Pause.

Martha (*looks at* **Otto**, *smiles*)   Still got the flat?

Otto   I'll keep that whatever happens.

Martha *smiles.*

Otto   I'll never take a rented room.

Martha *nods.*

Otto   You're hardly ever here, are you?

Martha   No – but it's enough.

Otto *looks.*

Pause.

Otto   I'm hardly ever home myself.

Pause.

'Course, I've not got anyone else yet. Though that'll soon change!

Pause.

Come home with me, I'll forgive you and we can start a new – romance.

Pause.

All right then, don't. (*He gets up to go.*)

Martha   You're still the same, aren't you?

Otto   Thank God.

Martha   You haven't changed.

Otto   I have, but that's none of your business.

Martha   Point taken.

Pause.

Otto (*almost at the door*)   You're still my wife, you know. If I demand my marital rights, you'd have to do it.

Martha   But you won't demand them.

Otto   No.

Pause.

Otto   Can I drop in again?

Martha   If you're in the area.

Otto   Right. Just to see how you are. Bye, then.

Martha   Bye, Otto!

Otto *goes.*

Martha *looks in the mirror.*

Scene Two: Concrete

At the doorway of a building-site hostel, a large hut provided by the firm for its workers. From inside, voices, card-playing, drinking, etc. and music. **Otto** *in his overcoat.* **Ludwig**.

Otto   I've come to fetch you, we're going home.

Ludwig *looks.*

Pause.

Otto   Your mum'll be coming home as well.

Ludwig *looks.*

Otto *looks.*

Pause.

Otto   This is no life here.

Ludwig   It suits me.

Otto   Barrack life. It's nothing but a place to crash out, and you call yourself my son. You should be ashamed of yourself, when you're used to better.

Ludwig *nods.*

Pause.

Otto   You're not of age yet, I can insist you come with me, if I want.

Ludwig   Sure.

Otto   Supposing I do? (*Looks at* **Ludwig**.)

Pause.

You can lead a horse to water but you can't make it drink. (*Short pause. Looks.*) It's more convenient anyway, we don't have to bother making up the sofa every night and there won't be any more holes in the wall from your drawing pins, which you were always being told about.

Ludwig   Sure.

Pause.

Otto   Come on home. Enough's enough.

Ludwig   No.

Otto (*looks, feels caught*)   I was only kidding. It was a trap.

Pause.

Ludwig   Are you all right?

Otto   You can see for yourself.

Ludwig   And mum?

Otto   Her as well.

Ludwig   Still seeing her, are you?

Otto   Why not, if she's coming back.

Ludwig   Right.

Pause.

Otto   This is a fucking dump.

Ludwig   I've got an apprenticeship, and I've got money.

Otto *laughs.*

Pause.

Otto   I won't ever be able to show you off if I've got to say his lordship my son's a bricklayer – I'd sooner say nothing at all.

Ludwig   Do that, then.

Otto   Getting cocky?

Ludwig *shakes his head.*

Otto   That's all right, then. I've still got parental authority, and nobody can take that away from me. (*Short pause.*) Well,

I'd say that's enough talking. Pack your suitcase, if you have one, and we'll be off. You've got five minutes.

Ludwig   I'm not going.

Otto   I'll give you such a clout.

Ludwig   If you hit me, I'll tell my mates.

Otto   Yes, you'd do that to me, your own father.

Ludwig   You started it.

Otto   All right, I'll fetch the police.

Pause.

You can have the living room all to yourself, as your own room and nobody will interfere. I'll leave you the TV – it'll be your kingdom. I'm all right with the bedroom and my workroom. We share the kitchen – neither interferes with the other. That'll be agreed in advance and sworn to.

Ludwig   And what about Mum?

Otto   She might be held up a bit.

Pause.

Don't let your old father down, you'll be sorry when he's dead and gone. That's a well-known fact.

Ludwig   You're not dead and gone. But I'll come and see you if you like.

Otto   Don't want any visitors, thank you. I can do without them. (*He goes.*)

Ludwig *watches him go – he is uncertain, but then he goes back inside the hut.*

Scene Three: Mirror Mirror

In the flat. It is oddly different. Spick and span, but unlived-in. **Otto** *has arranged it this way. As he couldn't manage the flat on his own, he* *has moved everything into one room: the kitchen. One can see it's the only place that looks lived-in. He sleeps there, he's put the TV in there, everything. But even the kitchen is too big. In fact, he lives only in the small space around the kitchen sofa, where he sleeps. So it is only a place where he sleeps. Everything else is distant, untouched and large.*

Otto *sits in front of the TV: Robert Lembke is just presenting the humorous* What's My Line. *Throughout,* **Otto** *talks grimly to himself. He has lost weight – if that can be shown on stage – and has had a haircut.*

Pause.

Otto   The humorous *What's My Line*, presented by Robert Lembke. What am I? I am an arsehole. – Sorry, I beg your pardon, what was that? – I'm an arsehole. – Skilled or unskilled? – As you like, I did a carpentry apprenticeship and now I'm a semi-skilled worker at BMW and I screw sixteen screws into the BMW 525. – Are you a car worker? – Yes, a car-screw in-screwer, a screw-screwer – a screwologist. – Are you a screwdriver? – Yes, the contestant is a screwdriver. – If you wouldn't mind, Herr Meier, show us your hands, please. – Yes, gladly. – Here you see, ladies and gentlemen, the distinctive screw hands, one with three fingers and the other one with two fingers. The remaining fingers are double the size of the normal fingers and are optimum for the operation. Please, Herr Meier, would you show us the typical hand mime. (*He mimes crippled hands, then screws.*) Thank you very much. Goodbye and a big hand for Herr Meier, the human screwdriver!

He applauds himself.

Pause.

Now he talks to himself seriously.

I am a worker. W-o-r-k-e-r! Not a doctor, not a lawyer, not an accountant, not a minister and not a factory owner.

Pause.

I can't put up with myself. Funny. Even if I wanted to.

Scene Four: The Show-off

Otto *and* **Martha** *in a little coffee house.*

Martha　It's nice you've come.

Otto　Wanted to see how you are; it's been a fortnight, you never know what could've happened. I almost didn't dare.

Martha　Why?

Otto　What if I'd met the other bloke?

Martha *looks.*

Otto　You like the job?

Martha　No, the job's awful, but they'll transfer me, if there's a vacancy – nothing exciting: selling slippers.

Pause.

Otto　If I said: come back, everything's just as it was before, you still wouldn't come?

Martha　No.

Otto　Well, if you don't like going out to work – you don't have to work when you're with me.

Martha *smiles.*

Otto　You don't want to turn the clock back?

Martha　No.

Pause.

Otto　You've got further since we split up, I've got less. That's not right. I was a happy man before, now I sit at home at night, having all kinds of ideas, going out of my head.

Martha　Why?

Otto   For instance, I talk myself into thinking I'm going blind.

Martha   Why should you go blind?

Otto (*really showing off*)   That's what I ask myself; but I talk myself into it. I imagine what it would be like if I was on my own in a very lonely mountain hut, somewhere high up, and suddenly I wake up in the morning and discover I'm blind – like the Count of Monte Cristo from the bird droppings that fell from the eagle's nest into his eyes, and there's not a single person about or a telephone to contact anybody. (*He laughs at his own idea.*) In the hut I find my way by touch, right, but I've got to get out and down the mountain, because I've only got enough food left for one day, but I'm blind – so how can I find my way down to the valley? It means certain death, out there in the wilderness, I'd get lost, fall and nobody would hear me. But if I stay in the hut, I'm finished just the same . . . (*He laughs.*)

A short pause.

I'm sorry you've gone.

Martha *looks.*

Otto   Will you let me again?

Martha *looks.*

Otto   Have you let him?

Martha *looks.*

Otto   It doesn't have to be right now, just some time.

Martha *looks.*

Pause.

Otto   I went with a whore. It cost me fifty marks, couldn't manage anything, though. So I asked for half my money back. But she said no and kept it all.

Martha   Waste of good money.

Otto *nods.*

Martha (*deliberately*)   Tossing yourself off is cheaper.

Otto (*looks, understands the attack*)   Right.

Pause.

Supposing we started from the beginning again?

Martha   Well, start.

Otto   Together, I mean.

Martha   That's ridiculous. You know that very well.

Otto   You don't have to split up just 'cause a man smashes the flat up once.

Pause.

You still want to go out to work?

Martha   I never did till now. But it's better than staying home. 'Cept at night my feet feel as if they had a hundred litres of water in them.

Otto   You never want to come back?

Martha   I've bought myself a little radio, that helps. (*Stops talking.*)

Otto   You never will, then?

Martha   Don't ask stupid, questions. I just don't know.

Otto   Who is he?

Martha   Who?

Otto   The other bloke.

Martha   Just like you. (*Laughs.*)

Otto   You're kidding.

Martha   He is.

Otto   Couldn't you find anybody better?

Martha   He's married, like me, but he doesn't tell his wife what I tell you.

Otto   Where's he from?

Martha   Works for the same firm. What I thought was this: if I really want to see it through, I must accept some help, otherwise I'll go back to you and I don't want to. So we got to know each other.

Otto   You'd never have talked like this before.

Martha   Before is before and now is now. Sure, sure. (*Looks at* **Otto**.) You let yourself be spat on – but once is once too often, Otto.

Otto   Bitch.

Martha *looks.*

Scene Five: Me

Otto *in the kitchen. Night. He is reading.*

Otto (b*egins talking to himself*)   If only I knew you still loved me, Martha, if you knew what I'm really like, then I'd try and make a go of myself. – What am I really like? For instance, it's really hard for me to read for a long time. I want to read now on my own, right, and I discover it comes very hard to me, right, not because I can't read, but it's really hard for me to read for a long time, though not for a short time . . . You coming back? No.

Goes to the door; he is uncertain, looks out through the spy-hole, opens it quickly.

Pause.

Closes the door again – there's nobody outside.

I'd better go to bed.

Scene Six: Who's Who

A Sunday afternoon. **Otto** *has tidied up in the living room; he is sitting there with* **Ludwig**. *They drink coffee and schnapps.*

Otto   Nice you found your way here at last.

Ludwig   I said I'd drop in.

Otto   Good to see you. Cheers!

Ludwig   Cheers!

They drink. Pause.

Otto   Still want to be a bricklayer?

Ludwig   Yes, Dad.

Otto   For your whole life? You know what that means?

Ludwig   Work.

Otto   I'd have preferred to see you in a bank.

Ludwig   But I earn more as a bricklayer than a bank messenger.

Otto   As a worker you're treated like shit, covered in dirt from morning till night. If you go into some restaurant the waitress knows straight away what you are – from your hands.

Ludwig   But you're only a worker as well, semi-skilled at that.

Otto   Afraid so. Remember when you said: I'd rather be dead than be like you?

Ludwig *nods.*

Pause.

Otto   Why would you rather be dead than be like me?

Ludwig   I can't tell you.

Otto   Because I'm a nobody you can't look up to?

Short pause.

Ludwig   But you like to be as you are, don't you?

Otto   I'd like to climb out of my skin, if I could.

Pause.

That's no excuse. I feel as if I was standing at the bottom of a hole, and I want to climb up there to the light, ten metres above me. But the sides are completely smooth and I can't find a handhold. (*Laughs.*) When I have a drop too much, I feel like taking a razor blade and opening myself up from top to bottom, then I imagine somebody else stepping out of my skin, somebody who's really me, whose way was blocked.

Ludwig   The frog who was a prince.

Otto   You're making fun of your father?

Ludwig   No.

Otto   I don't mind. I want you to be spared all that. A man needs something he recognises himself by, that he can be proud of.

Pause.

A man among the mass.

Ludwig   You're not the mass, you're less.

Otto   True, because we don't reach the goals we could reach.

Ludwig   So?

Otto   When you just become a bricklayer, Ludwig, with the best will in the world, you'll find you'll become exactly like me and you'll remember my words. Eventually you'll know everything about the job and you'll see how many other bricklayers there are in this world and that it's nothing and that there's a whole life somewhere else. (*Nods.*) And then you'll become exactly like me, I promise you.

Ludwig   No.

Otto *smiles.*

Ludwig   I won't just become a bricklayer, but also a human being.

Pause.

Otto   Maybe.

Pause.

Ludwig   What stops you from becoming one yourself, if you're dissatisfied?

Otto   Dreams.

Ludwig   Sure. Poor Dad.

Otto   Do you ever find you talk to yourself?

Ludwig   No.

Otto   I do. I invent things. (*Laughs.*)

Ludwig   Like being rich?

Otto   Not so much rich as recognised, successful.

Ludwig   But even if they weighed you in gold . . .

Otto (*laughs*)   . . . like the Aga Khan . . .

Ludwig   . . . you'd still be the same.

Otto   But the gold would set me up.

Ludwig *looks at his father.*

Otto   I often thought, you know, I'd give all the years still left to me for one . . .

Ludwig   One what?

Otto   God, I'd like to be taller by ten centimetres and so good-looking all the women would be running after me, and whichever one I fancied I'd only have to smile at her once and she'd fall for me, and I'd have lots of friends 'cause I'm rich, and keep them all. And travel round the whole world and wherever I went they'd welcome me – no worries, no loneliness, no bad luck, just freedom.

Ludwig   And when that year was over?

Otto (*looks*)   A long year. (*Short pause.*) I went with a whore, you know. By rights I shouldn't tell you, but today it doesn't matter.

Ludwig   Bastard.

Otto (*laughs*)   Your mum doesn't like me any more. So I've got to help myself. She's got somebody else, that woman.

Ludwig   Why don't you go and see her again?

Otto   She'll throw me out.

Ludwig   You've already been there?

Otto   But I don't dare to any more.

Ludwig   Why not?

Otto   He's always there.

Pause.

Ludwig   I've got to be going. (*Looks. Gets up.*)

Otto   Stay another ten minutes.

Scene Seven: Goodbye

*In **Martha**'s rented lodgings, after intercourse, both in bed. They talk very quietly.*

Otto   You've got two men. (*Short pause.*) I haven't got any woman at all.

Martha   Find one.

Otto   No one will have me except you.

Martha   I don't believe you.

Otto   It's true.

Martha   Silly women.

Otto   I have to depend on you. That's pretty bad.

Martha   More fool you.

Pause.

Otto   Does he know about me?

Martha   Of course he does – I told him.

Otto   What did he say?

Martha   What's he supposed to say? He's married, too. Like I told you.

Pause.

Otto   How does he do it?

Martha   What?

Otto   From behind?

Martha   Stop talking like that, Otto.

Otto   Same as me, or more expert?

Martha   Stop it.

Otto   Same as me?

Martha   Yes.

Otto   Bitch.

Pause.

Martha   You're still the same.

Otto   You sheltered me, now I'm naked.

Martha   That's unfortunate.

Otto   But it's too late.

Martha   Let's talk about something else. How are things at the firm?

Otto   Like always. Rough.

Martha   You always look on the black side.

Otto   I'd just love to creep inside you and never come out again. Childish, isn't it?

Martha *laughs.*

Otto   You pull me right inside you and I disappear!

Martha *laughs.*

Pause.

Otto   What's going to happen now?

Martha   I'm being transferred to another department next month.

Otto   She just can't think straight – that's not what I meant.

Martha   It's important to me.

Otto   You never feel you want to come home again?

Martha   I do.

Otto   I need you.

Martha   That's not true. You're a clean, tidy person and don't make a lot of work. And Ludwig has gone all domestic just recently, even wanted to wash his own pants if I'd let him. When everybody's gone, housework's not got much point.

Otto   The woman with a bad conscience, that's what you are now, am I right?

Martha   That'd just suit you. Whole mornings I just sat there and snivelled like a dog, not because of anything – there wasn't any reason – but I just sat down at the kitchen table after I'd done my housework and waited till the tears started to run, understand? (*She laughs.*) They'd tell me off at work if I sat down there and cried, but I don't feel the need to any more, because I've got to earn money to live.

Otto   You've no womanliness about you any more. You sound like a man.

Martha   Well, go and get yourself a woman.

Otto   You don't respect me any more, do you? Because he's better.

Martha   I'm telling you, Otto: go on talking like that, and as sure as this is your first time in this bed it'll be your last.

Otto *laughs.*

Pause.

What if I changed so much you didn't recognise me any more?

Martha *looks.*

Otto   That'd serve you right.

Martha   I'm getting up now.

She does so. **Otto** *just looks.*

Scene Eight: Being Human

Otto *alone in the kitchen late at night. He is drunk, and looks untidy.*

Otto (*to himself*)   I'm longing, Martha. I'm standing far off; looking. My skin is bronzed, I'm doing hard physical work and I'm sweating. Suddenly you come running along, looking for me. When you see me, you come up to me, you're trying to tell me something. But you get frightened. I've got large eyes, a handsome face, free of fear and ignorance. But it's still me.

By the time **Otto** *has finished he has a crazy, stupid face. He is turning the pages of the magazine in front of him. Then he opens his* *trousers and starts to masturbate – spiritless and limp. Shortly afterwards tears are starting to run down his cheeks. He cries.*

Scene Nine: Ending

In **Martha***'s rented room,* **Martha** *and* **Ludwig** *embrace.*

Martha   Has your dad sent you?

Ludwig *shakes his head.*

Martha   Only, I haven't seen you for ages.

Ludwig   Well, you just suddenly vanished.

Martha (*laughs*)   I had to find another room, your dad wouldn't leave me in peace.

Ludwig   Aren't you ever going home again?

Martha *shakes her head.*

Ludwig   Me neither.

Pause.

Ludwig *looks around.*

Martha   This is not the sort of life you might want for yourself – but us old women . . .

Ludwig   Don't be silly, Mum.

Martha   To an employer I'm an old woman . . . with no career to fall back on. (*Laughs.*) If the Kaufhof hadn't taken me on, in the shoe department . . .

Ludwig *laughs.*

Martha   I sell slippers all day. I have my counter which I'm responsible for. They don't let me do the cash-register yet, but they will when I've proved myself.

Pause.

Martha   Sometimes I'd love to just get up and go home.

Ludwig   In that case I'd come home, too.

Martha (*nods*)   When I have no strength any more, 'cause I can't manage things . . . (*Laughs.*) Though it's not hard work. I just arrange my counter so it looks nice and invites you to buy, as they say. If anybody asks for information, I give it. If somebody buys something, I wrap it and take it to the cashier. If we sell out, I go down the basement and fetch fresh supplies. New stock comes in once a month. (*She cries.*)

Ludwig   Go home again, Mum.

Martha   Somebody like me should stay in the place she's used to. I didn't know that. Sometimes I stand there and my whole body's juddering.

Pause.

I'm not used to anything. That's what it is. Though it's really so simple. Sizes are no problem – not with bedroom slippers. Half a size bigger than normal . . . (*She smiles.*) In the evening I sit feeling as if I'd done a marathon run all day long.

Pause.

Then your dad arrives and wants to discuss things for hours when I'm dead tired and have got other things to worry about. Though at the moment he doesn't because he doesn't know my new address yet. (*Smiles.*) Woe betide you if you tell him . . .

Ludwig *shakes his head.*

Martha   I even said I'd got somebody else so he'd leave me alone. (*Smiles.*)

Ludwig   Have you got somebody?

Martha   Fool. Where would I get anybody that quick?

Ludwig *laughs, relieved.*

Martha   And what about you – are you happy?

Ludwig   It's better than not working.

Martha *smiles, nods.*

Ludwig   You don't love him any more – Dad?

Martha   What does that mean – love him? I've put up with him, your dad, these last ten years, but that's quite normal.

Ludwig   That's not love.

Martha   Who knows? – Let's talk about something else. (*Laughs.*) I can't bear to see another pair of slippers. Not even these, which I've brought from home in case you thought I'd –

Ludwig   – nicked them from the Kaufhof. (*Smiles.*)

Martha   They've promised me if there's a position they'll transfer me to another department. To the food hall. That's what I'm hoping. I think that's more in my line, more interesting.

Ludwig   My job's quite interesting.

Martha   Because you're learning something. That's the difference.

Pause.

Martha *wipes a tear from her face.*

Ludwig   Don't, Mum.

Martha (*nods*)   No, course not. What a nuisance. (*Pause.*) Yesterday I even went to the cinema. For the first time. You know what happened? After the show, I was just looking at the photos in the display cabinet – this man about my age started to chat me up: did I want to have supper with him? (*Smiles.*) I didn't answer him, of course, and walked off.

Ludwig   Good for you.

Martha   He was quite attractive.

Ludwig   Shall we move into a place together?

Martha *smiles.*

Ludwig   I can't stay where I am now. It's the firm's place, and it's only for guest workers; and if they do make an exception you're supposed to be eighteen.

Martha   You got courage, that's good.

Ludwig   Give me your hand.

Martha *does so.* **Ludwig** *presses it.*

Martha   Ouch!

Ludwig (*laughs*)   Sure.

Pause.

Let's move in together or else I'll tell Dad your new address. (*Laughs.*)

Martha   Blackmail!

Pause.

In a few months maybe, when we're both independent. I'm not able to look after you yet. I've got to think of myself first and I'm just not used to that.

Ludwig   And Dad?

Martha (*shakes her head, calm*)   Got to do the same.

Ludwig   What?

Martha   Same as us: learn.

Desire

translated by

Anthony Vivis

Characters

Hilde, *a strong woman of forty*
Otto, *her husband*
Mitzi, *a plain woman in her thirties*
Fritz, *a young man, Hilde's brother*

Author's Note

The action takes place mostly in a garden centre; as well as in a cemetery and flat.

Since standard language is grey but a 'regional voice' colourful, the characters speak with an accent, which does not have to be a localised dialect. A 'standard English' equivalent of '*Hochdeutsch*' is certainly preferable to any attempt at reproducing Bavarian. (In the world premiere, the cast came from Saxony, Lake Constance, Switzerland and Westphalia. A process of careful amendment resulted in each character having his or her 'own voice'.)

Although the contemporary references in the play prevent it sounding 'old', an appropriate shift back in time, to produce an effect of distance, is desirable.

Act One

Scene One

Hilde *and* **Otto** *in their double bed. They are tired. It's dark.*

Otto *is audibly making an effort.*

Hilde (*after accepting things passively for a while*) If you're slogging your guts out all day, you can't be a sexpot all night.

Otto I'm not asking you to be, but – (*Making more effort.*) – there's lots of ways to please a man.

Hilde And there's lots of ways to please a woman.

Otto By leaving her in peace, you mean?

Hilde By showing her some respect.

Otto (*without sounding sorry*) Now he don't want to any more.

Hilde It doesn't have to be now, not going to go out of fashion, is it?

Otto That's what you always say.

Hilde Do yourself up, then, and stop shoving it at me.

Otto Call it a day, you mean?

Hilde I didn't say that.

Otto Thought it though.

Hilde I'm too tired to think.

Otto You never think what I might want. (*To himself, as if quoting.*) – 'What about that blow job, then?' – 'What, when I've already cleaned my teeth?'

Hilde Come off it, I've never said that.

Otto Never done it, neither.

Hilde   'Course I have.

Otto   Back when Noah was a lad.

Hilde   You can't force it, just has to happen.

Otto   Only it never does happen.

Hilde   Not tonight.

Otto   My point exactly.

Hilde   Didn't you hear me say in the bath: 'God, I'm so tired, and my back aches!'?

Otto   No, can't say I did.

Hilde (*after a short pause*)   Anyway, it's Thursday today, and Friday's one of our busiest days.

Otto   Okay. Point taken. Sleep well. (*He is sulking.*)

Hilde (*after a short pause*)   No need to sulk.

Otto (*brooding*)   I wouldn't mind coming in behind, like other blokes do, blokes what do what they want with their wives.

Hilde (*talking to him like a child*)   But Otto, it's so nice in front.

Otto   So you always say.

Hilde   I didn't go to the toilet today. I'm all blocked up.

Otto (*childishly*)   I'm all blocked out, you mean?

Hilde   My heart's wide open for you.

Otto   Big deal. (*He gives it another try.*)

Hilde (*after a longish pause*)   Leave it for now, Otto. He's none too keen anyway, and it's not my fault.

Otto (*quite affectionately*)   Silly bitch.

Hilde (*companionably*)   I do love you, even if I don't shout the house down when we make love.

Otto   Right.

Hilde (*contented*)   Glad you understand.

Otto *has meanwhile gone to the lavatory to masturbate, which he does while grimacing in the mirror.*

Hilde (*calling out*)   Now what are you doing?

Otto   Got a bit of meat stuck in my dentures. Just fishing it out.

Hilde   Lovely those pork schnitzels today, wasn't they?

Otto   Dead right.

Hilde   Night, then.

Otto   Night. I'm just coming. (*He catches his semen in a tissue, wipes his penis meticulously, and mops up a few drops on the turquoise floor tiles. Then he throws the tissue into the lavatory pan and flushes it. He breathes heavily.*)

Scene Two

Hilde and **Otto** *outside their garden centre.*

Fritz (*holding a small suitcase*)   Great to see you – both of you.

Hilde   Great to see you. (*She hugs and kisses him.*)

Otto (*grabbing his hand*)   Fritz! Great to see you!

Hilde   Here he is, then. So glad you could make it.

Otto   Nice you made it early. We didn't expect you till later.

Fritz   They let me out at seven.

Otto   Get a reasonable train, then?

Fritz   Through train. Only one stop.

Hilde   We been dying to see you. You put on weight.

Otto (*after sizing* **Fritz** *up, risks a joke*)   Made a new man of you, that holiday camp.

Fritz   I've put on eight kilos. I'm quite a flabby guts now.

Otto   It's the way they look after you in those places now. (*Laughing.*) Think yourself lucky they got beyond galley slaves. They never put on weight.

Fritz *also laughs.*

Hilde   Not short of nothing, are you?

Fritz   Don't think so, no.

Otto (*patting him on the shoulder*)   Once we get you back to work, you'll soon lose the flab.

Fritz · Thanks for putting me up, the both of you. Don't know what I'd've done otherwise.

Otto *nods.*

Hilde (*quickly*)   In you come, then, and make yourself at home.

Fritz (*takes a bar of chocolate from his pocket and holds it out*) This is for Susi.

Hilde   She's at school. We told her you've been in America but was feeling homesick. (*Stupidly.*) Stops people talking, you know.

Otto (*smiling*)   So you'd better eat that yourself. American chocolate bars look different. (*He gives him back his chocolate.*)

Fritz *nods.*

Otto   The world's a different place altogether since you been away. Have a look round, see what we been up to while you was in – America.

Hilde   He's not been away that long.

Fritz   Two years and ninety-three days.

Otto   What a memory! (*Looking straight at him.*) We'll soon have you good as new!

Scene Three

A room furnished simply, with an old-fashioned wardrobe, and a large mirror.

Fritz (*slowly and deliberately moves his things into the empty wardrobe, stares several times at his own reflection in the mirror, grins and makes slight movements – all this is very brief and hardly noticeable. Meanwhile, to himself*)   Socks . . . down here. – Shirts in here . . . no, on second thoughts, they'll be better here. We never wear these. – Do for work, though. Over here, you. – Dead right. – No good there.

Otto (*knocks, then comes in*)   How's it going then, Fritz?

Fritz   Okay.

Otto (*inspecting the wardrobe*)   Always tell a soldier from the state of his locker.

Fritz (*laughing*)   That's army talk. (*Taking a bottle out of his suitcase.*) Brought this to celebrate.

Otto (*laughing, he looks at the label*)   Asbach Uralt. 'In Asbach Uralt resides the spirit of wine.' (*Quickly.*) Got your pills, have you?

Fritz   Here.

Otto (*just looks*)   And you got to keep taking them, right?

Fritz   I do.

Otto (*having a good look at the packages*)   Them doctors will know what's best for you.

Fritz (*not hiding anything*)   That's one of the conditions they always lay down. When they let somebody like me out early.

Otto   Right.

Fritz   They're worried you'll reoffend if you don't take them.

Otto *just looks.*

Fritz   So you get sedatives, to keep you on an even whatsit, to start with anyhow.

Otto (*not sure of his ground*)   Drugs to inhabit libido, so Hilde said, that's what you'll be needing.

Fritz (*nodding*)   Too right, that's what they're called, libido-inhibitors.

Otto (*looking straight at him*)   Well, yes, takes all sorts . . . (*A short pause.*) Keep taking the tablets then, that's the ticket, so's you don't cause no trouble.

Fritz   Dead right.

Scene Four

The dining room, late evening. **Hilde**, **Otto** *and* **Fritz**.

Otto *is having a drink.*

Hilde   Go on drinking like that, Otto, and you'll be paralytic.

Otto   What are bottles for? – He brought the bugger!

Fritz   Celebrate being back, I thought.

Otto   Dead right. Put your tubs out when it's raining, as they say. Down the hatch!

Hilde   No need to overdo it, though.

Otto (*going one better than* **Fritz**)   Many women, many words; many geese, many turds.

Hilde   Oh Christ, he's off. Tomorrow is another day, don't forget.

Otto   We're out the house by four.

Fritz   Wake me and I'll be there.

Otto   You're my wife's brother, no two ways about that. Counts for something, that does. So you'll be getting five hundred quid cash down and all found.

Fritz   I'll put it towards my motorbike.

Otto   Fair enough.

Hilde   Just to tide you over, Fritz – temporary, like.

Otto   Once he's settled in, we'll see how we go. (*A short pause.*) The whole cemetery's more or less my baby. Sooner or later we'd've had to take on an extra pair of hands.

Hilde   Saves you taking on some stranger, don't it; this way you keep it in the family.

Otto   So long as he fits in, that's the main thing.

Fritz   I'll fucking fit in – no worries.

Otto   Down to you, Fritz. Took some sorting, I can tell you. It was quite a decision, this was.

Hilde   Think Fritz don't realise that?

Fritz   Dead right I do.

Otto   Just want everything above board and shipshape. Or you're fucked – know what I mean? (*A short pause.*) To realise my long-term thingamy I'll need a nifty pair of hands.

Fritz   These are.

Otto (*smiling at him*)   That I believe.

Hilde   Careful . . .

Otto   Only joking. (*More seriously.*) Listen: your standard stiff gets its standard wreath, which I buy wholesale, then jack up the price by forty per cent.

Hilde   We run quite a production line here.

Otto   There's nothing much to do except make money. Some of your stiffs are dead choosy, though – thank God. They won't all settle for a wreath costing a hundred and ninety-five marks including VAT. The stiff goes: 'Thing is, when I was alive, I always had to shop at Bilka, and even now I've snuffed it I still have to go for a cheapo send-off.' You got to give these 'roses from Holland' a good talking-to, so's they don't hang their heads when the coffin goes down. That's not much of a send-off, now is it? Seen my new air-conditioning unit?

Fritz   Can't say I have.

Hilde (*enthusiastically*)   It's brill, Fritz. You press this button and next day you've got three hundred and fifty lilies fresh as the morning God made them. Or you don't press it and you haven't got three hundred and fifty lilies. They're on stand-by till you switch them on, see. Cost 280,000 marks, the whole unit did. Tomorrow, let's say five people die – no worries: overnight spring will be sprung for them. And if nobody dies for a week or two, we switch to the ice-age setting. You can play summer, autumn and winter to your heart's content – or, more to the point, your market's, your customer's content.

Otto   Dead right.

Hilde (*enthusing – in standard English*)   Even nature has to bend to market forces once in a while. After all, she's only human.

Otto (*nodding*)   Or, as our Mitzi says, we keep people company on their final journey.

Fritz   Who's this Mitzi?

Otto   She's a genius, that's who.

Hilde   Dead right.

Otto   'Herr Holdenrieder,' she goes, 'what the customer wants, the customer gets, okay?' Looks straight at them, she does, and got second sight when it comes to wallets. Sees life as it's really lived, does Mitzi. (*A short pause. He has another drink.*) You and Mitzi'll get on like a house on fire. None of your tricks, mind – (*Moving his hand back and forth.*) – heave out your how's-your-father and she'll do a runner.

Hilde What did I tell you – pissed as a newt.

Otto Fat lot you know about sex! (*To* **Fritz**.) In a civilised society like this we're allowed to talk man to man. But seriously, mind: you give our Mitzi the once-over.

Hilde Christ, you aren't half pissed. This is the trouble, Fritz. Loves his garden body and soul, but drinks like a fish.

Otto Them plants of mine would peg out if they wasn't watered. I'm head plant, see, and under me they's all sub-plants.

Hilde For Chrissake, Otto – time and place!

Otto Dead right. (*A little pompously, to* **Fritz**.) Honest as the day is long, that's me, Fritz, okay?

Fritz That makes two of us.

Scene Five

Fritz *and* **Mitzi** *in the hothouse.* **Fritz** *is sitting on a bale of garden peat, breathing with difficulty.*

Mitzi (*shouting*) Herr Holdenrieder, quick, your brother's feeling funny. (*Back to* **Fritz**.) Nice deep breaths, now. That's the main thing.

Otto (*coming over*) What's up, then?

Mitzi Look – your brother's feeling funny.

Otto Brother-in-law, not brother. – What's up with you?

Fritz Can't get my breath.

Mitzi Some sort of collapse or something.

Fritz Can't swallow.

Otto Why not?

Fritz (*hand on throat*)   All jammed up.

Otto   Open wide and say 'aah'.

Fritz   Aah!

Otto (*peering into his mouth*)   Tonsils as big as your fist. That's what it is, your tonsils. Must've caught something. Must be a bit run-down, like women always are. Get indoors and we'll take your temperature, then we'll know.

Mitzi   Talk sense. He's straight down the doctor's, he is.

Fritz   No doctors. Don't need no doctor.

Otto   Don't you worry now, Fritz, we'll soon sort you out.

Mitzi   If it was me I'd see a doctor.

Otto   But it isn't, is it? (*Grinning.*) And a good thing too, eh, Fritz?

Fritz   Dead right. No doctors.

Otto   Fetch our thermometer. Middle drawer, kitchen cabinet.

Mitzi   I'd go to the doctor's.

Otto (*grinning*)   Stick to your subject, Mitzi. Flowers is what you know about, not men.

Scene Six

Bedroom. Night, but not totally dark. **Hilde** *and* **Otto**.

Otto (*genuinely unsettled*)   Seemed a good idea at the time. Now we're right in it.

Hilde   Nobody can help catching the flu. anybody we took on could've caught it. Nobody's to blame. It'll soon go away.

Otto   It won't go away. You'll see. What he's got will never go away.

Hilde   Trust you to look on the black side.

Otto   Affects your whole health, that kind of business. I mean, it upsets your whole system.

Hilde   I'm not saying there's no side effects, am I? You got to make allowances, that's all.

Otto   Don't seem fair we're lumbered with all this. Getting it all dumped on our doorstep.

Hilde   If we hadn't taken him in, so's he's got family behind him, he might've taken an overdose.

Otto   Well, for his type, maybe there's something to be said for it. (*Catching* **Hilde**'*s eye, he swallows self-consciously, then sniffs.*)

Hilde   That's no way to talk about nobody, let alone my brother.

Otto   I just don't see how a bloke gets them urges, why he's got the way he is.

Hilde   He's never attacked nobody. Never laid a finger on nobody.

Otto   Yes, but he needs one hand free so's he can – (*He moves his arm back and forth.*)

Hilde   You just watch it, Otto.

Otto   Why d'they keep banging him up, then?

Hilde   He couldn't stop, could he, that's why. He can't keep his lusts under control

Otto   Lusts, my arse! He's abnormal, he is.

Hilde (*with conviction*)   He's turned over a new leaf now. The important thing is to keep reminding him and set him a good example.

Otto   Whatever you say, he's a marked man. That type of behaviour can't never be cancelled out. (*A short pause.*) You just think about it – (*Another short pause.*) Let's say I walk down – (*A short pause.*) – the street to the corner, and then – (*He makes some movements in the air.*) – well, you know, and afterwards I come back home. (*Another short pause.*) Not the same bloke, am I?

Hilde   'Course you are!

Otto (*vehemently*)   On the outside, maybe, you stupid cow, but *inside!* What d'you reckon's going on inside him when he has to down a pound of tranquies a day so's he don't cause no trouble.

Hilde   Anti-testosterone drugs, that's all they are.

Otto   Oh, that's all right, then. (*Gives* **Hilde** *a look.*)

Hilde   Now let's get some shut-eye. Night, then.

Otto   What's he up to now, I wonder?

Hilde   What he's supposed to be up to – sleeping off his flu, I expect.

Otto   Tossing hisself off, more like – jerk, jerk, jerk. (*Laughing to himself.*)

Hilde   He'll be sleeping as sound as little Susi, you mark my words.

Otto   I wouldn't be too sure. Maybe I can see more than you can, that's all. (*A short pause.*) Night-night.

Scene Seven

Fritz's *room, daylight.* **Otto** *is looking hard at* **Fritz** *and* **Hilde**.

Otto   We been thinking, Fritz. You're best off going to the doctors what know you, and get them to examine you, see what's up with you. Okay?

Fritz   It's flu, that's what it is.

Otto   There's no telling with you, though, it could be anything.

Fritz   It's only flu, I'll be right as rain soon.

Otto (*loudly*)   Says you.

Hilde   I believe him.

Otto   Why not? But believing's one thing. Knowing's another. (*More personally.*) You just imagine what complications might set in if you fall ill.

Fritz   Think I'm going to snuff it from a touch of flu?

Otto   Won't be told, will he?

Hilde   Look at it Otto's way, Fritz, he's responsible for you, see.

Otto   Dead right.

Fritz   I'll be fine by tomorrow.

Hilde   Let's let him get a bit of rest.

Otto   When you're ill you need looking after. He can't be a couch potato here all day. (*A short pause.*) We're not the fucking NHS, are we? We got work to do.

Fritz   Don't worry on my account, I'm used to looking out for myself.

Hilde   Didn't mean it that way, did you, Otto? He's concerned about you, that's all.

Otto   Dead right. Seeing as how we get eight burials a week.

Fritz   I'll be on my feet again in no time.

Hilde   That's the ticket.

Otto *gives* **Hilde** *a hard look and nods, then goes out.*

Fritz   Why don't he like me?

Hilde   Don't mind him, he's an old worry-guts, that's all.

Fritz   I like him.

Hilde   We're quite a good team, though, aren't we?

Fritz *smiles and nods.*

Act Two

Scene One

In the cemetery. A grave and some wreaths. **Hilde** *and* **Otto**. *We can see that they work well together even when they're quarrelling.*

Hilde He's better again, so stop moaning.

Otto Those red blotches haven't gone, though.

Hilde They're pimples, aren't they, he had them when he came.

Otto They've only just struck me.

Hilde Well, they haven't me.

They carry on working . . .

Otto Okay, then, let's agree they pimples. (*Staring at her.*) Why's he got pimples?

Hilde Oh, God, I –

Otto Leave God out of this. He's a man but he's got pimples.

Hilde Our Susi's got pimples.

Otto Because she's a child, because she's pubertal. Your brother pubertal, is he?

Hilde Mentally maybe. With habits like his he might well be a bit backward.

Otto Sure – his sort probably are backward, all right. (*Loudly.*) But that's not the main issue here. It's abnormal, pimples on a man that age, believe you me.

Hilde Keep your voice down.

Otto There's nobody here for miles around. And the stiffs aren't listening in. (*A short pause.*) Who knows what else he might be suffering from?

Hilde   Talk sense.

Otto (*in standard English*)   All I'm asking is: what kind of pimples are they? And my answer is this: I'm a man who thinks things through, Hilde, so get used to the idea, okay? (*A short pause.*) He had the flu, right? Who else got it? You didn't, I didn't, even our Susi, who brings anything that's going home from school, she didn't get it neither. Only he got it. But I'm not talking sense, not according to you? (*A short pause.*) Until the balloon goes up, when it's far too late.

Hilde   What balloon?

Otto   He always locks the bathroom when he's in there.

Hilde   Why shouldn't he?

Otto   Fine so far as it goes – but in this particular case not so great. Why does he do it, then? I been thinking it through, and I can tell you exactly why. When he cleans his teeth, see – and he does do his teeth, he picked up the personal cleanliness habit when he was banged up, see – as I was saying, after he's – (*He makes teeth-cleaning movements.*) – he spits out down our toilet – (*Huffing, and nodding.*) – like this, see – and what I want to know is this: is he spitting blood, has he got bleeding gums?

Hilde (*very practical*)   You've got partial dentures. Fritz and me've still got all our own gnashers.

Otto   Fat lot women know about anything. If he'd got dentures in place he wouldn't never get bleeding gums, almost never anyway – only if he got something stuck between his gum and the plate, let's say – but in that case – (*Making a movement.*) – you flip it out just like that.

Hilde   You do talk some rubbish sometimes.

Otto   He's got pimples, but I'm talking rubbish, am I? He was banged up, but I'm talking rubbish. He's got to gobble pills but I'm talking rubbish. (*Staring hard at her.*) You think the kind of life he's led goes unpunished? You ought to be thankful you married a man what thinks.

Hilde (*puffing, speaks softly and sincerely*)   Ever since he was a lad my brother's been up to these tricks – (*She makes certain movements.*) – but that's all. How could he've caught anything getting up to his tricks? You think that one through if you're so clever.

Otto   What d'you think you're doing?

Hilde   Showing you how he – you know.

Otto   What filthy tricks have you been learning, eh? (*Imitating her.*) What's got into you?! Just look at yourself – go on, look! Would you have ever got up to them tricks in public with your husband standing beside you before that – person – moved in here?

Hilde   I was trying to show you for real, that's all.

Otto   I can use my imagination, thank you, if it stops my wife getting up to tricks like that.

Scene Two

The hothouse. Hot and bright. **Fritz** *and* **Mitzi**. **Mitzi** *is staring hard at* **Fritz** *while he works.*

Mitzi   I've brought that bumf from the jobcentre for you, like I promised. (*Reading the preface.*) Might help you plan your future.

Fritz *nods.*

Mitzi   'The key to your future lies in retraining.' (*She reads on.*) 'If your current career path fails to provide you with specialist training, you can apply for in-service retraining with a view to obtaining a better job with qualifications. See pages 4 to 7.' (*She thumbs through the leaflet.*) 'Hitherto, Herr D – real name changed – had been working as a building labourer. Then he enrolled in a twelve-week retraining apprenticeship for machinery used in construction work. The Employment Office paid him a retraining allowance throughout this period, which amounted to ninety per cent of his former net earnings. Today he is employed as a bulldozer driver.'

Fritz   There's loads of job prospects, that's for sure.

Mitzi   You got to put out feelers, that's the main thing.

Fritz   No telling what might happen once you start.

Mitzi (*nodding*)   You don't have to hide nothing from me. I know it's not just the flu you've had. I know you've been inside and all.

Fritz   There's no way you can know that.

Mitzi   Think I'm blind, or what?

Fritz (*crossly*)   Okay, if you know, you know. I don't give a shit what other people know about me. I know what I know.

Mitzi   I'm not prying or nothing. But the way I look at it is this: they don't send you to prison for no reason. And if you're not told nothing, you start imagining things a lot more worse than what really did happen, see.

Fritz   Bollocks.

Mitzi   Always see the downside, don't you? (*A short pause.*) The very first time I saw you I thought to myself: he's nice, I thought.

Fritz   Thanks for bringing the brochure.

Mitzi   Maybe you need a holiday. A change is as good as a rest. The Bavarian Tourist Office is offering a week in the Costa del Sol for six hundred marks, including flight and full board.

Fritz   That's not bad, six hundred marks.

Mitzi   I got a colour brochure at home, it's got all the holidays in. Play your cards right, and I'll bring it in tomorrow. (*She smiles.*)

Fritz *just looks.*

Scene Three

Otto *and* **Hilde** *in twin martial beds.* **Otto** *is reading an illustrated magazine.* **Hilde** *is staring at him.*

Otto (*reading*)   'My name is Elke. I'm twenty-two years of age. Only my doctor knows the truth. I'm often in tears these days.' (*He looks at* **Hilde**.) 'I got infected in Spain.'

Hilde (*quietly*)   My brother's never been to Spain.

Otto (*reading on*)   'The skin rash came seven months later. Seven months after my affair with Pedro. A beautiful boy. I met him on the Costa del Sol. I would have forgotten him by now but then I got this awful rash.' (*He turns over a few pages.*) 'My name is Dieter. I got infected in Kenya.'

Hilde   My brother's never been to Kenya.

Otto (*reading*)   'I went on holiday with some lads I know. The girls were really nice. My wife will never forgive me. But she is standing by me. I'm truly sorry, but what good is that?' (**Otto** *gives* **Hilde** *a look.*) And so on and on and on. (*Reads on.*) 'My name is Detlev. I got infected in prison. You're so alone inside. I had a moment of weakness. Now I'm infected. Only somebody who's been in prison can know what I'm going through.'

Hilde (*exhausted*)   My brother is not a poofter.

Otto   You must have a lot of trust in him.

Hilde   Why shouldn't I trust him? (*Exhausted.*) As I've already tried to explain.

Otto   I heard you. Okay, so he wanks a lot. But maybe his sex life is a bit more complicated than you might think.

Hilde   Trust you!

Otto (*sulkily*)   Night, then, or have you thought of something else you could do with tonight?

Hilde *just stares.*

Scene Four

Fritz *and* **Mitzi** *in a paddle boat on a hot day.* **Mitzi** *is giving* **Fritz** *a hard time.*

Mitzi   I bet you're an amazing lover, though. Am I right? Or am I right?

Fritz   Always asking questions, aren't you?

Mitzi   I'm not forcing myself on nobody. Don't need to, that's why.

Fritz *just looks.*

Mitzi   Not exactly a bodice-ripper, are you?

Fritz   Afraid not.

Mitzi (*pursuing him*)   What are you, then?

Fritz   What you want me to be?

Mitzi   Search me.

Fritz (*suddenly*)   A sadistic sex monster, that's what I am. So now you know. Now you'll keep well clear.

Mitzi (*deliberately*)   I read this article about sadists once, in *Quick*. I wouldn't do that if I was you. I don't like it.

Fritz   Who does like it? Still do it, though, don't you?

Mitzi   What did you do, then, when you did it?

Fritz   What'd it say in *Quick*?

Mitzi   Said they lash the victim with a whip, then, once they see blood, they can have sex with you.

Fritz   Sounds familiar.

Mitzi   That what you done, then?

Fritz   Dead right, that's for sure.

Mitzi (*choosing her words*) I mean, you can do special things for somebody you specially like, if you know what I mean. But that's going a bit far, for me, anyway.

Fritz (*jauntily*) First, they had to take their clothes off, then I'd prick them, see.

Mitzi What do'you prick them with?

Fritz Pins.

Mitzi Where?

Fritz Belly and breasts.

Mitzi How deep, then?

Otto Till I drew blood.

Mitzi (*nods, then swallows*) Then what?

Fritz Then I'd lick up the blood and then I could shoot off. (*A short pause.*) So now you know. You did ask.

Mitzi So that's why they sent you to jail, right?

Fritz (*with some relief*) Dead right.

Mitzi Thought it must be something of the sort, only I'd never have thought you capable of that, know what I mean?

Fritz (*carefree*) Good job nobody knows I'm a vampire killer. I leave bite marks all over my victims' naked bodies. 'Oh, Granny, what big teeth you've got!' (*Laughs hugely at this.*)

Mitzi (*with great concern*) Somebody needs to persevere with you, that's what I think.

Fritz Could be a long job, that.

Mitzi And unless you go in for all this sadism stuff you can't come, right?

Fritz I got to abstain, else it could all blow up again, see, then I might not know where to stop.

Mitzi   And if you don't know where to stop?

Fritz   Phew. Wouldn't like to say.

Mitzi   Soon be bleeding, would I?

Fritz   Slippery with blood you'd be.

Mitzi   That what they put you away for, then?

Fritz (*jauntily*)   Dead right, slish slash.

Mitzi   I don't think you can enjoy the pricking and that, even if you like somebody a lot.

Fritz   You're not supposed to enjoy it, that's the whole point.

Mitzi (*inquisitively*)   I've never met nobody like you.

Fritz (*childishly*)   Me neither.

Scene Five

The cemetery. **Otto** *is cutting back some ivy which overhangs a grave. He is deeply obsessed about his fantasies and suspicions, but* **Hilde** *prefers to keep out of it all.*

Otto   Let's trace the course of his spunk, what we might call his off-duty paras (*Laughs.*) then, shall we, through our house.

Hilde *just looks.*

Otto   Thing is, you see: he'll shoot his load just like that, walking or standing, if he forgets to take his pills, which is only human after all, and it's all over in seconds when you get the urge, see.

Hilde   Oh yes?

Otto (*undeterred*)   Oh yes, matter of moments sometimes. And he's not fussy where he shoots off – standing or walking – once he's ready to come. Has he got a tissue handy? If he has, he'll chuck it away once he's used it. And if he does, where does he chuck it, mmh? Does he chuck it really away or what? Let's say he hasn't got no tissue handy, but he smears his spunk on the nearest wall, sofa, curtain, whatever. (*Breathing heavily.*) So – now there's a whole load of off-duty paras lying in wait, see, till some victim or other happens to come along, with a scratch, let's say, and picks up the infection. Our Susi for instance. Who's just scratched herself playing, let's say. See what I'm driving at? Off-duty paras, broken skin, bingo. Bacteria in the bloodstream, right.

And who knows how often a bloke like that can jack off, else he wouldn't have to gobble pills to damp his drives down, would he? Get the picture? In court, this judge says: 'You must take medicine so's your sexual goings-on don't cause havoc everywhere.' There's no saying where he's left his stains. (*Looks hard at* **Hilde**.) Right. Your go.

Hilde (*keeping her distance, factually*)   I read somewhere if the virus is exposed to the air it dies.

Otto (*laughing*)   Dies of fresh air? Are you serious? Christ, first I've heard of anything dying from air.

Hilde (*serious and logical*)   Otto, my brother's only crime against us so far is to've had five days off ill. He's got plenty on his plate as it is. Don't paint the kettle any blacker than it is.

Otto (*gives her a look, then nods*)   You mustn't stop people thinking or they'll soon be barking. (*Disturbed.*) And the way I look at it is this: when blokes like us come, usually we can catch it in some sort of (*Lengthening the word.*) re-cept-ac-le. You don't just shoot off out in the open, or where you live, I mean, you (*Swallowing.*) have more consideration, see. We're not some kind of tomcats, are we, what just shoot off wherever they are, standing or moving, and make a stink? And that's why so many tomcats get neutered, see. Admittedly they haven't neutered your brother, but he's got to gobble down these libido-inhabitors, right? (*Openly.*) You reckon I ought to be on libido-inhabitors, too? Mmh?

Hilde   No, no, not you.

Otto (*gives her a look, then swallows*)   Because I'm a normal male, that's why. Dead right. (*Exhausted, he talks semi-nonsense.*) Anyway, tomcats do it on every street corner. They never stop. If it's not number two, it's number one.

Hilde   Otto, am I the receptacle for your number two?

Otto (*glaring at her*)   If I'm speaking out of turn, I beg your parsnip, okay? But what you got to remember, Hilde, is this: your husband's a thinking man.

Hilde   That's the ticket.

Scene Six

*At **Mitzi**'s place. She is knitting. **Fritz** is on the sofa. He stares hard at her. The further out she ventures, the deeper he retreats into himself. Neither can reach the other.*

Mitzi (*worked up*)   Prick. For Christ's sake, prick me. (*She stares hard at him.*) Go on, prick me. (*Getting into her stride.*) Hurry up, then, prick me as much as you want. (*More savagely.*) Prick! (*Almost in desperation.*) Go on, you bastard, prick me! For Christ's sake, get pricking, bugger you! (*She sighs, looks straight at him, then hurls herself on him.*)

Fritz (*helplessly getting out of her way*)   I don't need nothing what has sex in it.

Mitzi (*demanding*)   Prick me, I said.

Fritz (*desperately*)   I daren't prick you, or they'll lock me up again.

Mitzi (*excited*)   What if I tell the judge: 'He pricked me because I wanted it?'

Fritz (*barely audible*)   Nobody wants it.

Mitzi   There's always a first time. (*Desperately loud.*) For Chrissake, prick me!

Fritz (*desperately worried*)   Get off of me!

Mitzi   Prick me, I said, you useless pile of shit. (*Helpless and in agonising despair.*) Please prick me.

Fritz *just stares at her.*

Mitzi (*after a pause, gasps for breath*)   You're the shittiest arsehole I've ever met.

Fritz (*helplessly backing away*)   Christ, Mitzi, you frighten the life out of me.

Mitzi (*changing tack*)   You just watch what you say to me.

Fritz   To be honest with you, I don't want to prick you.

Mitzi   Call yourself a sex monster, you're just chicken. (*Stares at him, full of hate.*) What a good little Mummy's boy we are then, eh? Piss off out my house, pillock, before I get the law in.

Fritz (*shouting*)   What for?

Mitzi   Where you're concerned they need a 'what for'?

Fritz, *helpless, hits her , . .*

Mitzi (*shaking herself, energetically*)   You see! That's how quick there's a what for.

Fritz *stares at her desperately, tries to move off.*

Mitzi (*grabbing hold of him*)   You stay here, you wait till they come for you. (*Grinning.*) Or if you prefer: be a good boy! (*She reaches for his penis.*)

Fritz *tries to break free, but can't. He hits out at her.*

Mitzi (*won't be shaken off*)   Now we do it, right?!

Fritz   Talk sense, woman. Get off me, you cunt!

Mitzi (*excited*)   Somebody needs to get through to you, right? Come on, let it all out! Give me all the shit inside you. I can take it. Fuck the cunt! (*She struggles to get him.*)

Fritz (*knocks her almost senseless to the ground*)   Talk sense, get off me, I daren't hit you, my cock's my property, bang, bang, bang, you're dead.

Mitzi (*on the floor, quietly, all but finished*)   Somebody got to talk you down, right? New experience for you, isn't it: a woman what's strong and will put up with anything for love. Like what you see, do you? Look how you've made me look. Go on, look at me! After all the blood and bruises, I've deserved some loving, right? You've roughed me up enough, now make love to me. (*In full flood.*) Fuck me senseless, please, now, now, please!

Fritz *stares at her like something in a horror film.*

Mitzi (*softly*)   First the roughing-up, then the making love.

Fritz (*all but finished*)   First the roughing-up, then the finishing off, if you don't shut it.

Mitzi   I don't believe this. You can't just knock me about. I've earned some loving, haven't I? Are you listening to me? Make love, I said, make love. I get the same amount of love as I got punches – it's only fair, right? Nobody smashes a qualified florist in the face and gets away with it, okay? I'm asking you nice. (*Worn out.*) Love me now, or I call the law. Love me!

Fritz *first just gapes, then breaks free, half crazed, and runs off, as if escaping a mugger.*

Mitzi (*on her last legs*)   Love me, I said. Love me. Love me. Love me. Love me. Love me. Love me. Love me. Love me. Love me. Love me. Love me. (*This can go on for some time.*)

Scene Seven

The drive-in entrance to the garden centre. **Otto** *sees* **Fritz** *and* **Mitzi** *coming in.*

Fritz (*as* **Otto** *gives him a look*)   Fell off my moped, didn't I?

Otto   What about Mitzi?

Fritz   She was riding pillion.

Otto (*staring at her*)   Bloody hell.

Mitzi (*curtly*)   These things do happen, don't they?

Otto (*nodding, to* **Fritz**)   Switched from hand-jobs to games for two players, then, have we?

Fritz   Felt like catching a flick, didn't we?

Mitzi   There's no need to make comments, Herr Holdenrieder. Just be thankful we turned up for work in this state.

Otto   Hasn't robbed you of the power of speech, then, your accident?

Mitzi   Why should it?

Otto   My point exactly. (*Stares hard at them both.*) Jesus Christ. (*Grinning, he goes off.*)

Scene Eight

Hilde *and* **Otto** *in bed at night.* **Otto**, *very worked up, keeps staring at* **Hilde**.

Otto   Lost your tongue all of a sudden, then?

Hilde   Okay, so they fell off the moped.

Otto (*grinning*)   But the moped hasn't got a scratch. (*A short pause.*) My God, he must've fucked the arse off of her. Just

you look at her. I mean, have we ever . . . Are we ever in
that state when we've made love?

Hilde   No.

Otto (*almost enviously*)   Shit, I got to hand it to him, that
brother of yours.

Hilde   I know a – different – side of him.

Otto   Fine, okay – but life is full of surprises, right? (*With a
hint of envy.*) I ought to report him over this. That'd make
him sit up and take notice.

Hilde *just looks.*

Otto (*clinically*)   He'll've bonked her rigid, that's for sure.
Now, the thing is – if he's bonking her, he's not taking his
pills, right? And if he don't take his pills, he'll be infringing
his probation. With me so far? And if he don't comply with
his probation order, he'll have to be banged up again.

Hilde (*really meaning it*)   Honest, Otto, the more you talk
the more you frighten me.

Otto   Somebody's got to shovel up the shit that's left
behind. (*A short pause.*) Don't worry, I won't report him. Just
thinking aloud. But when he don't take his pills you can see
what happens if you look at Mitzi. (*With real passion.*) He
wants watching, he does. I'll have to make double sure he
takes his pills while I'm there to watch.

Hilde   Talk sense.

Otto   As long as he's not neutered he's a person like you
and me, and that's dangerous. (*A short pause.*) And even
castrations's never foolproof. Human nature! Or take pigs.
Your pig-castrator pops along and slits the scrotum so's the
balls flip out. But some pigs won't have it. On the quiet they
withdraw their balls back into their belly, see (*Grins.*), and
tuck their testicles out of harm's way. And it spoils the meat,
when that happens. There's even a special word for it,
because it happens so often.

Hilde *just looks.*

Otto (*nodding*)   These male pigs what refuse to be castrated they call them *nutroasters*. Because the meat is hard and bitter, see.

Hilde   My brother is not a porker.

Otto (*feverish, almost trembling*)   Fine, okay – just thinking aloud, wasn't I?

Scene Nine

Otto and **Fritz** *are having a pee in the pub lavatories.* **Otto** *is looking at* **Fritz**.

Otto   Goes straight to your bladder, beer.

Fritz   Dead right.

Otto   I could still drink you under the table, though. I've had eight pints to your two.

Fritz   I'm not supposed to drink.

Otto   Beer won't go with those – (*Laughs and moves.*) – appetite suppressors of yours.

Fritz   Dead right.

Otto   Don't matter to me, either way.

Fritz   I stick to what the doctors tell me.

Otto   Once them doctors get hold of you, you're dead meat.

Fritz   Seeing as I'm not ill, though, it's different.

Otto (*looking straight at him*)   I reckon I'd take a fucking overdose if I was in your shoes.

Fritz (*as if paralysed*)   Oh well, life is what you make it.

Otto (*grinning*)   Don't suppose there's much life in your doodah no more . . .

Fritz *has finished peeing, and does up his flies.*

Otto   Don't be so shy, let's have a look, then. We do everything else together, so it can't hurt.

Fritz   Okay, then, if you want. (*He lets* **Otto** *see his penis.*)

Otto (*taking a look*)   Looks quite normal to me.

Fritz *nods.*

Otto   Thing is, I thought all those medicines would shrink it, see. Till it was as small as a kid's dick. But it's full-size.

Fritz   It always is that size.

Otto   Right. (*A short pause.*) And you take them regular, do you, your pills, like women?

Fritz   Certainly do.

Otto (*nodding*)   But I still wouldn't change places with you. (*Abruptly.*) And there's still no cure for Aids, right?

Fritz *just looks.*

Otto (*abruptly*)   Just my little joke.

Fritz (*expansively*)   You can't spring many surprises on an ex-convict like me.

Otto   Let's hope it's one surprise you don't never get.

Fritz (*good-naturedly*)   I had loads of tests – in prison you do. You get regular check-ups inside. I bet you've never had an Aids test.

Otto   Why should I?

Fritz (*grinning*)   Behave ourself, then, do we?

Otto (*indignant*)   Fucking hell – I hope not!

Fritz   Just wondering. Who does?

Otto *gives him a look.*

Scene Ten

In a beer garden, where the beer is overflowing. Late.

Mitzi   We ought to be getting home, Frau Holdenrieder. I really think we should.

Hilde   You tell him, maybe you'll have more effect.

Mitzi (*gently*)   No harm done having a pint or two. But if you go on like this, there's no telling.

Otto   Did somebody speak?

Mitzi (*bravely*)   We want to go home, Herr Holdenrieder.

Otto   Did somebody speak?

Mitzi (*bravely*)   We want to go home, Herr Holdenrieder.

Otto   Just finish my pint first. (*To* **Fritz**.) Here's to it.

Fritz (*unsure*)   Yeah, cheers.

Otto (*stupidly drunk*)   Take off your clothes and you're bollock-naked, right?

Hilde   Right. (*A short pause, then harshly:*)   We want to go home. Now.

Otto   Well, well, if you'd seen what I've seen. (*Meaningfully.*) Phwoar?! Well, they do say: 'Look at a man's nose and you seen his dick.' That right, Fritz? I'm not telling you nothing you don't know, eh, Mitzi, you've had hands-on experience.

Mitzi (*curtly*)   I beg your pardon!

Otto   And all passions can be indulged with no worries, because he's got a spanking new Aids test. So far from him infecting us, we got to watch we don't infect him!

Fritz (*very embarrassed, to* **Hilde**)   Say something!

Otto   Go on, tell me something I don't know.

Hilde   You're drunk again, you old piss-artist. Give us the car keys.

Otto   My car and who drives it, I decide.

Hilde   Half the car belongs to me.

Otto   Half the car belongs to her and half the firm. Half everything belongs to her. So that means she only half (*A hand movement.*) belongs to me.

Mitzi   We'd rather not know about that, Herr Holdenrieder. (*Shuffles towards* **Fritz**.) You say something. You're a man, too, aren't you?

Otto   Not half. Know what I mean? (*To* **Mitzi**.) Would you let me, then, Mitzi, if you weren't bonking Fritz here – (*Grinning.*) – the beast from behind bars?

Fritz (*embarrassed*)   Beast from behind bars now, am I?

Otto (*with his hand between* **Mitzi***'s thighs*)   I asked you a question! Would you let me, a normal male, if he hadn't got in first?

Mitzi (*looking at* **Hilde**)   Herr Holdenrieder, you're going too far.

Fritz (*abruptly*)   Take your hand away.

Otto (*furious*)   Thank you very much, but this is my firm and I'm still boss, okay? (*He goes on groping* **Mitzi**.)

Fritz (*to* **Hilde**)   Sorry, there's nothing I can do.

Hilde   Pissed again, the senile old goat.

Otto   What am I?

Hilde   A senile old goat.

Otto   You can't say that in public.

Hilde   What's public about the place if everybody else has left?

Otto (*trying to be meaningful but sounding idiotic*)   Maybe the trees have ears, who knows? (*To **Mitzi**.*) If it wasn't for my old woman, I'd still be up for anything going. If you follow my meaning. Just like young Fritz here. Does as he pleases, he does, even if he do get banged up for it. (*Warming to his subject.*) But he's no *nutroaster*. He won't have his manhood tampered with. Not even by these (*Mimes copulation.*) ball-breaker tablets he got to swallow. (*Violently.*) A man's always got ways and means, eh, Fritz? Am I right? Men will be men, right? And if they got any sense women'll stand by them, because they know leaving a real man is going to spell trouble, okay? (*Gasping for breath, he stares hard at **Hilde**.*) Though when you're married, that's the first thing to go: your manhood, know what I mean?

Mitzi (*to **Hilde***)   If things get any worse than this, we're in dead trouble.

Fritz (*almost begging*)   For Chrissake, Otto, belt up before it's too late.

Hilde (*in desperation*)   Let him alone, he's my husband, let him have his say.

Otto   Dead right – anyone what's got ears – fucking listen! You stink of corpses and cash dispensers. (*Violently desperate.*) Cash dispensers and corpses. (*Gasping for air.*) You fucking listen to me, Fritz!

Fritz (*helpless, shattered*)   Belt up, Otto. You're a married man. (*Loudly.*) Act according.

Hilde (*bravely*)   Otto, for the sake of the one last thread holding us together, listen to Fritz and give me the car keys.

Otto   What the fuck is holding us together? Bar desperation.

Hilde *glares at him.*

Otto   She don't say nothing because she's scared.

Mitzi   She don't say nothing because she's had enough, Herr Holdenrieder.

Otto   She can give as good as she gets, can that Hilde of mine.

Fritz   As one man to another, Otto, shut the fuck up. (*Desperate.*) I tell you as a mate, she's had it up to here.

Otto   I had it way beyond here yonks ago. (*To* **Hilde**, *violently.*) What you ever do 'cept lie back on your fat fanny? Once a week I got to, and twice a week I'm allowed to, if I keep my nose clean. The rest is past history. (*Pants and sweats, desperate.*) All that turns you on now is doing me down. For behind I'm too big, for in front I'm too small. (*Violently.*) When will you give yourself to me with the back door left open? (*Desperate.*) Because up to now it's always been barred and bolted.

Mitzi (*mainly to* **Fritz**)   But even when you do give yourself it's still not right.

Otto (*will not be talked out of it, to* **Hilde**)   Even shitting's more fun than fucking her. At least I've got the paper to read.

Mitzi   Oh, my God!

Fritz (*helpless, almost in tears*)   I feel ashamed to be with you.

Otto   You've no need to feel ashamed. You can still show yourself in public, right? As for mine (*Looking down at himself.*), you don't bear looking at, you limp wimp. (*He pulls out his penis, stares at it and then at* **Hilde**.) It's all her fucking fault!

Fritz   Otto! Bloody belt up! You're well out of order. (*To* **Hilde**.) I done what I can.

Hilde *glares hard at* **Otto**, *then tries to jump on him to do up his flies, but he stops her.*

Mitzi *just stares, trembling with fear.*

Otto   What's up then, Mitzi? Used to a twelve-bore, are you? (*He means his penis.*) Look at him looking! (*In despair.*) Let me go round the table and ask everyone present: is this piddly little prick too big for her stonking great arsehole?

Mitzi *is paralysed.*

Hilde *is dumbfounded.*

Otto (*to* **Fritz**)   Well, go on, get yours out. Even after all those pills you're still twice as big as me.

Fritz   You can't do this, Otto. Not even to a mate. (*He shouts in desperation.*) Act your age.

Mitzi *is paralysed, feverish, out of breath.*

Hilde *is also paralysed rigid.*

Otto (*violently*)   Cocks out! Now you seen mine, show me yours. Come on, out with the fucker! (*He chases* **Fritz**, *grabs hold of him, pulls his trousers off, lifts up his shirt, etc.*)

Fritz *stands there shaking, naked, miserable.*

Silence. The women gape in disbelief at the two penises. With an involuntary gesture, **Hilde** *folds her hands over her lower belly to protect it.* **Mitzi** *is shuddering in feverish excitement. A pause.*

Fritz (*in shock*)   God Almighty, Otto! (*Pulls his trousers up.*)

Hilde (*breaking away from the others, icily*)   Car keys.

Otto (*handing them to her*)   Dead right. (*He also gets dressed.*)

Once again, silence, paralysis, disbelief and amazement. Then they run about like frightened hens, shambling and stumbling in confusion. **Hilde** *finally moves off.*

Otto (*watching her go, desperately to* **Mitzi**)   You're my only comfort, Mitzi.

Mitzi   I don't feel so good, neither. (*To* **Fritz**.) Give us a hug, then.

Fritz   Hug your fucking self. (*Shouting out.*) Hilde, it's me, your brother, wait for me! (*Runs after her.*)

A pause. **Otto** *and* **Mitzi** *stare at each other.*

Otto   I'm never allowed to do nothing, Mitzi.

Mitzi (*embarrassed, exhausted*)   Things can't be that bad, surely.

Otto   They are, though, Mitzi, believe you me. And my brother-in-law's right. I'm well out of order.

Mitzi (*shrieking*)   Fucking limp-dick! (*Genuinely stupid.*) A woman needs more than roughing up, Herr Holdenrieder. But that's all he's capable of. I should fucking know.

Otto   All he's capable of?

Mitzi (*violently*)   Yeah, he's just a big-mouth. He can't even stick a pin in you properly, he's too shit-scared.

Otto   Not even a pin?

Mitzi   Nah.

Otto   Don't worry, I will. (*He pulls a badge from his hat or her skirt.*)

Mitzi *shrieks in high-pitched lust.*

Otto   Not capable?

Mitzi (*shrieks*)   Not capable!

Otto   Not capable of this, neither?

Mitzi (*excited*)   No, nothing, never!

Otto (*suddenly colossal*)   Mitzi, I like you.

Mitzi (*unsure*)   I like you, too, Herr Holdenrieder.

They fall in a heap and fuck until they lie there gasping next to each other. Silence.

Mitzi (*coming out of her ecstasy, released, very slowly*)   We've let the sow out the sty now, Herr Holdenrieder. We got to get back to reality now, or people'll notice.

Otto (*happy*)   Right.

Mitzi   The first time don't count, does it, Herr Holdenrieder?

Otto   Special, though, the first time. (*Beaming at her.*) Mitzi, I love you.

Mitzi   Cut the crap, people never mean that stuff.

Curtain. Interval.

Act Three

Scene One

A really ghastly breakfast, complete with boiled eggs. **Otto** *and* **Hilde** *are both a bit frayed at the edges. There is a very long pause before* **Hilde** *chokes out the first sentence. She stares at* **Otto** *disbelievingly. He pretends to be busy with his breakfast.*

Hilde (*gasping for breath*)   Humped yourself back to health, then?

Otto (*his face red*)   I'm not giving up my Mitzi, I need her. I'd rather do a deal on the business, before I give up my manhood.

A pause. **Hilde** *is paralysed.*

Hilde (*defiantly*)   You can't be manly with me, you mean?

Otto (*tonelessly honest*)   We've been together an awful long time.

A long pause.

Hilde (*just staring*)   So? What now, then?

Otto   My work's here and my bed's with Mitzi.

Hilde   And your food?

Otto   I can eat at McDonald's. (*A pause.*)

Hilde   I ought to disown you.

Otto   For love? What's the point?

Hilde   Love you call it?

Otto   Not (*Stiffly.*) a criminal offence, is it?

Hilde *stares hard, then laughs hysterically.*

Otto (*stares back, venomously*)   You're a frustrated old bag.

Hilde (*at once*)   Oh, really? Whose fault's that, then?

Otto   Beg pardon?

Hilde *stares straight at him.*

Otto, *embarrassed, elaborately cleans his mouth, then gets to his feet and goes out.*

Hilde *watches him go, catches her breath, and in trying to calm herself down achieves the opposite.*

Scene Two

In the hothouse. It is hot and bright. **Hilde** *and* **Mitzi**. **Mitzi** *is beetroot colour, as if caught red-handed.* **Hilde**'s *face is almost green. The two women are repotting cuttings. They work expertly. From time to time, however, one of them breaks off and stares at the other for a long time from embarrassingly close quarters.*

Hilde   All I can say is this, Mitzi: you're abnormal, you are. High time you faced up to that.

Mitzi *just looks.*

Hilde   It explains why you feel drawn to my brother. Like attracts like.

Mitzi *(glares at her, paralysed)*   I don't feel abnormal.

Hilde *(nodding)*   There you are, you see. *(A short pause.)* Now if we were all a bit younger, well now . . .

Mitzi   I'm thirty-eight.

Hilde   Exactly. The very age you suddenly start going like this.

Mitzi *(indignant)*   Like what?

Hilde *(nodding again)*   I'm a bit chary of going into details, it's all a bit personal for my taste, but let's take a for instance – my Otto, we'll say – do you, you know *(Lowering her voice.)*, let him do anything he fancies?

Mitzi *just looks.*

Hilde (*nodding*)   My husband's losing weight these days, he's as thin as a rake. Don't you forget he's a father of children. The fact that he's neglecting his business and that he's drinking a beer for breakfast nowadays – these are things I'd rather not mention.

Mitzi   He used to drink beer before.

Hilde   Only once in a blue moon, though.

Mitzi   Point is he's surprised himself. He can't believe he's experiencing a second big romance.

Hilde   You, I suppose?

Mitzi   That's what he says.

Hilde   And what do you say? (*A short pause.*) Believe me, just because you stick your bum in his face doesn't make it a big romance. (*Puffs.*) A big romance is about building up a business, having a family and being happy.

Mitzi   As I see it, a big romance is about forgetting everything outside it.

Hilde (*nodding*)   That I can well believe. (*A short pause.*) I mean, don't you feel a twinge of conscience every time you look our Susi in the face? A child you're depriving of her father?

Mitzi   I haven't seen Susi for ages now.

Hilde   Well, you look into her eyes and examine your conscience. (*A short pause.*) We do live in a permissive age, Mitzi, I'm well aware of that. (*Catching her breath.*) As aware as you are. But God has a very watchful eye. Are you a believer, by the way, Mitzi?

Mitzi   Think so.

Hilde   In that case aren't you afraid of what He might do? Or do you think God's all for women putting it about a bit?

Mitzi   What do you mean?

Hilde For a grown woman you ask some very naive questions. You'll soon see. I'm telling you as a friend, mind.

Mitzi What do you want me to do?

Hilde Give Otto up, leave this firm and make a new start somewhere else.

Mitzi The next world, maybe?

Hilde Suit yourself.

Mitzi I'd rather take an overdose.

Hilde (*at full volume*) But he's my husband, you silly bitch, the father of my child, your boss.

Mitzi (*shouting back*) But I love him. Otto! Otto, my love, where are you?

Hilde (*impassively*) Sorting the rhododendrons. I do forgive you, Mitzi, don't think I don't. I do understand that a garden centre's a special sort of place. Everything's burgeoning, with new life bursting out of every tub, and there you are, stuck without the consolation of – what shall we call it? – seed. And then there's the cemetery. What with death one side and life the other, it's a wonder people don't go mad. But enough's enough.

Mitzi Not for me it isn't.

Hilde *glares.*

Mitzi (*cheekily*) Why can't we share him? (*Cutting.*) You're not that keen on the other anyway.

Hilde (*blushing scarlet*) I've no need to share anything with you, Mitzi. I'm not that desperate, not by a long chalk. Make no mistake. You're still my employee, don't forget, not the other way round. I only need to point my bum at Otto once and he'll forget you exist.

Mitzi Pull the other one. (*A short pause.*) Do you even know what an orgasm is?

Hilde   'Course I know.

Mitzi   I never stop coming, so Otto says.

Hilde   Bully for you.

Mitzi   For a man it's the absolute high point when a woman comes –

Hilde   – says Otto.

Mitzi *glares.*

Hilde   Congratulations!

Mitzi   Maybe – if you don't mind me talking woman to woman a minute – you should talk to a gynaecologist if you're drawing a blank in bed. Have you got a good one, or do you want mine's number?

Hilde *can't take any more, very flushed, twitching nervously.*

Mitzi   Gynaecologists can work wonders, you know. And, of course, maybe you're pre-menopausal, Frau Holdenrieder. Don't worry, there's loads of hormones on the market. They can prolong youth a good ten years.

Hilde *stands over* **Mitzi** *threateningly.*

Mitzi   What's up now, then? It's you I'm thinking of.

Hilde (*losing her temper*)   You dirty little cunt!

Mitzi (*with a stiff upper lip*)   Insults like that come at a price. But from your sort, of course, they're only to be expected.

Hilde   What sort am I, then?

Mitzi (*very superior*)   A frustrated old bag who couldn't rouse her adorable husband for all the tea in China.

Hilde (*venomously*)   And how do you rouse him?

Mitzi (*still superior*)   By knowing his wants and giving him what I got.

Hilde   All you got?

Mitzi   I'm not answering stupid questions. (*Turns on her heel.*)

Hilde (*glares, then suddenly throws a flowerpot at her as she disappears, her head held high*)   See if I care!

Scene Three

The ritual, the room and **Fritz**. **Fritz** *suddenly seems to have developed a lot of pimples, grown tubbier, lighter in complexion, and even younger.* **Fritz** *moves himself and the furniture in his room according to an unseen plan. The pattern is, it appears, completely preordained; if the table, for instance, is even a centimetre out of place – according to the invisible plan* **Fritz** *has mapped out – it drives him to the brink of despair. What matters most here is that* **Fritz** *takes the task extremely seriously – he feels agony if something goes wrong, and gets desperate.* **Fritz** *is trying to bring so much order into his room that he can always, wherever he stands or walks, see himself in the wardrobe mirror . . .*

Every now and then, in a remote corner of the room, **Fritz** *makes a movement – he will suddenly lift his pullover, for instance, or open his overcoat (assuming he has put it on) – stare in the mirror, catch sight of himself, react in alarm, then laugh with relief, grin and immediately stop. All the time he is grunting, croaking and groaning. This whole sequence can take a full five minutes – an eternity in the theatre.*

Fritz (*grinning at the mirror*)   Leave your traces, cover your tracks. That's the secret, Herr Fritz, that's all you need to know. And God help any bugger what comes too close (*Pretends to be firing a pistol from his flies.*), bang bang, you're dead. (*Enjoying this, he repeats the action, 'gunning down' everyone he can 'hit' in the auditorium; then right in front of the mirror.*) We fooled the fuckers, eh, Fritz, the culprit's conned the boys in blue. Nifty footwork, Fritz. (*Acts as if he is going to do something.*) We're going to shoot our way out, see, but nobody's going to get hurt. No, no, life will be respected. (*He acts out 'real*

*passion' which comes to nothing, then performs his own 'awakening',
after which he shakes himself awake, and runs to the door.)* Open
that spyhole! Come on, open up! (*Acts as if he is in a prison
cell.*) Life goes on, desire drains away. Cheer up, it may
never happen. Now, big smile for the mirror.

Scene Four

A tea break, out in the open air among gravestones and flowers. **Otto**,
Hilde, **Fritz** *and* **Mitzi** *are all wearing very light clothes – they
are all hot and hungry.*

*Painterly and exuberant, reminiscent of peasant genre paintings, this
three-minute eating scene contains long pauses with a lot of ambiguity
between what is said and not said. Oppressive heat, thirst.*

Fritz (*grousing as he gobbles*)   Nice bit of nosh this. (*The others
say nothing. Not noticing, he makes a joke.*) Home-made or picked
up at McDonald's, that is the question. Good job I know my
sister, eh. (*Grins.*)

Hilde *blushes scarlet. The others just stare, without saying anything.*

Otto .   If nobody's got nothing to say for theirselves, we can
cut the tea break short and get back to work right now. (*He
looks at his watch.*) It's an ill wind that blows nobody no good.
(*Gets to his feet.*)

Fritz (*defiantly*)   I was enjoying my snack.

Mitzi (*curt, breathless, self-conscious*)   Frau Holdenrieder has
got cooking off to a fine art, as we don't need reminding.

Otto   Dead right. Who's first back to work? Follow me.
(*He walks off listlessly.*)

Fritz (*gapes, not understanding, grins*)   Ah. Include me out.

Scene Five

*Otto and **Mitzi** in **Mitzi**'s flat. She wants to make it 'as good as possible'. He wants to be 'unforgettably good'. All this is complete nonsense because neither has anything to offer the other. They are both frustrated and ill: a pair of combatants who are wrapped around each other as if by accident, lying locked together in a coital embrace. A slow, edgy scene.*

Otto   Don't suppose I could get in a bit further, could I?

Mitzi   You're in all the way as it is.

Otto   Right, I'd better shoot, then.

Mitzi   Bang bang.

Otto   Nice? Or not?

Mitzi (*listless, sad*)   Sure. Lovely. (*A short pause.*) Ow.

Otto   Am I hurting?

Mitzi   Yes.

Otto   Thank God for that. You can still feel something. (*A short pause.*) Okay, that's your lot.

Mitzi   Don't tell me: bang bang, I'm dead.

Otto   What you mean?

Mitzi   He only ever wants to go bang bang.

Otto   Who's he, the cat's father?

Mitzi   Him down there.

Otto (*grinning*)   I scored a penalty in your ovaries.

Mitzi   Hooray.

Otto   You really are a cunt, Mitzi, but I still like you.

Mitzi   Okay, on your bike. (*Tries to detach herself.*)

Otto   Stay where you are. (*He pins her down – a brief struggle.*)

Mitzi (*as hysterical as she was with* **Fritz**)   Get off me, Herr Holdenrieder, and piss off out my place or I'll call the law.

Otto (*brutally*)   Mitzi.

Mitzi   Don't you Mitzi me. Piss off, or I'll throw up.

Otto   It may not have been the best bubbly but it still cost a packet.

Mitzi   Look, okay, I was out of order. Stay if you want.

Otto   Randy little bitch, aren't you, Mitzi? (*A short pause.*) But take my word for it: you haven't got a cat in hell's chance with Fritz.

Mitzi   I know, I know. But thanks anyway.

Scene Six

In the cemetery, on a sultry day. **Mitzi** *and* **Hilde** *are arranging wreaths near an open grave.* **Hilde** *looks exhausted, emptied, out of control.* **Mitzi** *is prettier than usual, superior and a bit silly. A long, hot scene, with a lot of friction.*

Hilde   Mitzi, I'm not in the habit of begging. But I'm begging you. Will you let me?

Mitzi   I should beg your husband, if I was you. Maybe you'll have better luck.

Hilde   I do know what's what.

Mitzi   And I don't, I suppose? (*They work on in silence.*) If I was going through what you're going through I might start wondering what I'd done wrong.

Hilde   Wondering don't help in a case like this.

Mitzi   No, because he loves me, that's why, and nothing's going to alter that.

Another silence. **Hilde** *is fretting so much she might explode.*

Hilde   Mitzi, I'm begging you on my knees. For the last time: give me back my husband and the father of my child. Please. I can't manage without him.

Mitzi   Get up, Frau Holdenrieder, you'll get dirty down there. Please get up. Now I'm begging.

Hilde   Is that all you got to say?

Mitzi   I did say please. Please get up.

Silence.

Hilde (*very quietly*)   Slag.

Mitzi   Oh, nice. You go down on your knees and beg. Then, when you don't get your own way, you start calling people names.

Hilde   If only you understood.

Mitzi   I've no reason to be ashamed of my feelings. Nor Otto neither. When you're dying of thirst you take any water what's offered you.

Hilde   And what's offered me, you scrubber?

Mitzi   Right, that's it. I can stand so much. I'd be well within my rights to leave without giving notice and bring an action for slander.

Hilde   And what about me? What do I do?

Mitzi   Love's not illegal, nor's feelings. And anyway, I'm late. In fact, I've missed a period, if you must know. So maybe you're depriving a small child of its father, and all.

Hilde (*glaring at her*)   I'm not having any of that. Just you remember, Mitzi, I'm not having no scandals. I'd rather hack it out your belly.

Mitzi   Talk sense for once. Think yourself lucky I'm not taking you serious.

Hilde *draws breath, then stares at* **Mitzi**, *her eyes filling with tears. She runs off, stops near another grave, and supports herself there. We* *can see her back shaking.* **Mitzi** *watches all this, a smile playing on her lips. She goes on working. Silence.*

Hilde *turns round, comes back, stops in front of* **Mitzi** *and looks her straight in the face.*

Hilde (*rooted to the spot*)   It'll never work. What the pair of you are cooking up together. Surely you can see that, Mitzi.

Mitzi   Anything can work if you really want it to.

Hilde *glares at her, turns on her heel, feels humiliated, runs off again, then stands stock-still a little way off.* **Mitzi** *goes on working until she has finished.*

Mitzi   Right, Frau Holdenrieder, all done. Like it? (*They exchange looks. A short pause.*)

Hilde   Don't leave me on my own like this, Mitzi.

Mitzi   I'm not, Frau Holdenrieder, we can walk back together.

Hilde   I don't want to walk with you, I want to talk to you.

Mitzi   But surely, we've said everything there is to say, haven't we?

Hilde (*almost to herself*)   Suppose so.

Silence. **Hilde** *suddenly makes a dash for* **Mitzi**, *which knocks her over. As she screams,* **Hilde** *jumps on her. They wrestle.* **Hilde** *is stronger, she starts hitting out at* **Mitzi**. **Mitzi** *struggles to her feet.* **Hilde** *pushes* **Mitzi** *in front of her.* **Mitzi** *stumbles into the open grave. Screaming.*

Hilde *picks up a stone lying by the grave in both hands.* **Mitzi** *howls,* **Hilde** *misses, and the stone slips from her grasp. She picks up another one, which she tosses into the grave.*

Hilde (*gasping for breath*)   For once in your life behave yourself and stay down there and do as you're told.

Mitzi *just howls.*

Hilde   Not listening, the little cunt. You listen to me! I'm telling you for your own good. You stay in there and stop screaming the place down.

Mitzi   But I'm dying.

Hilde   You've only yourself to blame. If you won't listen, you got to suffer.

Mitzi   I did listen.

Hilde (*peering into the grave*)   Rest in peace, Mitzi, it's all for your own good.

Mitzi   Thanks but no thanks. (*She clambers out. The two women size each other up. Taken aback, helpless.*) I'm all cold.

Hilde *takes her in her arms.*

Mitzi   But you want to murder me.

Hilde   Silly girl, nothing could be further from my thoughts.

Mitzi (*vomiting*)   I think I'm dying.

Hilde   Surely you can take a joke, Mitzi. Lord God above, Thou hast led me even into the wilderness. Know, Lord, I no longer feel any wrath toward her that she did tempt my husband away from me by plonking her bum in his face. Forgive her, Lord, even as I forgive her. Peace be unto you, Mitzi! I'm just a poor sinful woman.

Mitzi (*desperate*)   What the fuck do you think I am?

Scene Seven

In the cemetery loo, **Hilde** *is giving* **Mitzi** *some hot lemon from a thermos. They are both very shaken:* **Mitzi** *about the incident,* **Hilde** *about herself.* **Mitzi** *does 'running repairs' to herself.* **Hilde** *is trembling all over, turned inside out. They both feel they have been hurled head first against a wall.* **Mitzi** *talks loudly and is bemusedly inquisitive.*

Mitzi (*barricaded into the loo, disturbed*)   Dying don't frighten me. I've faced so much, expecting the worst, and come off okay, so why should dying be any different?

Hilde   I don't wish to alarm you, Mitzi, but I've not got so much more to say and you're just not listening to me.

Mitzi   Why should I have to listen to you when nobody's ever listened to me?

Hilde   We all carve out our own path through life, Mitzi.

Mitzi   I want to carve out mine in my own way, thanks very much.

Hilde   Now is not the time to carve out anything. What you need to do now is button your lip till things cool off a bit. And if you're not careful, I'll help you do just that.

Mitzi   There you go again – threatening me. When you promised me you wouldn't (*Stares hard at her.*) Frau Holdenrieder, please, pull yourself together. Life ain't worth living without some passion in it, but you got to keep things in proportion.

Hilde   Oh, absolutely. You're dead right, there.

Mitzi (*hysterical but also inquisitive*)   You really did want to kill me just now, didn't you? (*Openly.*) Don't be afraid to say, Frau Holdenrieder.

Hilde   I'm so sorry.

Mitzi (*numb*)   I'd never've imagined anybody would try to kill me. That really is a new one on me.

Hilde   You're still alive and kicking, though.

Mitzi   But you did try. (*Almost relieved.*) Didn't you?

Hilde   I won't again. Ever. Promise.

Mitzi (*hysterical*)   But you don't love Otto – not physically – you ought to be glad he's got somebody what lets him – act out his iffy fantasies.

Hilde   But one has to see people as a whole. And marriage, too, for that matter.

Mitzi   But it's me Otto loves. I never forced myself on him.

Hilde   He forced himself on you.

Mitzi   Didn't leave me much choice, then, did he?

Hilde   It's not his style to leave people any choice.

Mitzi (*courageously*)   Once we can forget about. But if you try to murder me again, I'll report you. I'm human too, you know, and I've just as much right as anybody else to love and the law.

Hilde   And I haven't, I suppose?

Mitzi (*at full volume*)   You been married to my lover for more than ten years, so the question should have come up.

Hilde *just looks.*

Mitzi   Whatever must I look like? Do you think anybody's going to love me like I look now?

Hilde   You look pale and vulnerable, certainly, but some men find that very attractive.

Mitzi (*taking her voice down*)   Don't forget I'm not as strong as I might look.

Hilde   I've never thought anything bad about you.

Mitzi   Living on your own does make you tough, but it's not easy if you're a woman.

Hilde (*warmly*)   I'll never touch you again, Mitzi. I sort of sense that. Can you sense it, too?

Mitzi *just looks.*

Hilde   Far as I'm concerned, and it's me talking – Hilde Holdenrieder – you've no need to worry next time. If there is a next time, it's my Otto I'll be murdering.

Mitzi   You've got so violent these last couple of weeks I can't get my head round it.

Hilde (*honestly*)   Nor me.

Mitzi (*defiant, and close to tears*)   If it was your brother, not Otto, I'd fight back, because I love him, you wouldn't sling me in no grave and get away with it, I'd give as good as I got.

Hilde   You're in love with Fritz, aren't you?

Mitzi   Wish he'd respond. But he goes berserk when he sees that somebody cares about him.

Hilde   Right, he can't handle that.

Mitzi   You can say that again.

Hilde (*quietly*)   A woman always stays the same, whereas a man changes according to the woman he's with, so I read somewhere. (*A short pause.*) Try playing hard to get.

Mitzi *looks at her.*

Hilde *nods.*

Mitzi   I'd like to get off home now and have a long weekend. You need a good long look in the mirror, I reckon, after a day like this.

Hilde   Dead right, Mitzi. You've earned some time off.

Scene Eight

Working outdoors. **Fritz** *brings on some largeish fruit trees in tubs.* **Otto** *prunes them.* **Fritz** *then takes them back out.*

Otto   Complicated business, marriage, Fritz. (*A short pause.*) Everybody's got problems, not just you. (*Pause.*) Maybe you're better off single. You pick on some woman, scare the shit out of her, jerk off in front of her, then melt away on your trusty steed in a cloud of dust.

Fritz *gives a forced laugh.*

Otto (*sizing him up*)   But you're well in control of your urges, that's for sure. (*A short pause.*) Us two half kill each other and you just stand there watching.

Fritz   She is my sister, and I feel sorry for her.

Otto (*looking straight at him*)   Dead right. (*A pause, then all of a sudden.*) You don't fancy Mitzi, then?

Fritz *reacts nervously.*

Otto   Not even for a bit of you-know-what?

Fritz (*quickly*)   She's not my type.

Otto (*stupidly*)   Nor mine if the truth be known.

Fritz   But she's been around a bit.

Otto   Not half.

Fritz (*honestly*)   If a woman's straight up with you, that's what I respond to best. Turns me right on, that does.

Otto   Listen to you! You've been around a bit, too, by the sound of it.

Fritz *just smiles.*

Otto (*looking him up and down*)   Well, you look pretty stable. That the tranquillisers, is it, calming you down?

Fritz   Dead right.

Otto   Not what I expected at all. I thought we'd be forever trying to calm you down, see, because you'd be so worked up, and that. (*Sizes him up.*) But bugger me if you're not placid to start with.

Fritz   I've always been on the quiet side, you ask my sister.

Otto   But inside you, everything's on the boil, yeah? Bubble bubble?

Fritz   The bubble's burst. More or less.

Otto   Now I'm on the bleeding boil instead.

Fritz   I know the feeling. Like banging your head against a brick wall?

Otto   Dead right. Ger-doing. Ger-doing.

Fritz (*clinically*)   In that case, you're buggered. That's one thing you learn pdq inside. Anything you really want isn't allowed, else you wouldn't be banged up in the first place.

Otto   What you really want is what instinct tells you to want. Repress your instincts and you're dead meat.

Fritz   Easy for you to say, you're normal.

Otto   Your sister thinks different.

Fritz   Because you like to play away, that's why. Only weak men go after other women, so my old mother used to say.

Otto *just looks.*

Fritz   There again, it's only natural. If I follow my instincts, I'll have the law on me, that's the downside.

Otto (*impassively*)   I'd take an overdose.

Fritz (*lightly*)   I don't need to take no overdose, just be a different person.

Otto   Can't be done. (*A short pause.*) If I pot up an asparagus it'll stay an asparagus and never become a Christmas tree. It can't change its nature, see – could die, I suppose – but that asparagus'll always be true to itself, because it got no choice.

Fritz (*cheerfully*)   But humans have.

Otto   Got roots too, humans.

Fritz   Not me I haven't.

Otto   You'll die, then, without enough water.

Fritz (*immobile, paralysed*)   Not me I won't.

A pause.

Otto I been thinking, Fritz – a character like you's got so much to battle against you must need help the whole bleeding time. (*A short pause, while he studies him closely.*) So, go on, tell me straight now – do you need my help?

Fritz (*lightly*) 'Course I do.

Otto Liar. You don't need my help. You don't need nobody. (*Looks at him hard, almost aggressively.*) I wish you did need my help more, things'd be a lot easier. I'm telling you this for your own good, mind.

Fritz (*disconcerted*) Well, okay then, sure, I do need your help.

Otto *nods, and looks straight at him.*

Fritz I'm not no asparagus, though, Otto, I'm a human being. (*A short pause.*) But even with plants you can graft one thing on to another. You know, I mean you can have an apple tree what has pears growing on it, see? (*He laughs.*) Happens all the time.

Otto But it's not in nature's scheme of things.

Fritz Bugger that. Nature's one thing, I'm something else.

Otto (*seriously*) But that's where you're going wrong, Fritz. That's why you'll end up totally fucked.

Fritz (*brightly*) When they let me out they said I should see everything in a positive light.

Otto (*nodding*) You or me, that's what I'm wondering.

Fritz (*looking straight at him*) What d'you mean?

Otto There is something wrong with you, even if it's not Aids. (*Smiling.*) Maybe it's something worse.

Fritz Like what?

Otto (*pernickety*) I got to think this through, don't rush me.

Fritz   If you're saying I don't fit in here, I'll push off.

Otto   You fit in good here. So good I'm not sure you can stay. Are you with me?

Fritz *just looks.*

Scene Nine

The bedroom and the kitchen. **Otto** *is just sitting there.* **Hilde** *is very obviously changing the bed linen, yet is still expecting him.*

Hilde   I still can't believe she just died on me. But I suppose even dying's something you can learn to live with.

Otto   People commit murder out of passion. That's just not you at all.

Hilde   Trust him to run his wife down.

Otto   You haven't got the puff for one thing.

Hilde   We was at each other's throats all day. Never let each other off of the hook, like we was hexed. She stuck to me like a bloody limpet.

Otto (*as if in a quiz*)   Did she want to die or did you kill her?

Hilde   She wanted to die, all right. I just made sure she knew what damage she'd done beforehand.

Otto   So you put a stop to my love?

Hilde   What happened is this: she slipped and ended up in this open grave, see, and I wouldn't let her out till she promised never to see you again.

Otto   Mitzi'd never promise that.

Hilde   That's why she's dead.

Otto   There was no need for that.

Hilde   But I had to do it. And anyway, I wanted to.

Otto   My God, poor Mitzi.

Hilde (*contentedly*)   If you ask me, she wasn't quite all there.

Otto   Meaning?

Hilde   A woman senses these things about another woman.

Otto   She was okay in bed.

Hilde   What a nice thing to say to your wife.

Otto   She was, though.

Hilde   Very deceptive, bed. I'm amazed you still can't see that.

Otto   I do love Mitzi. Just so's you know.

Hilde   We'll give her the best funeral she could ever dream of.

Otto (*uncertainly*)   She'll look lovely, with a wreath.

Hilde   What I thought to myself in this, see: I got to prove to my Otto there's more in life than offering your bumhole to a man and shouting the house down when you make love.

Otto   I wouldn't say no to a bit more shouting.

Hilde   No problem. You are my husband, and if somebody puts a spoke in my wheel and won't push off when I ask them nice, they'll have to pay.

Otto (*grinning*)   With their lives, seemingly.

Hilde   Too true.

Otto   Did she suffer?

Hilde   Can't say. First I saw HER, then YOU. I lashed out in between, and hit her. Then everything went blank.

Otto   Poor old Mitzi.

Hilde   Got the passion out my system, anyway.

Otto   Passion my arse, that's abnormal!

Hilde   Couldn't see nothing else for it, could I?

Otto (*happier now*)   Committed murder for love, then.

Hilde   That wasn't murder, it was self-defence.

Otto (*grinning*)   Banner headline: BLOOD, SEX AND TEARS.

Hilde (*meaning it*)   She's welcome to the tears.

Otto   How d'you feel about the blood, then, seeing as sex never softens you?

Hilde   What if the dead come back to life?

Otto   I wish poor Mitzi would.

Hilde (*desperate*)   I'm talking about me!

Otto (*looking straight at her*)   Don't just talk about it, do it.

Hilde (*nods*)   Look ahead, Otto, and make the most of me. (*She takes him in her mouth.*)

Otto (*making the most of it*)   Poor old Mitzi, thinking about me and suffering.

Hilde   She's not suffering, she don't use her head enough. Like when she said she's missed a period – if she still has them – she signed her own death warrant. I'm not having no scandals.

Otto (*grinning*)   If I turn you in, you'll go down for life. You're at my mercy.

Hilde   And I know you'll show me mercy – after all, you're my husband, Otto, and if I prove I'm putting up a fight for you, I'm sure that means more to you than turning me in.

Otto   Life you'd go down for and I'd walk away free.

Hilde   But with me you're so much freer, Otto.

Otto   Free to have a wank.

Hilde *just looks.*

Otto   You bite me and I'll bash you one.

Hilde   You don't want to go hitting a murderess, never know where it might lead.

Otto   Can't do much about it, anyway, can I? (*Enjoying the blow job.*) Well, you wanting me this bad is a bit sudden. (*Grinning.*) But maybe this murder of yours is nothing that serious, and we're making a mountain out of a molehill.

Hilde   Isn't a living wife better than a dead passion?

Otto *is lost for words.*

Hilde (*playing up to him*)   Committing murder must be a far greater proof of love than letting yourself be fucked up the bum. (*Wooing him, slowly getting undressed, he starts to weaken.*) If they're roused, people see everything different. Look on the bright side, Otto. The proof of the pudding . . .

Otto (*gasps, looks straight at her, nods, shouts out*)   Rest in peace, Mitzi.

Hilde   Dead right, come straight into me. (*Grabs at him and gets him.*) You see, Mitzi, it isn't just a bum you need to hold a man, but a brain.

Otto (*threateningly*)   I'm nearly there.

Hilde   Glad to hear it.

Scene Ten

Mitzi *at home, rather the worse for wear. Soft music. She is staring at a withered bunch of flowers.*

Mitzi (*writes, thinks, sniffs, waits, writes*)   Otto, my love, dying is a deep experience. Everybody should have this experience – it changes you. I know that now. But before Death took me, it asked me if I had one last wish and I said Otto Hildenrieder. Death didn't say, 'Never heard of him,' or

'But he's married,' or 'Sorry, he's just not your type.' Death said, 'Okay, have him.' And I thought: there's no time now. But straight off Death said, 'If you really want something there's always time.' So, Otto my love, I escaped Death and now here I am on my own in my flat. You don't call round, you never phone, where are you? I got away from Death by the skin of my teeth, open brackets, ask your wife, close brackets, but life does a dog leg around me when you're not there. I keep thinking about you, even though I've got a headache, three bruises and a swollen leg. It'll soon go down, I'm sure. I forgive Hilde because she's your wife. But I won't be sat on. I'm going to leave the firm and move into your heart. Let's go far away together, somewhere Hilde can't dig a hole under us.

New paragraph, underlined: 'I hereby give notice pursuant to the Paid Employment Act 1988 of one calendar month from today's date: September 30th.'

– In great hope and with my love, Mitzi Frey.

Scene Eleven

Hilde *and* **Otto** *in the bathroom – both knackered.* **Hilde** *is washing herself thoroughly.* **Otto** *has no compunction about cleaning his dentures.*

Otto   Mitzi's not dead after all. You just made up this murder story, didn't you? Pack of fucking lies!

Hilde (*tormented, but still indifferent*)   I wanted us to have a nice weekend.

Otto   Talk sense, woman. What about Mitzi?

Hilde   My little joke. And you enjoyed it. (*Aggressively.*) Well, didn't you?

Otto (*emotionless*)   We'll look a bit silly if she is expecting. Then we're right in it.

Hilde   She's not expecting. Menopausal, more like.

Otto (*unsuspecting*)   That's what she says you are.

Hilde (*exhausted*)   Typical. She'll stoop to anything, that one.

Otto   She won't get rid of it, she's told me.

Hilde   A leopard can't change its spots. Once a woman, always a woman.

Otto   Poor old Mitzi. If only she knew.

Hilde (*worn out, looks straight at him*)   Go back to her, why don't you? Mitzi's still alive. And eager to have you.

Otto (*emotionless*)   That's a bit below the belt.

Hilde *stares impassively.*

Otto *meets her stare, grins.*

Hilde   Do you despise me now? For my active imagination?

Otto (*trying to be manly*)   Come to bed and I'll tell you. If you're a good girl.

Hilde (*pretending to be 'manly'*)   Dead right.

Scene Twelve

Reunion. **Mitzi** *and* **Otto**. *In the hothouse.* **Mitzi**'s *face is swollen. She is covered with plasters, but still wearing make-up.*

Otto *doesn't look at her, he is more stupid than cruel. And he is deferential, as before.*

Mitzi   Otto, Otto, my love, it was her made me look like this.

Otto *prefers to look away.*

Mitzi   Is that all you can say to me?

Otto   Fill in a form. If you're off sick for long we'll have to get somebody else in.

Mitzi   Otto, I love you more than my life.

Otto   Sure, sure. But life's got to get back to normal some time.

Mitzi   Had enough of me?

Otto   What d'you mean by enough?

Mitzi   Enough's enough.

Otto   Maybe I've not got the same appetite no more, far as the physical goes.

Mitzi (*still trying to outplay him*)   Some man! Knuckles under to his wife and bottles up his passion.

Otto   Knuckles under, my arse! Maybe I just had a bellyful of dirty games with you.

Mitzi   Games? Dirty?

Otto   Come on! You're not going to deny you're a randy bitch what a man can do what he likes with.

Mitzi   Otto, you mustn't talk to me like this. What about that desert you was on about, and me your oasis?

Otto   Maybe I like the sand dunes better. (*Below the belt.*) Give Fritz a go, maybe he'll carry on where I left off.

Mitzi (*affronted*)   Otto, you don't talk to your Mitzi like this.

Otto   Everything's got its beginning and its end. That's life.

Mitzi (*cruel*)   Except marriage, eh? That goes on for ever. Go on, then, go back to your frustrated old bag, and wank away till your cock drops off.

Otto (*evenly*)   You cunt.

Mitzi (*after a pause*)   Otto love, please. Don't just leave me standing.

Otto   Matter of fact, Fräulein Frey, I'm not paying you to stand around. This is a normal working day and a normal weekday morning. And all you can do is waste time rabbiting. Whether I can spare the time to listen is another matter.

Mitzi *half-heartedly hits out at him.*

Otto *(grabs hold of her and smashes her into a corner)*   It's all over, okay! Once and for all! What you women get up to on your own don't matter a fuck to me. But never hit me, ducky, ever, or I'll show you *(Smiling.)* just how a real murder's done, okay, you stupid, randy little bag of shit.

Mitzi *(completely devastated, unable to go on)*   Christ, why are you so horrible to me? God, help me, please. *(She breaks down.)*

Otto *(deadly serious)*   Mitzi, this firm's got to get back to normal. It's been decided, there's no other way. Just accept it.

Mitzi *(confused)*   I'm giving in my notice.

Otto *(looks at her quickly, then nods)*   Glad you're being sensible at last. *(Goes out.)*

Scene Thirteen

Mitzi *and* **Fritz** *at work:* **Mitzi** *almost obsessively on the hunt,* **Fritz** *taking refuge in brutality.* **Mitzi** *very formal, speaking in a stylised accent.*

Mitzi   So you're not a real sex monster. You made it all up? Right?

Fritz   Right.

Mitzi *(after a short pause)*   But I'd've accepted it, Fritz. A lot sooner than exhibitionism in public, anyway. *(She smiles in a superior way at him.)* Really! I'm ashamed to know you.

Fritz (*without emotion*)   But that's all I am, a flasher. I can't
do any better than that. If I really was a sex monster,
leaving bite marks over naked corpses and that, they'd've
sent me down for life, not let me out on probation.

Mitzi   And we'd never have met.

Fritz   S'pose not.

Pause.

Mitzi   Not interested in anything normal, then?

Fritz (*straight out*)   I told you: I'm abnormal.

Mitzi   What, proud of it, are you? Being abnormal?

Fritz   I am how I am.

Mitzi   But you say it as if it was something to be proud of.

Fritz   I've been myself for so long I got used to it. (*A little
weary.*) By now if I did start behaving normal, it'd seem
abnormal.

Mitzi (*trying to flirt*)   And as far as us two go, you can't
come up with any ideas at all? Or can you?

Fritz (*emotionless and brutal*)   You'd better find somebody
else. I'm not keeping goal for Otto while he's playing away.

Mitzi (*genuinely desperate*)   Christ, what bastards you men
are. (*Pause. Then caustic, brutal.*) But you would like to jerk off
in front of me, right?

Fritz *just looks.*

Mitzi (*getting even more desperate*)   Maybe it would bring the
two of us closer.

Fritz   I don't want to get no closer. Why won't you see
that?

Mitzi   But people are social beings.

Fritz   Not me I'm not.

A pause.

Mitzi (*really acidic*)   Doesn't it make you feel lonely when you know I'm looking for love but I'm stuck here on my own?

Fritz   I'm not after love.

Mitzi   But I am.

Fritz   I feel sorry for my sister, that's all.

Mitzi   And who feels sorry for me? You didn't want nothing but you could've had the lot.

Fritz   I don't need nothing. I'm not Otto.

Mitzi   More's the pity.

Fritz   I wouldn't mind, only my sister's involved.

Mitzi   Somebody always is. You shouldn't take it so serious.

Fritz (*disparaging*)   Otto delivers the goods, eh?

Mitzi (*lying*)   Several times a day.

Fritz   I'd never've thought he had it in him.

Mitzi   Nor me.

Scene Fourteen

Work, work, work, nothing but drudgery. **Mitzi** *and* **Hilde**. **Mitzi** *is worn out, obviously under par.* **Hilde** *is working less, though she is fighting just as hard.*

Hilde (*crisply*)   Two heads is better than one.

Mitzi   What d'you mean?

Hilde   You ought to stay.

Mitzi   So you say.

Hilde   So me – and Otto – say.

Mitzi (*looks, then swallows, uncertain*)   It couldn't possibly work.

Hilde   It would for me. (*Woman to woman.*) I'd know where to draw the line (*Looks at* **Mitzi** *in a friendly way.*) if you stayed. So I wouldn't lose control again.

Mitzi (*offended*)   You certainly did lose control with me – in spades.

Hilde   But the good thing about it is we've cleared the air.

Mitzi   I see.

Hilde   To cut a long story short: I respect you as a woman and a person, and as for Otto –

Mitzi   That's all over.

Hilde   There would be a basis, then.

Mitzi   For me, but what about him?

Hilde   He'll try it on again, I daresay, but you've got the power to steer things your way.

Mitzi   Yes, but he'll catch me on the hop somewhere and you'll shove me in a grave again.

Hilde   I'm not shoving no one nowhere. I've come to trust you completely, and there's an end to it.

Mitzi (*with her last vestige of pride*)   I can't forget it even if I can finish it.

Hilde   Point taken.

Mitzi   What about Fritz?

Hilde   He's leaving us.

Mitzi *just looks.*

Hilde   He that travels far knows much. We're giving him a motorbike, so he can get about better.

Mitzi   Piss off quicker, you mean.

Hilde   Don't tempt providence!

Mitzi   That's good coming from you.

Hilde   Everybody has a date with destiny. Up it comes and says: 'Hello. Here I am. Destiny time.' I've said the same to myself about Fritz. One day, all of a sudden, some innocent young woman will come along and cleanse him of his dirty habits.

Mitzi *looks askance.*

Hilde   What Fritz needs is a big romance. Then everything will run like clockwork.

Mitzi   I'm not the one, that's for sure.

Hilde   My point exactly. You'd never hold him, believe you me. What Fritz needs is a woman who puts her foot down. So he asks himself: 'Why do I need to take my trousers down in front of complete strangers when I've got her?'

If he was with you, he'd soon be up to his tricks again – sure as eggs is eggs.

Mitzi   I'd never forgive him neither, not for that. (*A short pause.*) And I'll tell you for why: because what goes on within your own four walls, that's one thing. But if he suddenly goes out in the street and (*Lowering her voice, openly.*) masturbates, I couldn't be doing with that.

Hilde (*nods*)   It was him what started his habits and he's got to put an end to them.

Mitzi *looks blank.*

Hilde   He goes through life with these sexual hang-ups, and because he won't let them out in the open but keeps them bottled up, he puts people under pressure, see.

Mitzi   He never put any pressure on me.

Hilde (*smiling*)   It's his decision to leave. Why don't you ask him, you love talking to him.

Mitzi   I don't want your brother to go.

Hilde (*after a short pause, meaning it*)   Nor do I.

Scene Fifteen

The drive-in entrance. **Fritz** *and* **Mitzi**. **Fritz** *is packing his things onto the motorbike.*

Mitzi (*breathlessly*)   Maybe, if the time comes when you don't need to jerk off in public no more and I'm not eighty, we'll meet up again.

Fritz (*ashamed, but open because he is glad to be getting away*) First off, I got to get away, then we can take it from there.

Mitzi   You look after yourself, mind, because if things get tough you won't always find anyone stupid enough to love you. (*Laughing.*) Even if you're paraplegic, you can still show up.

Fritz (*grinning stupidly*)   But that'd be the end of all that business down there.

Mitzi (*very tenderly*)   Down there is one thing. Up here (*She kisses his forehead.*) is another matter entirely.

They look at each other. **Otto** *and* **Hilde** *come in. Embraces all round.*

Otto   Well, time for goodbye, I s'pose.

Fritz (*happy*)   Dead right. Bye, then.

Hilde   Drop us a line.

Fritz (*genuine, intimate*)   Watch this space, eh. 'A man's gotta do what a man's gotta do.' (*Grins.*)

Hilde   That's no man, that's my husband.

Otto (*good-naturedly stupid*)   What's all that whispering?

Fritz   Thanks for everything you've both done for me.

Otto   Think nothing of it.

Hilde   Any time you feel like calling in again, Fritz, just drop us a line or phone.

Otto   Dead right.

Fritz *revs up, moves off.*

Mitzi *bursts into tears.*

Otto   Seeing you in tears like this, a man could get really jealous.

Mitzi   Only thing I got, aren't they?

Hilde   Come on, Mitzi, we're no monsters. Fritz is miles away by now. (*Puts her arms around her, then quick as lightning reaches under her skirt and pulls.*)

Mitzi (*startled*)   For Christ's sake, Frau Holdenrieder!

Hilde *has what she was after:* **Mitzi***'s sanitary towel falls out.*

Mitzi *shrieks hysterically and tries to kick the ST away.*

Hilde (*very quietly*)   So I was right. You ought to be glad, Mitzi; having babies at our time of life is no picnic.

Mitzi *again bursts into tears.*

A long pause.

Mitzi *tries to stay upright,* **Otto** *waggles his head in a peculiar way,* **Hilde** *wants to slink away but can't. Paralysis.*

Otto (*after some time, very quietly*)   Get back to normal, then, quick march. Who's first back to work? (*A short pause, he is already worn out.*) Me.

Hilde (*to cheer* **Mitzi** *up*)   Me?

Mitzi (*very small*)   Me.

Slowly, and stumbling as if in a dream, they move off. When the stage is empty, curtain.

Through the Leaves

A play for two characters

translated by

Anthony Vivis

Characters

Martha
Otto

Scene One

In a room at the back of a shop. After the shop has closed. The clatter of crockery. Outside the door a dog is barking. **Martha** *and* **Otto**.

Martha (*giggles*)   Cheers!

They drink.

Otto   Quite a celebration.

Martha   If you spend time with me, you get something to remember me by. No expense spared. This is caviar – three marks eighty a jar.

Otto   Caviar! – Tastes like fish.

Martha   Fishes' eggs.

Otto   Small eggs.

Martha   The fish lays millions of these eggs. Put butter on as well – it brings out the flavour.

Otto   I didn't expect a bloody banquet!

Martha   You haven't seen anything yet. I can't cook properly here at the shop. You come up to my flat sometime, then you'll have something to get your teeth into.

She laughs to herself.

Otto   'Course, this isn't Russian caviar, though, is it?

Martha   No. (*Short pause.*) It's German – what else? Stick to the sausage if you don't like the taste.

Otto   It's not bad, but Russian's better.

Martha   Eaten a lot of real Russian caviar, then, have you?

Otto   It's a well-known fact.

Short pause.

Martha   Well, I like it.

Pause.

If you wasn't here with me tonight I'd go to the pictures.

Otto   What's on?

Martha   *Ben Hur*. It's an oldie, must be ten years since I saw it, but it's a film you never forget. You ever seen it?

Otto   No.

Martha   But you know the story?

Otto   How can I if I haven't seen it?

Martha   Shall I quickly tell it to you?

Otto   Not worth the bother.

Martha (*laughs*)   Dead right.

Pause.

Let me know when you've had enough and I'll clear away.

Otto   Go ahead, I've finished!

Martha   Nothing else you fancy?

Otto   Eat like a prince in the morning, a publican at midday and a pauper at night. – That way you live longer.

Martha   I'd better clear away now, then.

Clatter of crockery.

I've just started on something new.

Otto   What?

Martha   I'll give you three guesses.

Otto   Can't be bothered.

Martha   Because you'd never get it anyway. (*Short pause.*) A diary!

Otto *laughs.*

Martha   No kidding.

She rummages in her handbag.

Here. You can read what I've written so far.

Otto   A bloody novel!

Martha   I've written something about you.

Otto   What've you written about me?

Martha   I've written about you coming into my life. If you like, you can read what I've said.

Otto   Huh! (*Laughs.*)

Martha   Go ahead, read every word. I don't want there to be any secrets between us.

Otto   No point – I can see straight through you.

Martha   When something nice happens to us we need to keep hold of it, so we can remember what it was like.

Otto   I could never be bothered with 'composition'.

Martha   I loved it. But then I've got a lively imagination.

Otto   Me too. But not the kind you can put into words.

Martha   What are you trying to say?

Otto   Maybe I'll let you in on my secrets one day. If you're a good girl. But not just yet.

Martha   Suit yourself. Shall I put something on paper right now? (*Short pause.*) So it doesn't get forgotten?

Otto   You're only showing off.

Martha   Won't take a minute.

She writes something down in her book.

Otto   Each to his own.

He rummages about in his briefcase and brings out a magazine.

Martha   What have you got there?

Otto   Nothing. For men's eyes only.

Martha   It's full of women with nothing on!

Otto   It's none of your business, go on writing!

Martha   But I want to see what they're like. – I think she's the best-looking.

Otto   Not bad. I've had better.

Martha   Are they tarts, showing all they've got like this?

Otto   Fat lot you know about anything! They're photographers' models. Tarts my arse. Students, most of 'em – on tiny grants. So they do a few beaver shots on the side. That way they make enough to pay the next year's fees.

Martha   And how much do they make for these 'beaver shots'?

Otto   A thousand or more a time.

Martha   You wouldn't catch me exposing myself, not even for a thousand.

Otto   Nobody'd want shots like this of you. Just look at their bodywork.

Martha   This one here isn't much cop.

Otto   Takes all sorts.

Martha   If I had a beauty treatment and was fixed up with a nice wig like this lot you wouldn't be able to tell us apart.

Otto   I think I'd spot you, bet you anything.

Martha   Anyway, I wouldn't need to, I'm not that desperate.

Otto *laughs.*

Martha   Shall I read you what I've just put down?

Otto   Some rubbish.

Martha   But I've written it for you. Put that magazine away and I'll read it out to you.

Otto   You're only jealous of these birds. But there's no need. I don't hold with hand-jobs.

Martha   Why not?

Otto   Give me the real thing any time.

Martha (*clears her throat*)   January 10th: Today Otto came round and had his first meal with me. I served him cold meat and caviar. And straight away Otto complained it wasn't Russian caviar but only ordinary.

Otto   Dead right.

Martha   There's more to come! – I never dreamt my Otto would have such good taste. Now we're going to spend a nice evening together. (*She laughs.*)

Otto   You put down every blessed thing. (*A short pause.*) It's all rubbish.

Martha   And tomorrow I'll write down all the other things we got up to today. Only odd notes. But stuff I can make sense of.

Otto   I've got a better idea, come on.

Martha (*laughs*)   If you say so.

Otto   Get your clothes off, then.

Martha   And you.

Otto   A man doesn't always need to undress. But the woman does.

We now hear the dog barking more loudly and nearer.

Now that bleeding dog's trying to get in.

Martha   But he's not allowed to.

She takes her clothes off.

Otto   I might have known that bastard would start its tricks. Fucking nuisance. Where's the lead?

Martha   Over there.

Otto   Fucking bastard!

Martha   By the door.

Otto *finds the lead, goes out into the other room. The dog barks frantically as* **Otto** *lashes out at it.*

Martha (*to herself*)   That dog's my pride and joy but you can hit him if you want. Anyway, he's been barking at customers all day and annoying the neighbours. So he needs a bit of discipline.

Otto (*from outside the door*)   Belt up, you fucking bastard.

The dog growls viciously.

Martha (*to herself*)   He's not used to being locked out for so long, that's why he's acting up.

Otto (*recoiling as the dog is furious*)   Fuck off, you bastard!

We now hear the dog going on the offensive, and **Otto** *yells.*

Martha (*to herself, calmly, almost laughing*)   He won't take any rough stuff – he fights back.

Otto (*outside, battling with the dog*)   Piss off, you fucking monster! Fuck off, fuck you, fuck off! (*Shouts.*) Martha! Your fucking dog's sunk its fangs into me!

Martha (*runs out to* **Otto**, *shouting*) Bad boy, Rolfi, bad boy! Down, boy, heel! Get down this minute!

Otto *gasps for breath.*

Martha   And no more barking, or you'll have Mummy to deal with, then you'll be sorry!

The dog yowls contentedly and trots off.

Martha *and* **Otto** *come back into the room.*

Otto   It went for me, the bastard, tried to bite me!

Martha   If he's attacked, he'll fight back. And he knows straight away who trusts him and who's scared of him. (*She laughs.*)

Otto   I'm not scared. Next time I'll smash the bastard to fuck.

Pause.

Anyway, it's a bleeding pervert, that dog of yours. It goes between your legs, I've seen it.

Martha *laughs.*

Otto   Got a will of its own, your dog.

Martha   I'm freezing.

Otto   Come on, then.

They lie down on the divan.

Pause.

Martha   What's the matter?

Otto   Nothing. Just get rid of that dog.

Martha   January 11th: Though things got nasty later on, and it's all Rolfi's fault, for putting the wind up Otto. Now Otto's worked himself up into a towering rage against me and the dog. So he's out for revenge and he keeps telling me to get rid of Rolfi. But don't you worry, Rolfi. (*She giggles.*) You'll be safe with Mummy. Otto will be in for a nasty surprise if he's got any other ideas because he'll overstep the mark.

January 15th: My Otto calls in every day now. But he's a real shit, I'm afraid, there's no getting round that, and I don't know why he carries on like he does. I know it's crazy of him to be jealous of Rolfi but maybe that's just the way he is. But when he goes on about it the whole time and won't listen to me, but keeps spouting the same old rubbish and being horrible, he gets on my nerves and makes me all tense. Pity, really, because I am fond of him and I'd like to look after him. Otherwise, the weather is still freezing, and yesterday I was so upset about Otto going home I forgot to top up the oil for the night, so this morning the shop was an icebox and I was afraid the pipes must've frozen. But mercifully nothing happened, thank God! Sometimes I just think Otto has a screw loose. Let's hope things take a turn for the better soon. I'm keeping my fingers crossed!

Scene Two

At the shop. **Otto** *is in the back room, lying on the divan, smoking. He and* **Martha** *have to raise their voices to be heard between the two rooms.*

Martha (*at work*)   Tripery is a trade that'll never die out.

Otto   Meat – wherever you bloody look.

Martha   Bet you don't know all the cuts.

Otto   Couldn't be bothered.

Martha   If you knew a bit about the trade, you could come in with me. I could do with some help.

Otto   Do you think I want to be stuck in here all day flogging dog fodder?

Martha   I'd get you a delivery van and put you in charge of the buying. An hour or two at the abattoir in the morning and the rest of the day you could lie in the sun. If you're down the meat market early enough you get a much better idea of what you're looking for than if the meat's delivered to your door, like now. But you've got to know your meat. The buying can make or break you.

Otto   How much would I make?

Martha   We'd split everything down the middle.

Otto   I earn more now.

Martha   How much?

Otto   Never less than fourteen hundred.

Martha   Gross or net?

Otto   After deductions.

Martha   I earn more.

Otto   How much?

Martha   Two thousand in summer, and in winter it can be three thousand, and over. (*She laughs.*)

Otto   Liar.

Martha   I've got nothing to hide. Look at last year's books if you like!

Otto   What would I want with your fucking books?

Martha   And anyway I've got my independence, which is more than you've got.

Otto   Who needs independence? That won't pay the rent.

Martha   But you've never had it, though, have you, otherwise you'd talk different.

Otto   At work nobody tells me what to do.

Martha   Who said they did?

Otto   And if you get a lot of units completed you get a bonus – extra! Last month it came to sixty-five marks!

Martha   I wouldn't flog myself to death for sixty-five marks!

Otto   Because you haven't got a proper head for business. You've got to count every last pfennig.

Martha   But I work for myself.

Otto   Meaning I don't, I suppose? On that fucking packing machine every bloody twitch is registered and reckoned up!

Martha   I'd rather be my own boss.

Otto   It makes you sick. Earning all that money flogging dog fodder – it shouldn't be allowed.

Martha (*laughs*)   Silly sod, I don't sell just dog food, but all kinds of offal as well. I trained in butchery, served my apprenticeship – and butchering's a man's trade!

Otto   Dead right.

Martha   My parents started the business off, and I grew up in it. My dad even supplied a circus.

Otto   Ah, tigers now, is it – very impressive.

Martha   But now all the small circuses have gone bust, so the mantle wasn't passed on to me, as they say. (*She laughs.*) Nowadays circuses buy in bulk.

Otto   There isn't one fucking schnitzel in the whole bloody place!

Martha   Schnitzel isn't offal – the very idea!

Otto   You're not a real butcher because this shop doesn't stock real meat.

Martha   A tripery is an offal butchery. We specialise, that's all. It was my dad's idea. He knew which way the wind was blowing. Any time I choose I can switch over to normal butchering just like that. – I'm all geared up for it. But there's too many butcher's shops as it is. Whereas the tripery trade is falling off, so if you can stay in business you're made.

Pause.

Otto   But I don't care what you say; it's abnormal for a woman to be a butcher.

Martha   It's not abnormal, just more difficult. I've done it despite being a woman!

Otto   I'd rather be a man; there's a world of difference.

Martha   Well, I'd get on much better if I was, that's obvious. But by now the business is what my parents would call rock-solid. The turnover's going up all the time, the loans for the alterations are nearly paid off, and the flat –

Otto   – is owner-occupied – occupied by you and owned by the bank!

Martha   Liar! I've paid off a third and the rest's on a mortgage, which is less awkward and cheaper than paying rent, and this way I pay myself, not some other bugger!

She puffs hard, having really worked herself up.

Otto   The way she talks. There's nothing womanly about you!

Martha   I've always been used to speaking my mind.

Otto   But to be a woman you've got to act womanly. And these days you can never be sure.

Martha   What do you mean?

Otto   It's always cropping up – in sport, for instance, so you needn't look like that. All those Russian blokes pretending to be women, so they win more medals. We'd better lift up your skirt so we can sex-test you!

Martha   Dirty sod!

Otto (*laughs*)   Well, if I'm the only bloke who's ever taken pity on you, you do wonder.

Martha   I've had my chances, don't you worry. After all, I'm in the public eye all day. But why should I chuck myself away?

Otto   So how'd you get shot of your virginity, eh? Did it yourself one dark night when the priest wasn't looking?

Martha   Pig! It was so long ago I can't even remember.

Otto   Good thing too, at your age.

Martha   Point taken.

Pause.

When you're coping with a business all day, single-handed, there's precious little time for any private life.

Otto   No wonder you get funny ideas– with only dead animals for company.

Martha   Nothing interferes with my work. It's one thing I can be proud of. Everyone says so. It's no joke coping on your own, as a woman.

Otto   You've got a dog.

Martha   We've always had a dog.

Otto   It hates my guts, your bloody dog. (*He laughs.*) Because I'm here.

Martha   Point taken, but he's got to get used to you.

Otto   Rip my fucking throat out, given half a chance –

Martha   He doesn't mean any harm.

Otto   So you think I'm scared of it?

Martha *says nothing.*

Otto   Well, do you? Anyway, when they're fat they've got no muscle power.

Martha   Plenty of weight, though, and they use that.

Otto   Right then, I'll shoot the bastard.

Martha   You'd need a gun for that.

Otto   Dead right, and what's more I've got one.

Martha   Where?

Otto   Where it belongs – at home.

Martha   I say, we are well equipped.

Otto   Small calibre but maximum penetration.

Martha   Down the abattoir they got a gun that'll kill an elephant.

Otto   I don't need to kill no elephant.

Martha   You would if one attacked you.

Otto   Come off it.

Martha   What if one escaped from a circus, then what?

Otto   You got animals on the brain, woman.

Martha   I've got imagination, that's the point.

Otto   You know your trouble, you're on your own too much. Imagination doesn't come into it.

Martha   But now I've got you.

February 5th: Now I've got close to Otto, sometimes when I'm out in the street, I look to see if anyone's looking at me. I don't have a big effect, but people don't completely ignore me, either. Open brackets; men, exclamation mark; close brackets.

She giggles to herself.

I do wish Otto wouldn't be so ungrateful. After all, a woman does miss out if she's neglected love like I have. And I've only just realised that. Why is it, I wonder? Even so, I'm grateful to Otto for having come into my life. If he wants, he can stay, though he more or less lives with me as it is. But sometimes he gets all screwed up, then he starts on about Rolfi again and talking the most awful rubbish. Then he wants to know how I managed before he came on the scene. Sometimes I feel like telling him I played with myself, so he'll lay off Rolfi, but I just can't. Still, time will tell, as they say.

Last weekend we went to the zoo. My idea, because it's
years since I've been and at home all we do is argue.
Anyway, it was bloody freezing, and Otto was shivering
with cold, because he only wore a suit even though I'd
warned him. We can expect another overnight frost, so the
radio says. Temperatures eight to twelve degrees. Proper
wintry! Open quotation marks; icy nights; close quotation
marks. Sleeping badly these days. Funny, an old cow like
me. (*She laughs to herself.*) Just can't stop thinking about my
Otto. Though lately he hasn't been over every night. –
Where's he get to, I wonder? Is a big romance still possible
when you're past fifty, question mark. No sign of my Otto
today either – on my own again. So instead I'll make a date
with the Fred Rauch *Request* programme. Aren't I the lucky
one, exclamation mark.

Scene Three

Martha *and* **Otto** *making love.*

Otto   I can't love a woman who's having it off with a dog.

Martha   That's a lie.

Otto   Says you.

Martha   I ought to know.

Otto   The way it licks under your dress the moment your
back's turned, I noticed it the first time I came.

Martha   All dogs do that.

Otto   But this one does it because it's after something.

Martha   What exactly?

Otto   Keep still!

Martha   Ow. You're hurting me.

Otto (*pants*)   'Cause I was coming. But that's the last time I
try to teach you anything.

Martha   Easy enough to say afterwards.

Otto   I'm a man of my word, ducky.

Pause.

Martha   You don't know the first thing about women.

Otto   You know fuck all about men.

Martha   At least I'm willing to learn.

Otto   It's not something you learn; you're born with it.

Martha   There's just no pleasing some people.

Otto   But it's you I'm thinking about. Why else would I put myself out? But with that dog around it can't possibly work.

Martha   What can't?

Otto   It takes your mind off me.

Martha   He most certainly doesn't.

Otto   That's right, be obstinate instead of coming clean. But I know your game. Think I'm blind, or something? The way it hangs round you and licks you where it's got no business. And the way it hates me.

Martha   Because you're scared of him.

Otto   That's just an excuse.

Martha   I'm getting up.

Otto   Dead right – that's your lot.

Martha *gets up, puts her clothes on.*

Otto   I know your game!

Martha   You bastard!

Otto   Just nod.

Martha   Why should I?

Otto   Okay, let's drop it – it's obvious I'm right.

He turns away.

Wake me in half an hour.

Martha   Feel like a kip, then?

Otto   Forty winks – I'm knackered.

Martha   Fair enough – I'll repot the rubber plant.

Otto   Quietly, though!

Martha   Of course.

A short pause.

Otto   You've certainly got green fingers, I'll give you that.

Martha   But I've got a secret weapon. (*She laughs.*) I dig up earth from the field behind the church. Much better than anything you buy.

Otto   That's stealing.

Martha (*laughs*)   If you look at the field close up you'll see it's full of holes. My holes.

Otto   That's bloody stealing.

Martha   Nobody's going to miss a bit of earth.

Pause.

Otto   You're abnormal, that's what comes of being unattractive and living on your own.

Martha   We can't all be as much in demand as you.

Otto   It's because you're nothing much to look at. A woman's got to have something special to catch a man's eye.

Martha   Who said I want to catch a man's eye?

Otto   Who are you trying to kid?

Martha   Okay – what attracts you, then? If you don't mind me asking?

Otto I feel sorry for you.

Martha I don't need sympathy, that won't pay the rent.

Pause.

Come up to the flat and stay the night like a good boy.

Otto No.

Martha Why not?

Otto None of your business.

Martha Oh yes it is.

Otto Go on like this and you'll lose me completely.

Martha Got another woman, have we?

Otto A man's always got several irons in the fire.

Martha I see.

Otto I'm off to sleep. Wake me – at ten past seven.

Martha Dead right.

February 16th: Otto, where are you? Open brackets; longing for you; close brackets.

February 22nd: Sometimes I think: the doorbell will ring any minute and Otto will be standing there. Is he ever coming back? I'm determined to keep this diary going even if there isn't much to say right now. Business is booming. Today's takings: eight hundred and sixty-seven marks, sixty-three pfennigs. I hope to God Otto does come back. When you're not as young as you were it's no picnic finding a man you can get on with. I think he will come back. Got a touch of flu, and taking tablets for it. Pyramidon they're called, and not bad at all. Rolfi is being a handful, he's so thrilled to have me all to himself again.

She laughs.

The cheeky sod. Otto, I love you. Come back, exclamation mark, full stop.

Scene Four

In the shop.

Otto   We meet again.

Martha (*laughs*)   You're back.

Otto   Just a flying visit, see how you are.

Martha   Fine.

Otto   Me too.

Martha   You looked better when you left.

Otto   Life's for living.

Martha   You look half dead to me –

Otto   I need my freedom.

Martha   You've got it.

Otto   Never believe a word I say, do you?

Martha   I've got eyes.

Pause.

Come into the back room, don't stand there like a customer looking for a discount.

Otto   Okay.

They go into the back room.

You've kept that ashtray on the table specially for me, right, because you don't smoke!

Martha   Dead right. Jailbreaker.

Otto   Getting funny ideas because I'm back – typical.

Martha   I'm happy, that's all. You go away quite respectable and decent-looking and back you come looking like a down-and-out gypsy.

Otto   I've been living it up – three nights on the trot.

Martha   Wasting money.

Otto   My money.

Martha   All the same.

Otto   The first few nights I was at home with a telly and everything. (*He laughs.*) But I felt too tied down so I pissed off. Three days and three nights on a real bender, as they say. (*He laughs.*)

Pause.

Martha   And I thought my Otto must've got himself another girl. (*Short pause.*) Well, now you're back we'll soon have you good as new. Not to worry. A man needs to sow a few wild oats. No harm done. If you're short of cash I'll lend you some.

Otto   I never borrow from a woman.

Martha   Suit yourself.

Otto   I'm knackered.

Martha   Go up to the flat, have a good wash, get yourself something to eat out of the fridge, there's plenty there, get your strength back, then lie down and have a kip. And tomorrow it's back to work.

Otto   Dead right.

Martha   You've had your fun, let your hair down, and a good thing too. But now you need a bit of peace and quiet.

Otto   Coming up with me?

Martha   I can't shut up shop at eleven just because you come breezing in out of nowhere. In the lunch break I'll come up and cook us belly of pork with white-bread dumplings. And wake you up.

Otto   Don't fancy me, then?

Martha   All in good time. Look at yourself in the mirror – like a tramp. Make yourself presentable, then we'll see.

Otto   The way she talks.

Martha   Bit off more than you can chew?

Otto   I have been having some pretty tough away matches. (*He laughs.*)

Martha   I see. (*She laughs.*)

Otto *laughs.*

Martha   And how much did it all cost?

Otto   No tarts.

Martha   Look me in the eye.

Otto   No tarts – only ladies of a certain age.

Martha   A likely story.

Pause.

Otto   I'll come home, Martha, if you want.

Martha   What do you think? Here's the key, but for God's sake have a wash and take your things off before you get into bed and don't drink, not in this state, or you'll wet the bed again.

Otto   Bitch.

Martha   I know you.

Otto (*as he goes*)   Bitch.

Martha *laughs.*

Martha   February 25th: Otto's back. At last.

Scene Five

Martha *and* **Otto** *in the flat.*

Martha   Shrovetide Carnival will be over soon, and we'll have missed it.

Otto   Waste of fucking time.

Martha   You've got to try things out before you pass judgement.

Otto   And how much were the tickets?

Martha   That's my secret, because I'm treating us.

Otto (*reading*)   Tropical Ball. – That won't come cheap.

Martha   Who cares.

Otto   These balls can cost a packet, so I'm told.

Martha   We'll see. Anyway, I'm paying.

Otto   If we go at all, I'm paying. The man always does.

Martha   Up to you.

Otto   I'll only go if I'm paying.

Martha   Such a gentleman! – Life is for living.

She rummages about in some paper bags.

Otto   What you got there?

Martha   Wait and see!

Otto   A costume?

Martha   'Course, it's no fun otherwise.

Otto   I'm not going in fucking fancy dress, I don't hold with it. Besides, it isn't manly.

Martha   The proof of the pudding is in the eating.

Otto   What you going as?

Martha   Guess.

Pause. **Otto** *laughs.*

Martha   Going as a flower girl, aren't I? Any fool can see that. See? Eliza Doolittle. *My Fair Lady*! (*She laughs.*)

Otto *laughs in confirmation.*

Martha (*humming*) I could have danced all night . . .

Otto (*interrupts her*)   What am I going as?

Martha   Professor Higgins, of course!

Otto   Who the fuck's that?

Martha   Don't you know anything? A posh English gentleman!

Otto *laughs.*

Martha   Took me ages to think that one up. Here, you've only got to put it on, it's already made up.

Otto   Daft bitch, it must've cost a bomb.

Martha   It's only hired.

Otto   Where from?

Martha   A shop that hires out fancy dress. (*Short pause.*) Only shows what I can do when I put my mind to something.

Otto   But I've never been to a proper ball in my life!

Martha   Well, I have – even if it was years ago. We've all got to start somewhere. Hold on to me!

Otto   Think I'm scared or something?

Martha   What of?

She hums the song again.

March 1st: It was very nice really. Even though there wasn't that many people there, not for a ball. If I'd known, I'd have found another ball to go to. Still, not to worry. Otto can't dance, and now I realise that's why he didn't want to go. I danced with some other blokes and Otto went berserk. So I asked him why he didn't mention it before so I'd've known where I stood. And he said it slipped his mind. (*She laughs.*) I could still remember how to dance, even though it's been

years since I've done any. And when I didn't know the steps
I just hopped about like the others. Otto got terribly pissed.

April 12th: It's Otto's birthday tomorrow. Aries the Ram!
(*She laughs.*) Whereas I'm Leo the Lion (*She laughs again.*)
Thirty-eight, he says; question mark. I've got a surprise for
Otto; colon. One of these ultra-modern quartz watches with
a solid gold wristband; exclamation mark. All very up to
date – with no numerals on the face, just a little button for
the hour, minute, second, day and month – in fact the last
word in watches! (*She laughs*) He won't believe his eyes. Price:
one hundred and sixty-eight marks, ninety-five pfennigs the
watch, and ninety-three marks, ninety pfennigs the
wristband. Both from the jewellery section of a large
department store. On my way home I looked in a few more
watch shops – all much pricier. Dash; clever girl;
exclamation mark. Whatever will Otto say; question mark.

April 14th: Otto's birthday was a disaster. Even though I
could swear because I saw it in his; open brackets; stunned;
close brackets; exclamation mark; expression that it was a
tremendous surprise for him, all he actually said was:
fucking newfangled rubbish. And he liked his old one better
– which is dirt cheap and dead nasty.

Pause.

I told him you could always change it or get a gift token in
lieu. That made him sit up. Open brackets; no idea about
prices, Otto; close brackets. At first, he wouldn't even touch
it, but later on he picked it up and tried it out, and a good
thing too. (*She laughs.*) Now we'll have to see whether he
takes to it. Let's hope he wears it all the time, but if not,
never mind; open brackets; even though it wasn't junk and
cost me a packet; close brackets.

April 19th: There's just no point in going on like this. I keep
telling Otto but he won't have it. He will insist on being boss
and I won't stand for it. I'm a person too. I keep trying to
tell him but he doesn't want to know. I am fond of him but
he's got to learn not to enjoy trampling all over me – but do

something sensible; colon. Like giving me a hand. Business has really boomed this month; three exclamation marks. In the evening when I cash up, Otto just glares and goes red with fury. Yesterday's takings nine hundred and forty-five marks, twenty-three, only fifty short of a thousand. But instead of being pleased, the silly bastard nearly choked with rage. It's sheer envy, that's all. Otherwise we're both fine.

Scene Six

In the shop. **Martha** *at work,* **Otto** *in the back room. They have to raise their voices to be heard. The radio is playing folk music.*

Otto (*shouting*)   Got another beer?

Martha   Boozing again?

Pause.

Martha   If you've already drunk all five, there's none left.

Otto   Four – you can't count.

Martha   The other must be in the shopping, then, I bought five.

Otto (*fiddling about*)   Got it.

Pause.

Martha   Coming up when I've finished?

Otto   I can't come up every night.

Martha   Playing hard to get now, are we?

Otto   Something's cropped up.

Martha   What?

Otto   None of your business.

Martha   Not 'another woman' again? (*She stresses 'another woman'.*)

Otto   A better one, dead right.

Martha (*goes into the back room*)   I see.

Otto   You can't complain. I took pity on you, so belt up.

Martha   You said you'd turned over a new leaf for me.

Otto   I need my freedom, and nothing'll stop me getting it.

Pause.

You're insatiable, you are.

Martha   Okay, I'm insatiable.

Pause.

Otto   It's abnormal, itching for it as often as you do.

Martha   But if I love you why shouldn't I?

Otto   Not today. Let somebody else have a go.

A long pause.

Wait your turn. Just be thankful for the love you've had, it isn't everyone that gets it.

Martha   I'm not ungrateful, and I give you everything I have.

Otto   The last of the big spenders.

Martha   Some things you demand cost more than others.

Otto   Want me to go? It's always the man that leaves.

Martha   Then slinks back, crawling with lice.

Otto   Bitch.

Martha   Only stating facts.

Otto   All right. – Who forked out for the Tropical Ball – you or me?

Martha   I enjoyed myself and thanked you.

Otto   A hundred and sixty-three marks, all told!

Martha   Correct.

Pause.

Otto   This sort of talk won't get us anywhere. If that's your attitude, we'd better call it a day!

Martha   I haven't got an attitude. I love you, that's all.

Otto   You being an expert, I suppose.

Martha   No, but I am a businesswoman; you can't just push me around. Surely my independence counts for something.

Otto   I'm sick to death of your sodding independence. Do you think I haven't twigged you're Lady Muck and I'm a lump of shit?

Martha   I never said that.

Otto   Thought it, though.

Martha   Come up with me when I've finished. Like a good boy!

Otto   Obstinate cow!

Martha   Okay, I'm obstinate. (*Short pause.*) I bought a schnitzel, it'll go off if it isn't eaten.

Otto   Got a fridge, haven't you?

Martha   It won't keep long, even in a fridge.

Pause.

Otto   Here or not at all. I'm not going upstairs – I'm busy tonight.

Martha   Like hell you are.

Otto   Stubborn cow. Here or not at all.

Martha   Okay then, here – have it your own way.

Otto   Next time maybe I'll stay here longer.

Martha   Sure.

Otto   Let's get going then, I haven't got all night. Just knickers will do.

Pause.

What's up?

Martha   Nothing. You needn't bother, not tonight, I've changed my mind. You'd better go or you'll be late. Come on, be a good chap and shift yourself. I'm ready to lock up now.

Otto   But you haven't finished.

Martha   I'll check the rest tomorrow. You've obviously no time to lose.

Otto   Dead right.

He gets up to go.

Think it over.

Martha   Sure. See you.

Otto   Maybe.

He goes out.

Pause.

Martha (*to herself*)   What did I tell you!

April 30th: Again, Otto's been gone for over a week. I could see it coming, but what can you do? Though I didn't get so worked up this time, as it's happened before. But I do have to work out what to say if he rolls up again like last time. Has he got another steady woman after all? It hurts me inside to think about it, but I'd love to know what this other woman is like. Maybe I ought to spy on him when he knocks off from work one day? (*She laughs.*) If he really has got someone else, it's bad news. Then the dream will soon be over because this other woman is bound to be a doormat who'll put up with anything. Maybe he hasn't really got anyone but is only pretending, to make me jealous. Or just some old crone; exclamation mark. But I'd only feel jealous if I saw that this other woman he's got instead of me was a better catch. Otherwise, he's only himself to blame if he won't see the obvious. Business is bad; open brackets; a real scorcher; close brackets. Takings today: four hundred and eighty-seven marks, sixty.

Scene Seven

In the flat. Water is running into the bath.

Otto (*loudly*)   Get some clean underpants out ready for me!

Martha (*from outside*)   What?

Otto   Bring me some clean underpants, I said, or are you deaf?

Martha (*shouts back*) Just a minute!

Pause.

(*Coming into the bathroom.*) I'll put them on the radiator, so they don't get splashed.

Otto   Dead right.

Martha   Like me to scrub your back?

Otto   Needn't bother.

Martha   Some people don't know when they're well off. You've got a bath, a flat and someone to scrub your back. And where have you been bumming around?

Otto   Wouldn't you like to know.

Martha   I can well imagine.

Otto   Can you now?

He clicks his tongue.

Martha   Don't let's go on.

Otto   What are you staring at?

Martha   Nothing.

Otto   Like what you see?

Martha (*laughs*)   Daft.

Otto   You should've seen me in my younger days. What a physique! I was quite an athlete then.

Martha   Pity you don't do a bit more outdoor sport now, instead of you-know-what.

Otto   No blubber on me anywhere you look!

Martha   What about there?!

Otto   Where?

Martha (*in a posh voice*)   On your tum.

Otto   Don't talk cock, that's sheer muscle!

Martha   Want me to scrub your back?

Otto   Getting down to the bare facts, eh?

Martha *laughs.*

Otto   Gently does it!

Martha *scrubs his back.*

Otto   The Chinese have got bathhouses where they make a man feel really special when they bath him. They got a real feel for it, these geishas.

Martha   Well, I'm no geisha, ducky. But I will make sure your back's clean, that's more to the point.

Pause.

Right. Don't be long, supper's ready.

Otto   What is there?

Martha   A surprise.

Scene Eight

In the bedroom at night.

Otto   I'd let the shop and put my feet up.

Martha   You'd never live off it.

Otto   In that case I'd find myself a part-time job.

Martha   Give up my own business and take orders from some other bugger – I'm not that stupid.

Otto   The way she talks! You're totally unwomanly.

Martha   I've got a mind of my own, that's all.

Otto   But no feminine charm.

Pause.

Otto   I mean, how is a man supposed to feel when the woman he loves is a self-employed butcher who earns more than he does?

Martha   You might be pleased.

Pause.

I just don't feel right with you. And when I tell my mates at work about you they agree. (*Short pause.*) If you was nice-looking it'd be something.

Martha   If I was nice-looking I certainly wouldn't be as independent as this.

Otto   But more desirable.

Martha   Rubbish. You've got an inferiority complex, that's your trouble.

Otto   I've got no time for complexes.

Pause.

Martha   You've heard my offer, come in with me. I'll give you eight hundred and fifty marks all found. And if things improve, I'll pay you more.

Otto   I'd be worse off all round.

Martha   Only because you couldn't knuckle under to a woman boss.

Otto   It's abnormal, everybody says so.

Martha   I can't help that. Anyway, I love my work.

Otto   That's abnormal too.

Martha   You come in with me and you'll soon change your tune. Think it over: eight hundred cash down and all found.

Otto   Not likely. Like I said, I'm a man of my word.

Martha   May 26th: Otto's being awkward. Maybe he's got a hang-up about my looks. But he's no oil painting either. Though I'd never tell him so to his face, because he fancies himself. Otherwise I'm fine and so's Otto. He's moved in with me properly now. Exclamation mark. Maybe that's why we quarrel so much. He always thinks he's right, but usually I am. Simply because he always says the opposite of what I think, no matter what it is. He always makes out he's better than me, tramples on me. Maybe he's trying to break me down to build me up again? Or maybe he has to do this to prove himself a man, and maybe I should just turn a blind eye. Mental note: be more tactful; exclamation mark. Sometimes I feel I need to talk to somebody, but I realise I've got no female friends. I'd love to find one. Business is bad. Much too hot. Yesterday evening we went to the Löwenbräukeller, and sat in the garden. Very nice. Otto in a good mood. And not pissed. I'm very fond of him. Is he of me; question mark.

Scene Nine

In the shop. The back room.

Martha   In broad daylight, what if anybody sees?

Otto   Nobody'll see.

Martha   But I daren't risk it, it's Saturday morning – a customer might come in any minute.

Otto   You're scared, that's why.

Martha   What if somebody comes?

Otto   We jump to it, quick as a flash – now you see it, now you don't!

Martha   I can't do it, I'm not like that.

Otto   Ah well, point taken. I get the picture now. It's the same old story: a bloke in the background while the woman fucks around without so much as a backward glance.

Martha   Do you want the customers to turn nasty – and avoid me like the plague? The whole district's full of Catholics, they'd have my guts for garters.

Otto   Why do you want a man at all when you're married to the sodding business?

Martha   I do plenty for you.

Otto   Pity you can't show some humility.

Martha   Rubbish.

Pause.

Otto   Okay then, give us a blow job.

Martha   What's that?

Otto   The way a woman gives a man a treat. You don't need to undress, nobody'll notice anything. Except me.

Martha   What do I do?

Otto   Blow me, or don't you know how?

Martha   I've never tried it.

Otto   No time like the present.

Pause.

Martha   Okay, you win.

Otto   Dead right. Unzip my fly, then – gently does it. Bite me and I'll swipe you one.

Martha   Don't worry, I won't.

Otto   You'd better kneel down between my feet while I sit on the chair.

Martha   Okay.

Otto   And when I come, swallow it. No spitting it out.

Martha   But what if I feel too sick to get it down?

Otto   Make an effort; you're a woman, aren't you?

Martha   Sure.

June 9th: It's always my money we spend. Open brackets; except for the Tropical Ball; close brackets. But it isn't right. I'm not denying I earn more, even if he won't admit it, but all the same. He's so cocksure. I can't tell if he's given up his place, though he's always pissing off somewhere. He says he hasn't, but he is a liar sometimes. He's always making me feel small to prove he's a man and I'm not. So far I haven't managed to cure him of it. I shall just have to be even more tactful. But how can you go on giving when you're drained? Nobody's perfect, and Otto's not a bad sort. Just stupid. The fact that he dominates me and walks all over me doesn't make him superior; exclamation mark. I'm not much of an opponent. Though that doesn't stop him. Fighting me to the death. I'll give whatever ground I can. But there's things going on now I can't bring myself to write down; dot, dot, dot. I wonder what the future holds; question mark.

Scene Ten

In the living room. The television is on: the sports news.

Martha   We have to stand together, Otto, or we'll never get anywhere.

Pause.

Understand?

Pause.

All you do is work against me.

Otto   I'm trying to watch TV.

Martha   You live with me, eat with me.

Otto   I've still got my place.

Martha   Give it up.

Otto   Oh yeah, suit you down to the ground, that would.

Pause.

Martha   I realise now, there's a lot to love and a woman can't do without it. But you have to watch it or you'll get out of your depth in no time.

Otto   I don't, I'm a man.

Pause.

Martha   Early on, if you remember, I told you you could read anything I wrote in my diary. But you never have.

Otto   Not worth the bother.

Martha   But for a long time now I haven't wanted you to. And you've only yourself to blame.

Otto   A diary's private.

Martha   Maybe.

Otto   I can't force myself on anyone. I don't hold with it.

Martha   But lately I've written something specially for you.

Otto   My notice. (*He laughs.*)

Martha   Rubbish. A poem. The first I remember writing for years. Because I've been thinking about the two of us. Shall I read it to you?

Otto   Suit yourself.

Martha   I'd like to read it out loud. Turn the telly down.

Otto   I want to watch the sport.

Martha   It's my set.

Otto   Dead right.

He gets up and switches it off.

All ears.

Martha (*laughs*)   I haven't thought up a title yet: Night brought me your shadow. Here I stand and reach out but I am tiny. All the flowers will soon be blooming, even the ones on the balcony. I would like to be your wife for better or for worse. Stand by me when I'm tired at night, as I will stand by you. And where I have sown a seed for us, do not tread on it. Take care.

Pause.

The end.

Otto   It can't be a poem – it doesn't rhyme.

Martha   Still, you couldn't write one like me.

Otto   No.

Martha   June 12th: It was all a waste of time, no matter how hard I tried. A poem's got to rhyme, he's absolutely right, He doesn't feel at ease with me, he says, and it's my fault. Because it's abnormal being a woman butcher. Maybe he's right. But so what? I have to run the business as best I can. Open brackets; today's takings were down to six hundred and twenty-two marks eleven, but it's as hot as hell; exclamation mark; close brackets. I think I'll go on a diet for him. Then perhaps he'll stop pestering me about this butchery thing. Weight at present nearly sixty-five kilos. Aim to get down to under sixty. Though I have to be careful. I need all my strength for the work I do. But you've got to give up something for love. So I start on the fifteenth with a calorie-controlled diet. I look in the mirror a lot these days. (*She laughs.*) I look womanly all right, though I'm no sex bomb. (*She laughs.*) But there's no pleasing Otto. Though he can be very affectionate. When he's not totally pissed, just a bit woozy, that's when I like him best. Then it's lovely being with him. I've tried controlling his intake but suddenly he'll have one too many and all hell breaks loose. And he's just as rotten when he's sober because then he tramples on me. Stupid bastard. Otherwise everything's fine. Should we go on holiday together, I wonder; question mark. Open brackets; but who minds the shop; question mark; close brackets.

Scene Eleven

In the living room. **Martha** *under a sunlamp.*

Martha   You'll see what a difference a suntan makes.

Otto   And in the meantime I go blind.

Pause.

Now your eyes are shut and you can't see anything, I might slope off and never come back.

Martha   You'd soon be back!

Otto   Dead right.

Pause.

Using the sunlamp without the regulation glasses is strictly
forbidden!

Martha   But then I'd have white rings round my eyes and
people would see my tan wasn't real, only artificial.

Otto   But it'll affect your eyes.

Martha   You want me to put the glasses on?

Otto   Because of your eyes.

Martha   But you mustn't moan if they've got rings round
them.

Otto   No, because your eyes come first.

Martha   Are you concerned about me?

Otto   What concerns me is that you stick to the rules.

Martha *laughs.*

Martha   June 28th: Otto has pissed off again. But he'll be
back. I'm not at all worried. He'll roll up again in a day or
two. Once he realises how well off he is with me.

July 10th: Still no sign of life from Otto. Getting worried
now. I wonder if I should ring up his factory and ask if he's
still there? Let's hope nothing's happened to him. But I
doubt that, because then he'd need me and would've got in
touch by now. Will we ever see each other again; question
mark. Often think back to the old days; exclamation mark.
Did we go wrong somewhere? I suppose we did, but where?
Refusing to let him walk all over me wasn't a mistake.
Certainly, he could've felt big, but nothing more. I hope
he's all right. I am. And so's the shop. Rolfi's being a pest,
though. I often think about going on holiday by myself.
Ideal time of year; exclamation mark. And I dare say the
shop would survive, other businesses shut down for their
holidays and still get their customers back. But with a
sodding dog you're lumbered. Where can Otto have got to;
question mark.

August 4th: This is a photo of Otto and me at the Tropical Ball. Open brackets; as a memento; close brackets.

September 1st: Very lonely. Deep longing; full stop.